FOR FUN AND PROFIT

CRITICAL PERSPECTIVES ON THE PAST

A series edited by Susan Porter Benson, Stephen Brier, and Roy Rosenzweig

The Transformation of Leisure into Consumption

Edited by RICHARD BUTSCH

TEMPLE UNIVERSITY PRESS *Philadelphia*

Temple University Press, Philadephia 19122

Published 1990
Printed in the United States of America

The paper used in this publication meets the minimum requirements of American National Standard for Information Sciences—Permanence of Paper for Printed Library Materials, ANSI Z39.48-1984.

Library of Congress Cataloging-in-Publication Data

For fun and profit : the transformation of leisure into consumption / edited by Richard Butsch.
p. cm. — (Critical perspectives on the past)
Includes bibliographical references.
ISBN 0-87722-676-8 (alk. paper)
1. Leisure industry—United States—History. 2. Leisure—Economic aspects—United States. 3. United States—Popular culture—Economic aspects. I. Butsch, Richard, 1943- . II. Series.
GV188.3.U6F67 1990
338.4'77900135'0973—dc20 89-27699
CIP

CONTENTS

ACKNOWLEDGMENTS

On the long road to the completion of this book, many have encouraged and supported the effort. What perhaps most sustained me was the chain of colleagues and friends that I forged along the way. The idea grew from a session on commercialized leisure that I organized for the 1985 Social Science History Association meeting, with the intent of bringing together and enhancing the visibility of the relevant research. Kathy Peiss encouraged my efforts by signing on as one of the first contributors, suggesting others, and recommending the prospectus to her editor, Janet Francendese, who also provided encouragement.

Many scholars in history, sociology, and mass communication, leisure, and cultural studies, in the United States and Britain, offered encouraging comments on the book prospectus and suggested contributors. Jeanne Allen, Peter Bailey, Frank Couvares, Richard Gruneau, Richard Johnson, Stephen G. Jones, H.F. Moorhouse, Vincent Mosco, Richard A. Peterson, Roy Rosenzweig, and Todd Swanstrom provided helpful suggestions. John Clarke kindly helped to arrange my pleasant and productive stay at the Centre for Contemporary Cultural Studies in Birmingham, England, where Wyn Thomas and

Chris Wall proffered a home away from home. A paid research leave from Rider College made the sojourn possible.

The contributors to the book submitted first-rate, original scholarly studies and were patient in awaiting the book's appearance. Robert C. Allen, Susan Porter Benson, and anonymous reviewers commented helpfully on the manuscript. Patricia Sterling's copyediting saved us from our errors and clumsy phrases. Last, thanks to Ava Baron, who provided hope, faith, and guidance to what seemed at times an unending and fruitless journey to publication.

PART I
HISTORICAL AND THEORETICAL ISSUES

1

INTRODUCTION: LEISURE AND HEGEMONY IN AMERICA

Richard Butsch

In ways that are obvious even to the casual observer, leisure activities have become commercialized. Two centuries ago Americans purchased few leisure goods or services; many made their own music and toys for their children and drank homemade cider. Today, most of our leisure activities depend upon some purchased commodity: a television set, a baseball, tickets to the theater. We spend much of our free (nonwork) time watching and listening to programmed entertainment distributed by large corporations; we use sports and recreational equipment supplied by oligopolistic industries. Toys, now a multibillion-dollar industry, are produced by major corporations and retailed through national chains. As we have become more dependent on purchased goods and services for our fun, so too has leisure become a source of profit for corporate enterprises and an integral part of the economy.

This process of commercialization has been continuous but gradual and uneven. Although such activities as theatergoing were

Acknowledgments: For their helpful comments I would like to thank Ava Baron, Mary Blewett, Patricia Cooper, Stephen Hardy, Susan Klepp, Bruce McConachie, Roy Rosenzweig, and Todd Swanstrom.

already commercial in the eighteenth century, leisure-time pursuits did not depend generally upon purchased products and services until the late nineteenth century. Spalding and other sporting goods manufacturers promoted standardized game rules in order to sell their products. Many local entrepreneurs who had catered to class-specific markets were displaced by national oligopolies that market their wares to the "masses." Theater and vaudeville gradually came under the control of the Theater Syndicate and the United Booking Office, both of which determined what acts people would see across the nation. Mass media—magazines, movies, radio, television—were designed to appeal to large cross-class audiences. Even today, new forms of entertainment are created or existing ones colonized by leisure industries that concentrate and centralize production of leisure goods and services and, in turn, restructure leisure activities.

The contributors to this volume are interested in the reasons for and the consequences of these changes in the organization of leisure. Why has leisure developed in particular ways? Did impersonal social or economic forces, such as the dynamics of a capitalist economy, constitute the engine of change? Or did various groups seek to use leisure for their own purposes? As consumers of leisure products, have we lost control of our own free time? Does leisure represent the interests and values of participants—that is, is it an arena of self-expression? Or have capitalists or reformers designed leisure to control the behavior of lower classes?

All these questions center in issues of power, domination, and resistance that scholars have commonly considered in relation to labor but have only recently begun to address in relation to leisure. The study of leisure and domination has roots in several disciplines and diverse theoretical orientations in the broader literatures on mass culture, popular culture, and working-class culture.[1]

John Clarke's essay (Chapter 2) characterizes the scholarship on popular culture as torn between pessimism and populism. Pessimists focus on the rise of centralized, commercial production, use the term "mass culture," and call the consequent corroded form of society "mass society." Populists tend to prefer the terms "popular culture" or "working-class culture," to indicate a "people's culture." Over decades, fashion has favored one or another assessment.

Pessimists tend to worry about the deterioration of society. Some envisioned the masses as incapable of providing the intellectual leadership necessary for a civilization, at worst deteriorating into mob rule, as Edmund Burke feared from the French revolution; twentieth-century versions of these conservative-elite fears often point to mass media as the culprit.[2] Others were pessimistic for opposite reasons. As they attempted to account for the rise of fascism in the 1930s and 1940s, they feared that centralized mass media would contribute to the breakdown of community and provide a means for elites to propagandize the masses. Liberal theorists blamed radio and film for the demise of voluntary organizations and community, which made public opinion vulnerable to demagogues using the mass media for propaganda. Similarly, some Marxists blamed mass culture for undermining working-class consciousness. Both liberals and Marxists feared that mass media would undermine the collective action that they considered the foundation of democracy. Both regarded leisure founded upon mass media as diverting the masses' attention from political concerns.[3] Critics of these theorists have challenged their caricatures of the masses as passive and defenseless but cannot dismiss the serious implications of structural changes represented by centralized mass media.

Some of the research into the effects of mass communication began as an empirical complement to mass society theories, focusing on the transmission of messages and the effects of various forms of transmission; it neglected the listener's ability to interpret the message in his or her own terms. Not explicitly concerned with questions of domination, by default it assumed the audience to be passive receptors of propaganda.[4] While experimenting with variables of message transmission after World War II, however, social psychologists began to reveal the limited effectiveness of explicit messages. Research turned to consumers' "uses and gratifications," regarding the audience "as actively utilizing media contents, rather than being passively acted upon."[5] By exploring people's uses of mass media to satisfy their own needs, mass communications research reassured us that media did not enslave us, but its optimism virtually erased questions of domination and ideology from the agenda.

During the late 1960s and 1970s, a second look at effects moderated the celebration of audience expression by pointing up ways in which media *are* influential. Research indicated that when information rather than opinion is involved and when media sources are prestigious monopolies, audiences do incorporate implicit ideas into their own thinking. In the 1970s, Marxist mass communication researchers turned their attention to the structure of media industries. Emphasizing that capitalist concentration of cultural production increased domination, they provided evidence of those conditions under which media are effective in persuading audiences.[6]

In the 1970s a new generation of social and labor historians analyzed leisure as a medium of class domination and resistance, describing how leisure developed and changed in the nineteenth century and considering why it took particular forms. Some social historians began to study the aspects of social control in reform movements directed at the working class, exploring the ways that public services and facilities were developed and designed to control working-class behavior—for example, through the parks and playground movements.[7] Other historians criticized the social-control approach for ignoring working-class resistance to reforms and emphasized the working classes' creation of their own culture despite efforts by capitalists and reformers to dominate them.[8] By concentrating on single communities, these scholars could reconstruct the lives of ordinary people.[9] Some looked specifically at working-class leisure, showing that the reformers' efforts had met with significant opposition and limited success. Some found that early leisure entrepreneurs allied with workers by providing pleasures that reformers were foreclosing in public places.[10]

Much historical research made domination a central research question, but these studies end at the community boundaries and in the early twentieth century; they leave unexamined the national leisure oligopolies that were already forming, and they predate the retreat of leisure from the working-class community into more private settings. They analyze the nickelodeon, saloons, and amusement parks, but not the heavily capitalized chains of picture palaces, the radio, or the phonograph. These histories provide rich evidence of working-class agency, but they barely touch questions of structure that are important to an understanding of commercialized leisure. British cultural studies in the 1970s, focusing on working-class leisure in contemporary mass culture, did advocate a synthesis of structure and agency, but the most famous work celebrated agency in working-class youth's subversions of mass culture without looking at the structural limits created by leisure industries.[11] Some British historians, however, have combined economic history with the insights of social history to shed light on the changing relationships between entertainments and audiences.[12] Such studies, like the ones in this book, examine the contribution of both industries and consumers to the restructuring of leisure.

HEGEMONY AND LEISURE PRACTICES

With no single agreed-upon theoretical framework to comprehend the development and implications of commercialized leisure, scholars need to emphasize approaches that encourage dialogue among the various research traditions and that rethink their theoretical concepts. Such syntheses of social structure with human agency are not new to social theory. Peter Berger and Thomas Luckmann in the 1960s and Anthony Giddens in the 1980s emphasized the complementarity of structure and agency: people create and yet are created by society; structure provides the meaningful context whereby action is possible even as it constrains that action. In the 1970s Raymond Williams fashioned a similar approach directed specifically to culture and leisure.[13] Central to Williams's synthesis is the concept of "social practices," a term also used by Giddens.[14] The concept connects social structure with human agency by focusing on the activities people engage in: dining, playing cards, shopping. Practices are the intersection of structure and agency. People continually re-create structure through their participation in a practice; at the same time, the pre-existing conventions of the practice shape and constrain their behavior and also provide the framework within which they interpret the practice in their own way.

Studying leisure as social practices avoids the dilemma of having to choose between a totally constraining structure and complete free will. The study of leisure practices requires examining how the organization and form of the activity operates to constrain us and also how the organization is shaped by our very participation. To paraphrase Karl Marx, people act, but not just as they please; they do what they do under circumstances transmitted from the past. Moreover, looking at leisure as social practices shifts our attention from cause and effect to the process itself. By emphasizing process and change, an analysis of practices emphasizes that structures may be more or less determinant, more or less fluid, and agency more or less efficacious, without either resorting to structural determinism or ignoring structure altogether.

Practices need to be understood in terms of power as well. The concept of practices is well suited to a nondeterministic and historically dynamic concept of domination that we shall call "hegemony." Since that term has been used in various ways, its application to the study of leisure practices requires some clarification.[15] It has sometimes been used interchangeably with such terms as "class domination" and "ideology." Ideology, for example, implies a system of ideas, meanings, and beliefs, developed by or for the ruling class, which results in a "false consciousness" of subordinated classes. If we were dealing only with ideology imposed by a ruling class, then, Raymond Williams points out, it would be "a much easier thing to overthrow."[16] Hence, building on Antonio Gramsci's earlier formulation, Williams distinguishes hegemony from either ideological indoctrination or direct control of one class by another. Hegemony entails class domination through the *participation* of subordinate classes. In our daily work and leisure activities we participate in creating the conditions and social relations that shape our lives. As Williams explains, hegemony is "a saturation of the whole process of living . . . to such a depth that the pressures and limits of [social structure] seem to most of us . . . simple experience and common sense."[17] This directs our attention to practices rather than ideas—leisure rather than culture—as a medium of hegemony. A focus on hegemony encourages us to look for the forces and limits of control in the fabric of practices that constitute people's lived experience.

Hegemony varies in strength; it is never total, secure, complete but is susceptible to attack, degeneration, undermining, displacement. A practice is hegemonic to the degree that its structure is defined by elites, by centralized social structures, and even by the physical space and objects available for the practice—relative to being controlled by its practitioners. A group of children playing a street game without standardized equipment, grounds, or rules have greater power over their leisure practice (which is thus less hegemonic) than do children playing in a Little League game, whose equipment, organization, and rules are specified by centralized and commercial authorities (making it more hegemonic).

Thus, hegemony in leisure may be assessed by the degree to which practitioners of leisure are not the producers of their own leisure, the degree to which they are constrained by the conventions of the practice or limited by their access to the means of "producing" that leisure activity. Just as access to the means of production shapes the organization of production, access to the means of consumption shapes leisure. People's leisure choices are constrained by the skills, knowledge, space, equipment available to them.[18]

Understanding how leisure practices are structured is important to understanding how hegemony operates. We need to explore the ways in which leisure industries become embedded in the fabric of everyday life; the ways in which leisure practices are shaped with the participation of people, individually and collectively; and the ways in which multiple class interests are expressed through these processes.

A study of the commercialization of leisure reveals how that part of our lived experience supposed to be free of domination is transformed by capitalist development. The expropriation of the means of leisure is a prerequisite for commercialization. For example, when street entertainments are prohibited, amusement parks, theaters, saloons may become alternative leisure spaces, where people may pay to do many of the same things they had done previously in the street. A generation that grows up with purchased leisure may not develop the skills of self-entertainment. Expropriation and commercialization, then, with attendant centralization and standardization of leisure practices, may be mechanisms of hegemony.

But agency is not necessarily absent in commercial forms of leisure. How people use television in their homes may extend beyond the reaches of corporate domination. Hegemony is a historically specific and changing mixture of constraint and expression.

THE HISTORY OF LEISURE AND HEGEMONY IN AMERICA

Leisure practices acquire structure and meaning from their relationship with other human practices; moreover, they change over time along with other changes in the society. The commercialization of leisure represents the development of a new relationship between leisure and the economy, a historical process involving changes in hegemonic forms that are themselves linked to changes in politics, kinship, and economies. The history of leisure's development into a relatively discrete activity has not yet been written.[19] Indeed, one of the purposes of this volume is to emphasize the need for such a history. The following sketch necessarily presents generalizations and glosses over considerable variation between regions and practices.

The history of leisure practices in the United States can be conceived in three periods, with dividing lines roughly at 1830 and 1880. Each period is distinguished by its forms of hegemony. Each period also varies from beginning to end as processes develop from the previous period and into the next. A look at earlier forms of leisure and hegemonic control will provide background for the essays in this volume, which focus primarily on the decades since 1880, when commercialization began to predominate.

Traditional Authority

In the American colonies and early republic, work, leisure, and the household formed an unbroken web of life in small communities.[20] Manufacturing took place in small craft shops and was usually organized around a household system of production in which work and leisure were hardly distinguished. The print shop, for example, typically adjacent to or part of the master's living quarters, was social center as well as workplace.[21] Gambling and drinking were often built into the workday. Male workers commonly expected alcoholic beverages on the job as part of their compensation. In rural areas, liquor was itself often a part of subsistence production and integral to the American diet; it was either homemade or cheap enough to permit a common laborer to get drunk daily. Efforts by the state to tax whiskey resulted in the Whiskey Rebellion and repeal of the tax.[22] Even outside the workplace, work and leisure were intertwined. Holiday festivals were craft oriented; masters and journeymen paraded together for the republic and their crafts.[23]

The place, time, skills, and implements for participating in recreation were equally accessible to all. Space for outdoor diversions was seldom a limitation in rural society. Open land lay within walking distance for residents even of Philadelphia, the largest colonial city; semirural areas within the city served as pastures, gardens, playgrounds.[24] Yet even during this period, the leisure practices of the lower classes were not entirely of their own making. Local elites (religious, mercantile, and planter) ruled over preindustrial communities in which their economic and political dominance was supported by political and religious ideology.[25] In a society of small communities, their authority was enhanced by being local, direct, and personal.[26] Hence, local elites could directly or indirectly regulate much lower-class leisure. During the first half of the eighteenth century the public house (an inn offering food, drink, and lodging) was the focus of community life, often the largest public building in town. Because of its importance, the upper class saw to its licensing and exercised informal oversight.[27]

The reservation of certain recreational activities to the elites themselves provided an ideological justification for their station above craftsmen and servants. Mercantile and planter elites mimicked their English counterparts in practicing a culture of manners in which their "cultivated tastes" set them above the lower classes. For example, thoroughbred racing was an exclusionary sport that elites had already institutionalized by the early nineteenth century.[28] Theaters may have housed all classes under one roof, but the seating reflected the class hierarchy of the community, with elites in boxes, mechanics on benches in the pit (now the orchestra), servants and laborers in the gallery. As patrons and subscribers of stock productions in eighteenth-century cities, elites controlled the programs and personnel of companies whose members were considered their inferiors. By virtue of their social status, the upper classes also exercised some control over the audience. Others in the audience might interrupt and force changes in the performance by shouting, throwing things, jumping on stage, and even rioting—but within limits set by their "betters."[29]

This is not to suggest that such divisions were uncontested; there may well have been significant struggles. Cheap rum and proliferating taverns stretched and weakened elite oversight. Uses of Philadelphia streets and squares for popular gatherings were contested even in the eighteenth century.[30] Certainly class factions emerged amidst and after the Revolution. But relative to the next period, traditional authority seems to have held sway. The mid-nineteenth century was evidently much more turbulent.

Leisure and Class Struggle

Changes in the economic, political, and cultural landscape in the nineteenth century gradually eroded the patterns of traditional authority and supplanted them with class conflict. In this context, leisure as well as labor became an arena of class struggle, though the exercise of power remained local, direct, and personal.

Throughout the mid-nineteenth-century growth of industrialization, entrepreneurial capitalism prospered in family firms and among resident industrial elites. What Richard Edwards called "simple control" predominated inside the firm. The boss, typically either the entrepreneur himself or a member of his family, was "both close and powerful."[31] He controlled his workforce directly by intervening in the work process to discipline or to reward. Much has now been written about working-class responses to the rise of industrial capitalism. Journeymen formed organizations separate from their employers and engaged in more extensive strike activity as they saw their control over work and their opportunities for achieving master status shrink.[32] Working women rose up against the tyranny of factory discipline and deteriorating working conditions.[33]

Laboring classes found not only the means of production expropriated by the upper class but the time and place for leisure as well. Factory discipline excluded recreation and socializing during work hours, drawing a sharp boundary between paid and "free" time. But the long workday left little time for workers' amusements, and urban crowding in immigrant slums began to preclude traditional recreations. Likewise, the state increasingly restricted the uses of public space by the lower classes.[34]

As in the workplace, however, this upper-class control was not uncontested. Historians have begun to explore the class antagonisms revealed in the political and social activities of the working class. Artisan republicanism mobilized journeymen mechanics into political insurgency against traditional party politics.[35] Festivals in New York and Philadelphia in the mid-nineteenth century expressed working-class autonomy and class antagonism.[36] Audience sovereignty over theater performance also became a class-contested issue. New York elites gradually abandoned the notion, still held by workers, that the audience had the right to direct the performance. In the 1830s police began to be used to prevent riots, creating resentment among working-class theatergoers at such infringement on their "sovereignty" and culminated in a working-class riot at the upper-class Astor Place Opera House in 1849; twenty-two persons were killed. By the 1850s, the New York working class and elites had established separate centers of entertainment in the Bowery and on Broadway.[37]

Entertainments based on distinct ethnic and craft traditions developed their own class expression and trajectory.[38] Much of the existing literature on working-class leisure during the first half of the nineteenth century focuses on the practices of white adult males. As Christine Stansell has shown, many laboring women in metropolitan areas were caught in a struggle to make ends meet and had little time or money for recreational activities as such, though some young single women found pleasure in mixed-sex settings such as dance halls, and others engaged in church social functions.[39]

The working-class saloon in the latter part of this period appears to have been at the core of a white male working-class subculture. The saloon provided shelter, toilets, free lunches; it was a place for job seeking, politicking, unionizing, male camaraderie, and a variety of entertainments. Prizefighting, blood sports in which animals were pitted against each other, billiards, and gambling typically were based and organized in saloons.[40] Even Shakespeare, tailored to working-class audiences, was performed in saloons "as part and parcel of popular culture."[41]

Working-class theater thrived during this period. In most places outside the largest eastern cities, dramatic plays were surrounded by other acts as part of variety shows. In the 1830s, New York's Bowery entrepreneurs found it profitable to offer melodrama to audiences of single journeymen and semiskilled workers. From the 1850s to the 1880s, Pittsburgh's skilled ironworkers set the tone of that city's stage entertainment in the absence of an elite culture. Working-class domination of stage productions survived even later in the specialized Yiddish theater of New York's Lower East Side.[42]

But nineteenth-century working-class leisure did not grow unfettered. In place of the earlier period's ongoing regulation by local elites, middle- and upper-class reformers—often through state intervention—attempted at first to confine and later to shape working-class leisure. State licensing eventually restricted liquor sale to the saloon, removing it from the kitchen grog shop within working-class homes. Temperance crusades combined with employers' efforts to effect a reduction in drinking, though repeated assaults on the "iniquity" of the working-class saloon were less successful.[43] City police departments enforced new restrictions on public space and behavior; at the end of this period Philadelphia required parade permits for public gatherings.[44] The upper-class American Society for the Prevention of Cruelty to Animals (ASPCA), founded in 1866, advocated the prohibition of blood sports to discourage "gambling and misspent time of the working class."[45]

Still, research on the parks movements in the postbellum period highlights the limited success of reformers either in co-opting space for their own leisure or controlling the recreations of the working class. Efforts of the middle and upper classes to establish urban open spaces for their own use met with significant opposition and developed into struggles for space and public funds. Working-class politicians in Boston and Worcester, Massachusetts, for example, successfully altered city plans to allow for at least small parks in working-class neighborhoods. Even more dismaying for the reformers was their inability to control behavior in the parks. Urban workers simply ignored prohibitions on liquor and rowdiness and continued to enjoy their free time in their own fashion. By the Progressive era the parks movement had evolved (with only partial success) into park management and playground supervision designed to police working-class uses of the streets and to put workers' children under state control.[46]

Entrepreneurs serving a working-class clientele were allies of the working classes in defense of their traditional recreations. Owners of saloons typically lived in working-class neighborhoods and were themselves immersed in the culture of their customers. They sheltered and even sponsored many amusements attacked by reformers and the state. Amusement parks and dance halls gave freer reign to young workers than did reformer-sponsored facilities.[47]

The upper and middle classes not only attempted to control the working classes but imposed a Victorian ideology of self-control on themselves. Early in the period they conceived of recreational activities as means of self-improvement rather than relaxation. Parks were proposed as sylvan retreats for reflection and repose in nature, restorative antidotes to the degenerative effects of urban life.[48] Elites attended their own "legitimate" theaters for an "educative" experience.[49] Some founded athletic clubs as part of a new advocacy of exercise in the 1860s, which diverged from the parks movement's preference for contemplative recreations. After the Civil War exclusive sporting clubs of all sorts proliferated as badges of status.[50] Even baseball clubs, though less exclusive than some, were primarily organizations of middle-class professionals and merchants. These clubs promoted sports by lobbying for park space, financing facilities, and institutionalizing rules, leagues, and competition—all of which were steps toward the commercialization of sports and the growth of spectatorship.[51]

Leisure Becomes Consumption

As commercialization began in earnest, there occurred a shift from local leisure entrepreneurs to leisure oligopolies—in some cases stimulated by state policy—and with it a shift from labor- to capital-intensive leisure. Chapters 3–11 in this book illustrate the complexities of the forces that shaped recreational activities as these corporations built new marketing strategies to attract middle-class audiences and induce a culture of consumption.

The shift in hegemony and leisure practices accompanied the development of corporate capitalism after 1880. With their expanded capital and workforces, large corporate firms successfully combined mass production with mass distribution. Bureaucratic control of work displaced the personal style of direct supervision characteristic of the family firm. National mass markets superseded local markets.[52] Leisure industries prospered as higher wages and shorter hours (though they varied by race and gender) permitted workers to increase their consumption of commercially provided leisure goods. The work week in factories shortened gradually throughout the nineteenth century, then dropped rapidly in the early twentieth century from about sixty to about fifty hours.[53] Average annual earnings of employees improved steadily between the depression of the 1870s and that of the 1930s.[54]

From 1875 to 1918, working-class families increased the proportion of their income spent on items other than food, clothing, and shelter from under 10 percent to about 25 percent. This rate, sustained even through the Great Depression, had increased by the 1980s to over 40 percent as Americans shifted from "time-intensive" to "goods-intensive" recreation.[55] Expenditures specifically on leisure quintupled between 1901 and 1961, though reading material, sheet music, and musical instruments—the means of participatory entertainment—did not share in this growth. The phonograph, radio, and television increased their share of sales more than any other category.[56]

The federal government became involved not simply in controlling working-class leisure, as local reformers had done, but in stimulating its commercialization. Copyright laws of the late nineteenth century enhanced the commercial value of music, plays, and fiction. The government, rejecting a recommendation that it retain control of broadcasting, aided the creation of a radio patent pool and of RCA as a joint venture of General Electric, AT&T, and Westinghouse, thereby commercializing radio and future television broadcasting.[57] Such government intervention contributed to the twentieth-century move from locally backed live entertainment to recorded or amplified performances offered by national corporations through capital-intensive technology.[58]

L. Sue Greer (Chapter 8) describes a government policy of stimulating regional economies through recreational industries. By building roads, campgrounds, and other facilities and encouraging related local business, the U.S. Forest Service packaged the "forest experience" for tourists, thus effectively expropriating the forest from local residents and preparing the infrastructure for "sale" to a broader urban market.

Leisure industries of the mid- to late nineteenth century had catered to class-specific markets; local entrepreneurs successfully profited from fulfilling working-class demands for class-expressive recreation. But like the rest of the economy, leisure industries gradually came under the control of national corporations that created cross-class "mass" markets. Breweries in Chicago and Boston, for example, began controlling local saloons (though this development was interrupted by Prohibition).[59] Mass media had consolidated into oligopolistic industries by the end of the 1920s. Three recording companies rapidly gained control of the phonograph industry, even shaping the predominant technology into a playback-only device.[60] The movie industry was briefly dominated by the Motion Picture Patent Company and from the 1920s on by vertically integrated movie companies.[61] A decade after the beginning of radio broadcasting, CBS and NBC accounted for half the industry income.[62] The era of the mass market had entered leisure, creating "mass culture."

New marketing strategies went hand-in-hand with or preceded oligopolistic concentration. Stephen Hardy (Chapter 4) documents the standardization of sports rules and equipment as a product of the marketing strategies of nineteenth-century sporting goods manufacturers, who wrote and distributed rule books and sought product endorsement by professional leagues, teams, and star players.

Catering to the "masses" required a leisure firm to develop a marketing strategy and product that would appeal to many classes and groups at the same time. Ironically, the result was not a class-neutral product or marketing approach but one "with class," encouraging consumers' identification with the upper class and its luxury in an effort to promote consumption as a value. The entertainment industries in particular appealed to middle-class aspirations to upward mobility.

The first leisure entrepreneurs had sought to increase profits by expanding the markets for male working-class entertainments—the saloons and the variety and movie arcades where men engaged in rough, rowdy, and drunken behavior. The ideology of Victorian morality restricted both middle-class ladies of leisure and working-class women to home-based recreations. Continuing development of commercial entertainment, therefore, hinged on reintroducing women into public leisure. Working-class women first and then more affluent middle-class women and men had to be persuaded that certain public amusements were "respectable" in order to make such enterprises profitable. Kathy Peiss (Chapter 5) shows how such marketing strategies coincided with women's opportunity to throw off Victorian chains and regain access to public leisure at the turn of the century. Dance halls and amusement parks appealed to single working women who wanted to experiment with new definitions of propriety beyond the watchful eye of their parents. Vaudeville began as a respectable form of variety cleansed of the profanity and prostitution that accompanied saloon entertainment. Movie exhibition followed a similar trajectory from male arcades to working-class family nickelodeon to middle-class movie palaces. The nickelodeon was advertised as a place for wholesome family amusement.[63]

Bruce McConachie (Chapter 3) describes the gradual development of the notion of middle-class decorum as appropriate audience behavior. The rising status of touring star performers as larger-than-life heroes enabled them to silence an audience where the familiar local players could not. After the Civil War entire traveling companies displaced locally controlled stock companies and enhanced the power of national booking agents. Theaters began to control audiences by banning drink and prostitutes, and replacing pit benches with fixed orchestra seats. In the late nineteenth century a new generation of producers also promoted decorum by marketing a new form of realism; darkening the hall encouraged the audience to become silently absorbed in the performance, to identify with the star not as hero but as role model, and to aspire to the ownership of consumer products that would allow them to mimic life on the stage.

Movies continued this mode of marketing. Beginning in the 1920s they depicted grand homes and showcased elegant ladies in high-fashion clothes.[64] Douglas Gomery (Chapter 7) delineates a Chicago firm's development of movie houses that played upon middle-class aspirations of upward mobility. The "picture palace" made luxurious surroundings, servants, air conditioning, and extravagant stage shows—reflecting the world of the screen—affordable to the middle class. Using this approach, Balaban & Katz built what would become part of the nationally powerful, vertically integrated Paramount company by the end of the 1920s.

Such marketing was part of a general shift to a consumer culture among the middle and upper classes. Victorian values of self-denial and work gave way to ideas of self-fulfillment that sanctioned consumption as a source of identity.[65] With the demise of the family firm and the growth of an affluent middle class of corporate bureaucrats, upper- and middle-class males no longer aspired to achieving elite status through hard work. For them, leisure became less a means of self-improvement than a release from the bureaucratic work world. Advertising promoted the idea of fulfillment through purchases. In the early twentieth century, ads were already trying to arouse demand by associating products with feelings of well-being.[66]

Robert Snyder (Chapter 6) shows that the quest for a middle-class market resulted in the absorption rather than the abandonment of the working-class audience. Early twentieth-century vaudeville theater chains such as Keith's and Loew's provided something for all classes: Times Square theaters offered big-name acts in regal surroundings, while new acts could be tried out in neighborhood houses patronized by working-class audiences who exercised traditional sovereignty, chasing unsatisfactory performers from the stage. However by this time their judgment reflected not solely their own culture but the standards of big-time vaudeville. Thus was forged a mass audience ready to respond to mass-produced entertainment.

Leisure practices became increasingly capital intensive as recording and amplification technologies centralized the production of entertainment and replaced armies of entertainers. Early in the twentieth century, movies shared billing with live performers but soon outgrew and overwhelmed vaudeville.[67] Player pianos proliferated in middle-class homes; 2.5 million were produced before they were displaced by the phonograph and radio. But musical instrument production dwindled in the late 1920s as phonograph records, radio programs, and talking movies replaced live amateur and professional performance, and music listening increasingly supplanted musicmaking. Between 1926 and 1929, when the radio audience doubled, piano sales dropped from $94 million to $38 million, sheet music sales from $3.5 million to $2.1 million. The talking movie put out of work an estimated 18,000 musicians who had played for silent movies and vaudeville.[68]

Ellen Wartella and Sharon Mazzarella (Chapter 9) demonstrate that from college students of the 1920s to grade schoolers in the 1980s, a succession of media have been central to the development of youth cultures. Moreover, the mass media have acted as magnets, drawing time away from other leisure practices generally. Television in particular has become the "dominant activity" around which children's leisure is organized.

These home entertainments, to the degree that they privatize leisure and withdraw the household from the community, may weaken the subcultural bases of resistance to hegemony. Where reformers and police failed, television has succeeded in enticing the working class from the streets and saloons back into their homes. The proliferation of television in the 1950s was accompanied by a precipitous drop in movie attendance from its peak in 1946 to one-fourth of that level. At the same time, television has colonized leisure, its average use per household increasing from four and a half hours per day in the early 1950s to over seven hours per day by the mid-1980s.[69]

Nevertheless, such hegemonic processes are not simply dominating. Leisure commodities were not always unilaterally imposed but often grew from the symbiotic cooperation of consumers with corporations. For example, the hobby industry developed from small entrepreneurial efforts by hobbyists themselves to guidance by specialty publications, national organizations, and eventually the large hobby goods suppliers.[70] Subordinate groups, particularly youth, have appropriated commodities for their own subcultural expression, sometimes causing leisure industries to change course. When 1950s radio stations, desperately seeking replacements for listeners lost to television, began playing a broader range of music, American youth tuned in to rhythm-and-blues and fostered the creation of antiestablishment rock-and-roll, dismantling a thirty-year recording industry oligopoly.[71] Even after reconcentrating in the 1970s and 1980s, the record industry has repeatedly drawn upon subcultural, often countercultural, musical traditions. George Lipsitz (Chapter 10) shows how a reggae record and music video served to communicate antiestablishment messages to cross-cultural audiences. He argues that while a mass medium may heavily filter communication, it may nevertheless also distribute counter-hegemonic messages. Such was the case, for example, in the late 1960s when RCA both sought military contracts and marketed the iconoclastic music of the Jefferson Airplane.

Richard Butsch (Chapter 11) demonstrates that leisure practices are not entirely the impositions of monolithic capital, nor are they entirely the free expressions of consumers. In the early 1980s the world's largest consumer electronic corporations spent two billion dollars to make videodisc, a playback-only device, the established technology of home video. But the availability of movies on videotape, which could be rented from small retailers, movies on videotape, and the convenience of "time-switching" televised programming tipped the balance in favor of videocassette recorders, allowing consumers for the first time a degree of direct control over what they watched on television and when.

These examples demonstrate that though oligopolies wield imposing influence in shaping leisure, their control is not total. Resistance and class expression not only persist but are important sources for the innovations on which consumer industries depend. It is among subcultures that corporations seek new ideas for music, movies, television programs, toys, clothes—ideas that are not simply reflections of capitalism but expressions of people. In other words, the hegemony of commercialized leisure is dependent for its existence upon its own incompleteness. Hegemony grows from a symbiosis between corporate capital and consumers. Consumers participate in shaping new products and practices, which corporations in turn shape into profits and "mass culture."

Commercialization, then, represents a fundamental shift in the nature of hegemony, which now operates not through the traditional authority and personalities of local elites, nor through the power of capitalist employers, middle-class reformers, and state intervention, but rather through the impersonal, even apparently "natural" structures of corporate industries and mass markets. Class conflict, direct and personal in the nineteenth century, is submerged in relations between leisure industries and consumers. This impersonal hegemony was and is delivered not as law or the pronouncements of elites but through the forms of leisure commodities, which do much to shape leisure practices. Hegemony is the child of the marriage of corporate profits and consumer "fun"; social control and class expression are merged in the same practices. Understanding how hegemony is embedded in these practices is a necessary step toward appropriating our leisure for "recreating" ourselves.

NOTES

1. Among the diverse fields of research that bear on the topic, I concentrate on two lines of inquiry: mass culture theory with related mass communication research, and the new social historical research. In sociology the study of leisure has been marginal, although the sociology of culture is experiencing a renaissance. See John Wilson, "The Sociology of Leisure," *Annual Review of Sociology* 6 (1980): 37; John Clarke and Chas Critcher, *The Devil Makes Work: Leisure in Capitalist Britain* (Urbana: University of Illinois, 1985); Chris Rojek, *Capitalism and Leisure Theory* (London: Tavistock, 1985). Some scholars in the sociology of sport (e.g., Harry Edwards and Richard Gruneau) have applied political, economic, and cultural practices approaches that have raised questions about power and domination. See George Sage, "Pursuit of Knowledge in Sociology of Sport," *Quest* 39 (1987): 255–81. Some sociologists have applied the production of culture approach to show how the structure and concentration of industry have shaped popular culture. See Richard A. Peterson and David G. Berger, "Cycles in Symbol Production: The Case of Popular Music," *American Sociological Review* 40, no. 2 (1975): 158–73; Richard A. Peterson, "The Production of Culture," *American Behavioral Scientist* 19, no. 6 (1976): 669–84.

2. The long history of such concerns predates the twentieth century. For studies of mass culture critiques and mass society theories, see Alan Swingewood, *The Myth of Mass Culture* (Atlantic Highlands, N.J.: Humanities Press, 1977); Salvador Giner, *Mass Society* (New York: Academic Press, 1976); Martin Jay, *The Dialectical Imagination: A History of the Frankfurt School* (Boston: Little, Brown, 1973), chap. 6; Patrick Brantlinger, *Bread and Circuses: Theories of Mass Culture and Social Decay* (Ithaca, N.Y.: Cornell University Press, 1983). See also the debates in Bernard Rosenberg and David Manning White, *Mass Culture: The Popular Arts in America* (New York: Free Press, 1957); Norman Jacobs, *Culture for the Millions?* (Boston: Beacon Press, 1959).

3. William Kornhauser, *The Politics of Mass Society* (New York: Free Press, 1959); Giner, *Mass Society;* Jay, *Dialectical Imagination.* Fears of mass society were an integral part of many nineteenth-century theorists' dichotomies between traditional community and impersonal modern society. See the summary of classic social theories in Melvin DeFleur and Sandra Ball-Rokeach, *Theories of Mass Communication,* 3d ed. (New York: David McKay, 1975), 136–153. For a recent variation on the theme of community breakdown, see Robert Bellah, Richard Madsen, William Sullivan, Ann Swidler, and Steven Tipton, *Habits of the Heart: Individualism and Commitment in American Life* (Berkeley: University of California Press, 1987).

4. DeFleur and Ball-Rokeach, *Theories of Mass Communication,* 153–59.

5. On uses and gratifications research, see Jay Blumler and Elihu Katz, *The Uses of Mass Communication: Current Perspectives on Gratifications Research* (Beverly Hills, Calif.: Sage, 1974); Elihu Katz, Jay Blumler, and Michael Gurevitch, "Uses of Mass Communication by the Individual," in W.

Philips Davison and Frederick T. C. Yu, eds., *Mass Communication Research: Major Issues and Future Directions* (New York: Praeger, 1974), 12. Carl Hovland, Irving Janis, and Harold Kelley, *Communication and Persuasion* (New Haven, Conn.: Yale University Press, 1953), and Elihu Katz and Paul Lazarsfeld, *Personal Influence* (New York: Free Press, 1955), presented the results of systematic laboratory studies.

6. James Curran, Michael Gurevitch, and Janet Woollacott, "The Study of the Media: Theoretical Approaches," in Michael Gurevitch, Tony Bennett, James Curran, and Janet Woollacott, eds., *Culture, Society, and the Media* (London: Methuen, 1982), 13, 16–21. On media industry structure, see Graham Murdock and Philip Golding, "Capitalism, Communication, and Class Relations," in James Curran, Michael Gurevitch and Janet Woollacott, *Communication and Society* (London: Edward Arnold, 1977).

7. E.g., Paul Boyer, *Urban Masses and Moral Order in America, 1820–1920* (Cambridge, Mass.: Harvard University Press, 1978); Frances Fox Piven and Richard Cloward, *Regulating the Poor: The Functions of Public Welfare* (New York: Pantheon, 1971). See discussions of British use of the concept in A. P. Donajgrodzki, *Social Control in Nineteenth Century Britain* (Totowa, N.J.: Croom Helm, 1977).

8. William Muraskin, "The Social Control Theory in American History: A Critique," *Journal of Social History* 9 (Summer 1976): 559–69; Stephen Hardy and Alan Ingham, "Games, Structures, and Agency: Historians of the American Play Movement," *Journal of Social History* 17 (Winter 1983): 285–301; and Gareth Stedman Jones, "Class Expression versus Social Control? A Critique of Recent Trends in the Social History of 'Leisure,'" *History Workshop* 4 (Fall 1977): 162–70.

9. E.g., Alan Dawley, *Class and Community: The Industrial Revolution in Lynn* (Cambridge, Mass.: Harvard University Press, 1976); Daniel Walkowitz, *Worker City, Company Town* (Urbana: University of Illinois Press, 1978); John Cumbler, *Working Class Community in Industrial America: Work, Leisure, and Struggle in Two Industrial Cities, 1880–1930* (Westport, Conn.: Greenwood Press, 1979). These earlier working-class histories make only cursory mention of saloons, clubs, or other recreations, concentrating instead on work, family, and politics—in contrast to British historians' early interest specifically in working-class leisure. See "Work and Leisure in Industrial Society (Conference Report)," *Past and Present* 30 (April 1965): 96–103; "The Working Class and Leisure: Class Expression and/or Social Control (1975 Conference Report)," *Bulletin of the Society for the Study of Labour History* 32 (1976): 5–18. Studies introduced at the 1975 conference were eventually published as Eileen Yeo and Stephen Yeo, eds., *Popular Culture and Class Conflict, 1590–1914* (Atlantic Highlands, N.J.: Humanities Press, 1981).

10. Roy Rosenzweig, *Eight Hours for What We Will: Workers and Leisure in an Industrial City, 1870–1920* (New York: Cambridge University Press, 1983); Francis Couvares, *The Remaking of Pittsburgh: Class and Culture in an Industrializing City, 1877–1919* (Albany, N.Y.: SUNY Press, 1984); Kathy Peiss, *Cheap Amusements: Working Women and Leisure in*

Turn-of-the-Century New York (Philadelphia: Temple University Press, 1986).

11. Stuart Hall and Tony Jefferson, eds., *Resistance through Ritual: Youth Subcultures in Post War Britain* (London: Hutchinson, 1976). On advocating a synthesis of structure and agency, see Richard Johnson, "Against Absolutism," in Raphael Samuel, ed., *People's History and Socialist Theory* (London: Routledge & Kegan Paul, 1981); and Stuart Hall, "Cultural Studies: Two Paradigms," in Tony Bennett, Graham Martin, Colin Mercer, and Janet Woollacott, eds., *Culture, Ideology, and Social Process* (London: Batsford Academic, 1981).

12. Peter Bailey, *Leisure and Class in Victorian England: Rational Recreation and the Contest for Control, 1830–1885* (London: Routledge & Kegan Paul, 1978), chap. 7; Penelope Summerfield, "The Effingham Arms and the Empire: Deliberate Selection in the Evolution of Music Hall in London," in Yeo and Yeo, *Popular Culture*, 209–40; Paul Wild, "Recreation in Rochdale, 1900–1940," in John Clarke, Chas Critcher, and Richard Johnson, *Working Class Culture: Studies in History and Theory* (London: Hutchinson, 1979), 140–60.

13. Peter Berger and Thomas Luckmann, *The Social Construction of Reality* (New York: Doubleday, 1966), 53–61; Anthony Giddens, *Profiles and Critiques in Social Theory* (Berkeley: University of California Press, 1982), 8–11, 32–39. Giddens adds the element of power (see pp. 38–39), absent in Berger and Luckmann. For Raymond Williams, see "Base and Superstructure in Marxist Cultural Theory," in his *Problems in Materialism and Culture* (London: Verso, 1980), 31–49 (reprinted from *New Left Review* 82 (November 1973); 3–16; and Williams, *Marxism and Literature* (London: Oxford University Press, 1977). Richard Gruneau's analysis of sports in *Class, Sports, and Social Development* (Amherst: University of Massachusetts Press, 1983), chap. 2, builds on Williams's conceptualization in terms very similar to mine.

14. Giddens and Williams use the term "practices" without defining it. Louis Althusser used it in a specific technical sense, with different emphasis and implications; see his *For Marx* (New York: Vintage Books, 1970), 166–67. This is not the definition adopted here. Sociological social psychology's "situations" and Erving Goffman's cumbersome "situated activity systems" are similar to "practices" as I use it here, though without the dimension of power. See *Encounters* (Indianapolis, Ind.: Bobbs-Merrill, 1961), 94.

15. On interpretations of Antonio Gramsci's use of the term, see Williams, *Marxism and Literature*, 108–14; Thomas Bates, "Gramsci and the Theory of Hegemony," *Journal of the History of Ideas* 36, no. 2 (1975): 351–65; Carl Boggs, *Gramsci's Marxism* (London: Pluto Press, 1976), chap. 2. On recent historians' use of the concept, see T. J. Jackson Lears, "The Concept of Cultural Hegemony: Problems and Possibilities," *American Historical Review* 90, no. 3 (1985): 567–93; and the debate in *Journal of American History* 75, no. 1 (1988): 115–57.

16. Williams, *Problems in Materialism and Culture*, 39.

17. Williams, *Marxism and Literature*, 110.

18. As Gruneau, *Class, Sports, and Social Development*, 53, expresses it: "The effects of these differential resources can be measured in the greater collective power of some agents to 'structure' play, games and sports in certain ways and to contour the range of meanings and significations associated with them."

19. Clarke and Critcher, *The Devil Makes Work*, chap. 3, provides a history of British leisure and capitalism. On twentieth-century Britain, see Stephen G. Jones, *Workers at Play: A Social and Economic History of Leisure, 1918–1939* (London: Routledge & Kegan Paul, 1986). These sources and the research they cite reveal instructive parallels between British and American developments: e.g., in relationships between working classes, reformers, leisure entrepreneurs, and the state; in struggles over the uses of public space; and in the concentration of capital in entertainment industries.

20. In the mid-eighteenth century the largest city, Boston, had a population of 17,000. By 1820 only eleven towns had over 10,000 inhabitants and only four more than 35,000 (excluding suburbs); only New York exceeded 100,000. With its suburbs, metropolitan Philadelphia had 122,000. In 1820 only 7 percent of the population lived in urban areas of 2,500 people or more. See U.S. Bureau of the Census, *Historical Statistics of the United States, Colonial Times to 1970*, bicentennial ed., pt. 1 (Washington, D.C.: Government Printing Office, 1975), 11. Even factories remained a rural phenomenon. Primitive transportation isolated towns and regions from each other, even while they grew. See Caroline Ware, *Early New England Cotton Manufacture* (1931; reprint, New York: Atheneum, 1966).

21. Ava Baron, "Women and the Making of the American Working Class: A Study of the Proletarianization of Printers," *Review of Radical Political Economy* 14, no. 3 (1982): 23–42. Similarly, see Dawley, *Class and Community*, on shoemakers.

22. W. J. Rorabaugh, *The Alcoholic Republic: An American Tradition* (New York: Oxford University Press, 1979), 29, 53–56; Rosenzweig, *Eight Hours for What We Will*, 35.

23. Sean Wilentz, "Artisan Republican Festivals and the Rise of Class Conflict in New York City, 1788–1837," in Michael Frisch and Daniel Walkowitz, eds., *Working Class America: Essays on Labor, Community, and American Society* (Urbana: University of Illinois Press, 1983), 37–77. Festivals also had their dimensions of racism. See Gary B. Nash, *Forging Freedom: The Formation of Philadelphia's Black Community, 1720–1840* (Cambridge, Mass.: Harvard University Press, 1988).

24. Susan G. Davis, *Parades and Power: Street Theatre in Nineteenth Century Philadelphia* (Philadelphia: Temple University Press, 1986), 28.

25. Rorabaugh, *Alcoholic Republic*, 27–29; Davis, *Parades and Power*, 25, 26; Charles Sydnor, *American Revolutionaries in the Making: Political Practices in Washington's Virginia* (New York: Free Press, 1952).

26. Boyer, *Urban Masses and Moral Order*, 5; Stephen Hardy, *How Boston Played: Sport, Recreation, and Community, 1865–1915* (Boston: Northeastern University Press, 1982), 45.

27. Rorabaugh, *Alcoholic Republic*, 27–29. State regulation of places to drink is discussed in Rosenzweig, *Eight Hours for What We Will;* and Perry Duis, *The Saloon: Public Drinking in Chicago and Boston, 1880–1920* (Urbana: University of Illinois Press, 1983).

28. Melvin L. Adelman, *A Sporting Time: New York City and the Rise of Modern Athletics, 1820–1870* (Urbana: University of Illinois Press, 1986), 47.

29. McConachie, Chapter 3 in this volume; David Grimsted, *Melodrama Unveiled: American Theater and Culture, 1800–1850* (Chicago: University of Chicago Press, 1968), 74.

30. Rorabaugh, *Alcoholic Republic*, 32–34; Davis, *Parades and Power*, 34–35.

31. Richard Edwards, *Contested Terrain: The Transformation of the Workplace* (New York: Basic Books, 1979), 19.

32. David Montgomery, "Workers' Control of Machine Production in the Nineteenth Century," *Labor History* 17 (Fall 1976): 485–509.

33. Alice Kessler-Harris, *Out to Work: A History of Wage-Earning Women in the United States* (New York: Oxford University Press, 1982).

34. On struggles over the uses of public space in the nineteenth century, see Davis, *Parades and Power;* Christine Stansell, *City of Women: Sex and Class in New York, 1789–1860* (New York: Knopf, 1982). Traditional recreations involving gatherings of lower-class people were suppressed because they were believed to lead to politically dangerous disturbances. See Davis, *Parades and Power.*

In Britain the limits of space were made more acute by the enclosure of common land. See Robert W. Malcolmson, *Popular Recreations in English Society, 1700–1850* (Cambridge: Cambridge University Press, 1973), 107–10. Efforts of the state to limit uses of space are well documented. See Robert D. Storch, ed., *Popular Culture and Custom in Nineteenth Century England* (London: Croom Helm, 1982), chap. 1.

35. Sean Wilentz, *Chants Democratic: New York City and the Rise of the American Working Class, 1788–1850* (New York: Oxford University Press, 1984).

36. Davis, *Parades and Power*, 38–39. On racism in festivals, see Nash, *Forging Freedom.*

37. Peter G. Buckley, "To the Opera House: Culture and Society in New York City, 1820–1860" (Ph.D. diss., SUNY at Stony Brook, 1984), chap. 2; Bruce McConachie, "'The Theatre of the Mob': Apocalyptic Melodrama and Preindustrial Riots in Antebellum New York," in Bruce McConachie and Daniel Friedman, eds., *Theatre for Working-Class Audiences in the U.S., 1830–1980* (Westport, Conn.: Greenwood Press, 1985), 17–46.

38. Robert C. Toll, *Blacking Up: The Minstrel Show in Nineteenth Century America* (New York: Oxford University Press, 1974), chap. 1. On the division of the audience and the proliferation of entertainment forms, see Toll, *On with the Show: The First Century of Show Business in America* (New York: Oxford University Press, 1976).

39. Stansell, *City of Women*, 83–89. There seems to have been little investigation of free black leisure in the nineteenth century, although the study of slave culture was inspired by Eugene Genovese's *Roll, Jordan, Roll: The World the Slaves Made* (New York: Pantheon, 1974). Some discussion of free black leisure in Philadelphia can be found in Emma Lapsansky, "South Street, Philadelphia, 1762–1854: A Haven for Those Low in the World" (Ph. D. diss., University of Pennsylvania, 1975); Roger Lane, *Roots of Violence in Black Philadelphia, 1860–1900* (Cambridge, Mass.: Harvard University Press, 1986); and Nash, *Forging Freedom*.

40. Adelman, *A Sporting Time*. For a turn-of-the-century description, see Jon Kingsdale, "The Poor Man's Club: The Social Functions of the Urban Working-Class Saloon," *American Quarterly* 25 (October 1973): 472–89. On prizefighting, see Elliott J. Gorn, *The Manly Art: Bare-Knuckle Prize Fighting in America* (Ithaca, N.Y.: Cornell University Press, 1986).

41. Lawrence Levine, "William Shakespeare and the American People: A Study in Cultural Transformation," *American Historical Review* 89, no. 1 (1984): 34–66; and *High Brow/Low Brow: The Emergence of Cultural Hierarchy in America* (Cambridge, Mass.: Harvard University Press, 1988).

42. McConachie, "Theatre of the Mob," 19; Francis Couvares, "The Plebeian Moment: Theatre and Working-Class Life in Late Nineteenth-Century Pittsburgh," in McConachie and Friedman, *Theatre for Working-Class Audiences*, 47–60; Levine, "Shakespeare and the American People"; Mel Gordon, "The Yiddish Theatre in New York, 1900," in McConachie and Friedman, *Theatre for Working-Class Audiences*, 69–74.

43. Rosenzweig, *Eight Hours for What We Will*; Rorabaugh, *Alcoholic Republic*.

44. Davis, *Parades and Power*, 167–68; Hardy, *How Boston Played*, 46; Buckley, "To the Opera House."

45. Adelman, *A Sporting Time*, 241–43.

46. Boyer, *Urban Masses and Moral Order*, chap. 16; Rosenzweig, *Eight Hours for What We Will*; Hardy, *How Boston Played*; Dominic Cavallo, *Muscles and Morals: Organized Playgrounds and Urban Reform*, 1880–1920 (Philadelphia: University of Pennsylvania Press, 1981); Cary Goodman, *Choosing Sides: Playground and Street Life on the Lower East Side* (New York: Schocken Books, 1979).

47. Rosenzweig, *Eight Hours for What We Will*; Peiss, *Cheap Amusements*.

48. Boyer, *Urban Masses and Moral Order*, chap. 1, and 238–39.

49. Buckley, "To The Opera House."

50. Hardy, *How Boston Played*, 52, 139–45; Benjamin Rader, *American Sports from the Age of Folk Games to the Age of Spectators* (Englewood Cliffs, N.J.: Prentice-Hall, 1983).

51. Adelman, *A Sporting Time*, 123–26.

52. Alfred D. Chandler, Jr., *The Visible Hand: The Managerial Revolution in American Business* (Cambridge, Mass.: Harvard University Press, 1977); Edwards, *Contested Terrain*.

53. Benjamin Kline Hunnicutt, *Work Without End: Abandoning Shorter Hours for the Right to Work* (Philadelphia: Temple University Press, 1988), 1; also Daniel Horowitz, *The Morality of Spending: Attitudes toward the Consumer Society in America, 1875–1940* (Baltimore, Md.: Johns Hopkins University Press, 1985), xxvi.

54. Bureau of the Census, *Historical Statistics*, pt. 2, 164–65.

55. Horowitz, *Morality of Spending*, 121, 174–75. The terms "time-intensive" and "goods-intensive" leisure are from Steffan Linder, *The Harried Leisure Class* (New York: Columbia University Press, 1970).

56. John D. Owen, *The Price of Leisure: An Economic Analysis of the Demand for Leisure Time* (Montreal: McGill-Queens University Press, 1970), 84–86, 94, table 4-D; Jack Poggi, *Theater in America: The Impact of Economic Forces, 1870–1967* (Ithaca, N.Y.: Cornell University Press, 1968), chap. 3.

57. Laurence Bergreen, *Look Now, Pay Later: The Rise of Network Broadcasting* (Garden City, N.Y.: Doubleday, 1980).

58. On monopolies based on vertical integration and control of distribution networks in entertainment, see Poggi, *Theater in America;* Douglas Gilbert, *American Vaudeville: Its Life and Times* (New York: Dover, 1940); Mae D. Huettig, *Economic Control of the Motion Picture Industry* (Philadelphia: University of Pennsylvania Press, 1944); Barry R. Litman, *The Vertical Structure of the Television Broadcasting Industry: The Coalescence of Power* (East Lansing: Michigan State University Press, 1979); Steve Chapple and Reebee Garafalo, *Rock 'n'Roll Is Here to Pay* (Chicago: Nelson-Hall, 1977).

Early monopolies in mass media were based upon control of patents on technology. See, e.g., Llewellyn White, *The American Radio* (Chicago: University of Chicago Press, 1947); Ralph Cassady, Jr., "Monopoly in Motion Picture Production and Distribution, 1908–1915," in Gorham Kindem, ed., *The American Movie Industry: The Business of Motion Pictures* (Carbondale: Southern Illinois University Press, 1982), 26–68.

On the impact of concentration on British music hall and cinema, see Peter Bailey, "Custom, Capital, and Culture in the Victorian Music Hall," in Storch, *Popular Culture and Custom*, 180–208; Summerfield, "Effingham Arms," 209–40; Wild, "Recreation in Rochdale."

59. Duis, *The Saloon*, chap. 1. Cf. England's system of brewery-owned pubs, described in Christopher Hutt, *The Death of the English Pub* (London: Arrow Press, 1973).

60. David Giovannoni, "The Phonograph as a Mass Entertainment Medium" (master's thesis, University of Wisconsin, Madison, 1980), cited in Jeanne Thomas Allen, "Social Choice in Phonograph Design in the U.S. from Record and Playback to Playback Only, 1877–1929," paper delivered at the American Studies Association Annual Meeting, Miami, October 1988; and Roland Gelatt, *The Fabulous Phonograph, 1877–1977* (New York: Collier Macmillan, 1977).

61. Douglas Gomery, *The Hollywood Studio System* (New York: St. Martin's Press, 1986); Kindem, *American Movie Industry*.

62. Christopher Sterling, "Television and Radio Broadcasting," in Benjamin Compaine, ed., *Who Owns the Media? Concentration of Ownership in the Mass Communication Industry* (New York: Harmony Books, 1979), 67.

63. Peiss, *Cheap Amusements*, chap. 1; Lary May, *Screening Out the Past: The Birth of Mass Culture and the Motion Picture Industry* (New York: Oxford University Press, 1980), 28; John Kasson, *Amusing the Million: Coney Island at the Turn of the Century* (New York: Hill and Wang, 1978).

64. May, *Screening Out the Past*, 32, chap. 8.

65. On the change to a culture of consumption, esp. among middle and upper classes, see Stuart Ewen, *Captains of Consciousness: Advertising and the Social Roots of the Consumer Culture* (New York: McGraw-Hill, 1976); Richard W. Fox and T. J. Jackson Lears, *The Culture of Consumption: Critical Essays in American History, 1880–1980* (New York: Pantheon, 1983); Lewis Erenberg, *Steppin' Out: New York Nightlife and the Transformation of American Culture, 1890–1930* (Westport, Conn.: Greenwood Press, 1981); and Horowitz, *Morality of Spending*.

66. Ewen, *Captains of Consciousness;* T. J. Jackson Lears, "From Salvation to Self-Realization: Advertising and the Therapeutic Roots of the Consumer Culture, 1880–1930," in Fox and Lears, *The Culture of Consumption*, 1–38; Roland Marchand, *Advertising the American Dream: Making Way for Modernity, 1920–40* (Berkeley: University of California Press, 1985).

67. Robert C. Allen, "Motion Picture Exhibition in Manhattan: Beyond the Nickelodeon," *Cinema Journal* 18, no. 2 (1979): 2–15.

68. Jeanne Thomas Allen, "The Industrialization of Culture: The Case of the Player Piano," in Vincent Mosco and Janet Wasko, eds., *Popular Culture and Media Events*, vol. 3 of *Critical Communications Review* (Norwood, N.J.: Ablex, 1985), 93–109; Owen, *Price of Leisure*, 92; Arthur W. J. G. Ord-Hume, *Pianola: The History of the Self-Playing Piano* (London: Allen & Unwin, 1984), 46; Vern Countryman, "The Organized Musicians: II," *University of Chicago Law Review* 16, no. 2 (1949): 244.

69. "$4 Billion Plus B.O. Record Set in '84," *Variety*, 9 January 1985, p. 5; A. C. Neilsen Co., personal communication, 1986.

70. Richard Butsch, "The Commodification of Leisure: The Case of the Model Airplane Hobby," *Qualitative Sociology* 7, no. 3 (1984): 217–35; H. F. Moorhouse, "Organizing Hot Rods: Sport and Specialist Magazines," *British Journal of Sports History* 3, no. 1 (1986): 81–98.

71. Peterson and Berger, "Cycles in Symbol Production"; Richard Butsch, "Rock, Participation, and Mass Entertainment," paper read at the Popular Culture Association Annual Meeting, Baltimore, 1978.

2

PESSIMISM VERSUS POPULISM: THE PROBLEMATIC POLITICS OF POPULAR CULTURE

John Clarke

In this chapter I take up some of the issues raised by the commercialization of leisure in relation to theoretical and political debates about popular culture. "Culture" represents a wider framework within which the analysis of leisure can be situated.[1] "Culture" designates the social field of meaning production (sometimes called ideological struggle, signifying practice or processes of representation). It refers to the processes through which people make sense of themselves and their lives within the frame of possibilities offered by the society of which they are members. It is within culture that individual and collective identities and projects are formed. In Britain, "culture"—and the set of approaches known as "cultural studies"—has been the focus for analyses of ideological power, patterns of domination and subordination, and struggles to mobilize meaning around the social divisions of class, race, and gender.[2]

Acknowledgments: I thank Richard Butsch for encouraging me to think and write about these issues, and those who took part in seminars at the University of Sussex and the Economic and Social Research Council workshop on "Modernity, Culture, and Locality" for pushing me to think more clearly.

The view of culture as the site of struggle over meaning illuminates many issues concerning the historical and cultural specificity of "leisure" itself, not least the historical development of the spatial, temporal, and cultural separation of "work" (defined as wage labor) and "leisure" (defined as "free time"). A cultural history of leisure, for example, casts light not only on the struggles to "win" free time which accompanied the development of industrial capitalism but also the struggles to control the uses to which such free time could be put.[3] Cultural analysis, then, enables us to think about both the meaning of leisure and the meaning of activities or social practices within leisure.

The issues involved in the commercialization of leisure, highlighted by Richard Butsch in his introduction to this book (Chapter 1) have also been central to the study of popular culture. Investigations of contemporary culture have had to take account of the ways in which the means of cultural production and distribution have been both commercialized and centralized over the last century. By itself, this does not mean that social groups have become the passive recipients of centrally produced meanings, any more than the commercialization of leisure necessarily implies that groups do not choose how to "spend" their free time. But it does mean that the conditions under which social groups choose and create meanings are overshadowed by the concentrations of economic, cultural, and political power that the "cultural industries" represent.

The consequences for popular culture of these economic and political developments have been the subject of continuing debates. I outline here two major—and very different—assessments of the significance of those changes. The most obvious starting point is the ambiguity embedded in the very idea of what popular culture is.

In one definition, "popular" refers to cultures that arise from and "belong to" the people (the popular masses, the subordinate classes, or subordinated social groups). This is a historically derived reference, drawing on the distinction between "high" and "low," "elite" and "folk" cultures. This concept of the popular carries an implicitly (and sometimes explicitly) positive political affirmation of the validity of popular culture, relative to the dominant views and standards expressed in "high" or "official" culture. The most resonant expression of this view of popular (class-based) culture was provided by Edward Thompson in his introduction to *The Making of the English Working Class:* "I am seeking to rescue the poor stockinger, the Luddite cropper, the 'obsolete' handloom weaver, the 'utopian' artisan, and even the deluded follower of Joanna Southcott, from the enormous condescension of posterity."[4]

In a contrasting definition, "popular" describes a culture provided for the people but not produced or distributed by them. The first view sees popular culture as produced by the people; the second sees it as consumed by them. The first carries a positive validation of the "popular"; the second stresses the more passive implications of consumption as opposed to production. It opens up suspicion of the motives and intentions of the producers of popular culture and questions the political effects of cultures that do not arise from and belong to "the people."

Clearly, the tension between these two views is intensified in the study of contemporary popular culture, precisely because of the domination of culture by the institutions of mass cultural production and distribution, of which the mass media are the most striking example. The rise of mass cultural institutions means that the task of the political assessment of popular culture has moved away from the rescue and celebration of "popular" forms into the much more ambiguous issue of the "popular" in an era of mass cultural production. Political evaluation now has to confront the consequences of a culture whose dominant forms are mass produced and distributed and in which "popular" participation is primarily defined by the act of consumption rather than of production.

The analysis of contemporary popular culture has become increasingly polarized between two assessments of its political significance, whose proponents I characterize as the "cultural pessimists" and the "cultural populists." This chapter explores the focal points of these two positions before considering how they might be reconciled. I should confess that in discussing these as "polar" positions and emphasizing the ways in which they are opposed, I am undoubtedly less than just to some of their subtleties. Nevertheless, I think this "hardening up" of the positions does no injustice to the main direction of the arguments.

CULTURAL PESSIMISM

The pessimistic evaluation of contemporary popular culture focuses on the primacy of cultural production. It emphasizes the insertion of popular culture into a system where production is concentrated in a limited number of centers and where consumption takes place among a disaggregated populace at the periphery. In these broad terms, this pessimism carries more than a few echoes of earlier, culturally conservative analyses of "mass culture" and "mass society." It differs in the way that it locates the economic, political, and ideological impulses of contemporary cultural production within the processes of economic and cultural power in advanced capitalism. The imperatives of popular culture derive from the tendencies of the dominant classes toward economic concentration and ideological incorporation in contemporary capitalist societies.

"Culture" in capitalism has been commodified: that is, it has been brought into the realm of objects that are produced and exchanged under capitalist social relations of production. From being a practice "of the people"—a self-creating process—cultural production has been taken into the centers of economic power. Culture is profitable. For the cultural pessimists, this is the decisive shift. The "alienation" of cultural production from the people locates it decisively in the heart of the capitalist domination of the social world. Information, entertainment, the pleasures of leisure have all been subordinated to the processes of what Harry Braverman called "the universal market."[5] Access to and participation in them has been increasingly dominated by exchange relationships. People have to buy their way into popular culture, through the direct purchase of clothes, music, and sporting goods, for example, and through such indirect means as buying television sets. Popular culture now demands an entrance price.[6]

The starting point of this pessimistic evaluation is the massive concentration of cultural power that the "cultural industries" represent. Culture is not a marginal aspect of capitalist economies but a central object of investment and production. The enterprises involved in cultural production and distribution have followed the characteristic economic logics of capitalist organization: the process of concentration (the absorption and elimination of competition); the process of diversification (both horizontal and vertical); and the creation of new markets. What is more, they have followed those logics successfully, becoming not merely corporate giants in the fields of communications and culture but also dominant enterprises in the larger realm of multinational capitalism.

But these enterprises also represent a distinctive aspect of the capitalist economy in that they combine concentrations of economic power with concentrations of cultural power. They stand at the intersection of "the economy" and "daily life" (as it is represented by popular culture), linking the logics of capitalism to the realms of play, fantasy, imagination, and pleasure. Needs and desires are directed into the world of commodities, and each new need fuels the fires of capitalist expansion. But the logic at work here is not merely an economic one. The cultural industries are also driven by an ideological logic—the drive to reproduce the ideologies of domination that serve to hold the subordinate classes in their places.

This issue needs to be addressed in two rather different ways. The first concerns the way in which the "industrialization" of popular culture reproduces the social relations of capitalism; the second, the reproduction of specific ideologies. In the first, the transposition of popular culture into "consumer culture" moves cultural production into the cultural industries and changes the participation of subordinate social groups into the act (and relationships) of exchange and consumption. In this sense, the conditions of popular culture reproduce the dominant economic relations of capitalism and extend them to new spheres of life. As Stuart and Elizabeth Ewen argue:

> It is no accident that a *mass culture*—a social landscape marked by consumer industries, mass media and merchandising—developed just when a formerly rural or otherwise non-industrial people were being transformed into a permanent, mass industrial population. The panorama of a mass culture was a bridge between the aspirations of an old culture and the priorities of a new one.
>
> On a narrowly economic level, the origin of mass culture can be seen as an extension of the necessity to generate and maintain an industrial labor force and expand markets. Yet both of these imperatives were inextricably linked to cultural and perceptual processes of change. The creation of an industrial labor force and of markets necessitated an abolition of social memories that militated against consumption.[7]

The new popular culture involved the destruction of previously existing practices and relationships and confined "cultural practice" to the domain of consumption:

> The acceptable area of human initiative is circumscribed by the act of purchasing, given the status of *consumer* and audience. Within the logic of consumer imagery, the source of creative power is the object world, invested with the subjective power of "personality." ... Consumerism engendered passivity and conformity within this supposedly ever-expanding realm of the *new*, which put leisure, beauty and pleasure in the reach of all. Customary bonds of affection and interdependence, born of other circumstances, disintegrated.[8]

This new popular culture individualizes social relationships; turns social interactions into the impersonal act of exchange; and transposes relations between people into relations between things:

> It is a world defined by the retail (individualized) consumption of goods and services; a world in which social relations are often disciplined by the exchange of money; a world where it increasingly *makes sense* that if there are solutions to be had, they can be bought.[9]

A consumption-based popular culture both reproduces and reinforces the social relations of capitalism: it works through them in the sense that participation in popular culture increasingly rests on the exchange relationship, and its messages reinforce the "normality" of the presumption that life is like that. This point opens up the second sense in which the pessimistic reading of popular culture links economic and ideological domination, this time in its content rather than its relationships.

Popular culture is a field in which dominant ideological meanings are reproduced and relayed. The quotations from Ewen and Ewen make clear that one aspect of this is the insistence that satisfactions are to be gained through the act of consumption. Both in mass advertising (and its promises of fulfillment through the use of specific products) and the many forms of popular entertainment that celebrate the equation of success with ownership (from *Dallas* to game shows), the reassertion of the promises of capitalism is a dominant theme of popular culture. Similarly, many forms of popular culture celebrate the "naturalness" of competitive individualism as the elemental human condition.

Equally, popular culture is involved in the reproduction of specific sets of relationships within capitalist societies: forms of domination and subordination between classes, genders, and ethnic groups. It validates and recuperates existing forms of social divisions, rendering them invisible and naturalizing them. Television's *Miami Vice* replays the "border question" and the presumed dangerousness of Central and South America through its obsession with Hispanic drug smugglers. The discovery of the "professional woman" has nevertheless managed to keep alive some of women's "essential" qualities of emotionality, compassion, and care (as in the lawyers of *L.A. Law*). In these and many other ways, popular culture is enmeshed in the recirculation and revitalization of structures of social inequality. And in the process of revitalization, alternative possibilities are marginalized and demobilized.

This is a very truncated representation of arguments about the place of ideological domination in popular culture, and many discussions of it are considerably more complex than my summary suggests. Nevertheless, the range of view—from those that stress direct "reflection" of dominant ideologies to those that see popular culture as a ground in which dominance is "recuperated" against challenges to it—share a common view about the production of cultural meaning. It is one that stresses the dominance of the moment of production as against the structured secondariness of the moment of consumption. Meanings are inscribed and fixed in the act of cultural production and are presented to the consumers. Popular culture as mass consumption fuses the economic and ideological logics of contemporary capitalism and positions the "popular audience" both through its social relations and through the cultural meanings it relays.

The production of dominant meanings and the secondariness of consumption is the point of sharpest contrast between cultural pessimism and cultural populism. In the arguments of the cultural populists, the reproduction of dominant ideologies is an altogether more elusive process.

CULTURAL POPULISM

Whereas cultural pessimism sees the production of meaning as relatively closed at the point of production and therefore thinks of consumption as a relatively passive process, cultural populism starts from a more complex view of signification. It regards the production of meaning as an unstable process, drawing heavily on those analyses of signification that have stressed the arbitrary quality of signs. In particular, the arguments derived from semiology, and expanded in "poststructuralist" writing, that all signs are polysemic—that is, capable of multiple meanings—have been particularly influential. The emphasis of cultural populism is thus on the instability, or even volatility, of meaning: the same cultural object or social practice can be "read" (or invested with meaning) in different ways.

This approach has been influential in studies of youth subcultures and of the creation of subcultural styles, studies that have examined the processes by which the original meanings of commodities have been subverted or reworked in the creation of subcultural identities.[10] Dick Hebdige, for example, described the transformation of the motor scooter by British "mods" in the 1960s from a cheap and functional form of transport into a highly decorated symbol of collective mobility. In this view, consumption is an active, rather than a passive process. It involves the investment of the object being consumed with new significance; it plays upon the possible meanings of the object rather than merely receiving the meaning inscribed within it in the act of production. Meanings are constantly being re-created. Iain Chambers has offered an emphatic statement of this view of active consumption:

> Contemporary urban culture, then, is a complex cypher of its circumstances. Across its surfaces a popular semiotics daily mixes together real conditions and imaginary material. The vivid languages of the cinema, television, pop music and magazines are translated into personalized styles, manners, tastes and pleasures: under given condi-

> tions, in particular situations, we take reality to pieces in order to put it back together with a further gain in meaning.[11]

Where cultural pessimism sees consumption as an act that is subordinated to the conditions of production, cultural populism sees it as a distinct and separate social practice that takes place after the act of exchange. The "consumer" appropriates the commodity and then consumes it, investing it with meaning in the process. Allied to this separation of exchange and consumption is a theory of social difference that provides the cultural motivation for such subversive consumption. The "difference" here is the difference of a multiplicity of "social audiences" or groups of cultural consumers—differentiated by class, gender, ethnicity, sexuality, locality, and age. These social positionings provide the possibility of different "readings" of the same cultural practice or object. The working-class youth subcultures referred to earlier actively appropriated cultural commodities and invested them with meanings related to their distinctive social positioning. Cora Kaplan has explored the implications of this differentiated cultural positioning for such cultural texts as the prime-time soap opera *Dallas*:

> *Dallas* may, in part, be pleasurable to watch not because the fantasy it engenders fulfills our most unprogressive social and psychic desires, but rather because it allows us to make fun of them. Which is surely one way its makers intend it to grab us. Most of the mass popular narrative made today for an international viewing or reading audience has a deliberately ambiguous, even unstable, tone. Enjoy it as melodrama or as satire, *or both*, the texts seem to say. Make it part of whatever political paradigm you like, only enjoy.
>
> Yet that instability of tone exposes, deliberately again, the narrative conventions, encouraging viewers of all kinds to discuss the form and limits of serial soap as part of the pleasure of consumption. This self-aware element of soaps does not make the product radical, but it does tend to make its effects quite complicated and contradictory, harder to pin down as reactionary for all or every class, gender, age and race of viewer. Into that gap between plot and presentation ... the social and political context in which *Dallas* is seen by different cultural, class and national constituencies is inserted, and determines how it will, in the end, be understood.[12]

Two things are worth emphasizing about the view of popular culture offered here. One is a growing concern with the form as much as the content of popular culture, which has led to analyses of the "spaces" left open in its texts for readers to create their own meanings. Such arguments give further emphasis to the polysemic character of culture (suggesting that the reproduction of dominant ideologies is far from unproblematic), paralleled by a view of the audience as "knowing"—understanding the codes and conventions of the cultural forms it consumes and able to engage with them in a distanced and critical way. As Chambers has argued, popular culture is a field in which we are all "experts."[13]

In effect, then, the cultural populists have turned many of the central propositions of the pessimists on their heads. Rather than regarding the creation of meaning as limited to the moment of cultural production, they insist that the practice of consumption is also a process of signification. Where cultural pessimism identifies consumption as a passive position of structured secondariness, populism finds it an autonomous moment of active cultural creativity. Where pessimism tends to see the "consumer" as the dominant social role, populism sees "consumers" as differentially socially located, "reading" from their distinctive experiences. And where pessimism stresses the reproduction of dominant social relationships and ideology, populism celebrates the existence of difference, critical distance, and knowing creativity.

DOMINATION AND RESISTANCE

Weighing the merits of these two assessments of popular culture is a difficult task, as is trying to reconcile them. In comparing what seem to be their relative strengths and weaknesses for understanding popular culture, let me begin by raising two problems about the pessimistic evaluation.

First, a central strand of cultural pessimism is its emphasis on the integration of economic and cultural power achieved through linking the economic structures of the cultural industries with the reproduction of cultural domination. However this position is qualified, it nevertheless points to a structural tendency of popular culture to be a field in which domination is reproduced. The pessimistic "readings" of popular cultural forms, practices, and objects tend to emphasize the ways in which these work to insert subordinate groups into dominant relations and ideologies. The effect is to make popular culture a more or less "unproblematic" field and, in the "hardest" variants of this position, to stress incorporation as a functional quality of popular culture. Doing so minimizes some of the contradictory processes and consequences of popular cultural practice, and marginalizes the problems of how the "people" are inserted into popular culture.

This stress on incorporation or domination through popular

culture overestimates the unity of economic and cultural logics in advanced capitalism. The movement beyond the nineteenth-century bourgeois commitment to "improve" the masses, through rational recreation and rational reproduction, to a more "multicultural" commercialized popular culture suggests that the economic and cultural logics may not combine so directly. Indeed, the narrow economic logic of maximizing audiences and markets may run counter to the "political-cultural" interests of capital. The discovery of new "needs," new markets, and new ways to mobilize consumers may drive sections of capital to "market" cultures of protest and opposition: the counterculture, reggae, feminism, and so on. This raises a question about the sources of popular culture. It has constantly been revitalized not just (not even primarily) by the greater circulation of bourgeois cultural forms ("high culture") but by the adoption and adaptation of popular pleasures and practices from subordinate groups, of which the most consistent example has been the relationship between "pop" music and black musics. Similarly, the processes described by Stuart Hall as cultural "ventriloquism" in the popular media suggest that popular culture cannot be viewed as a field of monolithic domination and incorporation through the imposition of bourgeois forms and meanings.[14]

Second, I take issue with the tendency of the pessimistic view to elide the processes of exchange and consumption. There is rightly a concern with the historical subjugation of popular culture to the processes of the market and the growing domination of the exchange relationship. But cultural pessimism tends to assume a unity of production, exchange, and consumption that links consumption too tightly with the act of exchange. Purchase is not the same as use; exchange needs to be differentiated from consumption. Hence, cultural populism points to a significant weakness in the pessimistic view that the meaning of consumption is inscribed (and circumscribed) by the relations of production and exchange. The pessimistic view of the "passive" consumer is a direct consequence of this elision. I want to hold open the spaces between production, exchange, and consumption as allowing the possibility of difference in the social practices of consumption. Viewed abstractly, "consumption" designates social practice that takes place *after* the act of exchange and *outside* the exchange relation—a differentiation of time and place. In terms of the processes of capitalist economies, it is a "private" rather than a "public" practice and is subject to all the varied social conditions that characterize civil society (and all the forms of social differentiation and division therein).

Together, these two points suggest that cultural pessimism collapses the "economic" and the "cultural" too readily into a single unified system of domination. It closes the space in which it makes sense to talk about difference and resistance, which are the central themes of cultural populism.

Ewen and Ewen are scathing about such a search for "resistances";

> Too often, critics of capitalism turn away from the analysis of ideological power. It is as if the analysis would assert some kind of determinacy, foreclosing the possibility of resistance. Each time the question of hegemony is raised, a story of resistance is told, as if the very raising of the question of ideology threatens the populist fantasy of an autonomous and perpetually heroic "common folk" (read—sometimes—"working class").
>
> To demand that reality only be perceived in the frame of successful struggle, resistance and popular heroism is a dangerous and deceptive game to play. It may stand in the way of political thought and action. The social and historical dynamics of contemporary capitalism should not be obscured in favor of a "working class" that is at the same time downtrodden and autonomous; plundered yet ideologically self-determined. This is the stuff of Hollywood.[15]

This argument highlights the central political tension between cultural pessimism and populism: the relative weight of domination and resistance. The opposition of the Ewens to "heroic" conceptions of subordinated social groups is an important emphasis, but foreclosing the *possibility* of resistance by adopting an overunified view of ideological domination seems to me to be equally detrimental to "political thought and action." Resistance cannot be held "in reserve" as a concept, an afterthought to a story of otherwise successful capitalist domination. The spaces for its appearance (successful or not) must be included as integral elements of the story. Otherwise, we confront only the reality of capitalist domination and have nowhere (no material basis) from which to begin to construct alternatives—except in our imaginations.

This leads me to some of the problems that surround cultural populism in spite of its attention to the questions of resistance and refusal. The radical reevaluation of popular culture that cultural populism represents has both challenged some of the presumptions of cultural pessimism and set aside some of the central issues. I begin by returning to the intersection of the economic and the cultural in popular culture. Many of arguments I have drawn together as "cultural populism" have taken the separation of the economic and the cultural to its extreme conclusion—which is to focus on the cultural as an "autonomous" sphere. This extreme is reflected in the study of popular culture as a domain of texts, signs, objects, forms, codes, and the like, that are radically decontextualized from the economic relations within which they are produced, exchanged, and consumed.

Briefly, there are three significant consequences of such decontextualization. First, it separates cultural texts from their conditions of production within the cultural industries, and thus from the economic, political, and cultural imperatives that those industries condense (ranging from censorship through selection to construction). Second, it leaves to one side the whole issue of the dominance of the exchange relationship. By focusing on consumption, it allows the conditions of consumption (exchange) to remain an unexamined (and uncriticized) "backdrop" to the practices of consuming. In that sense, it has lowered its horizons to what happens within "actually existing" popular culture, rather than keeping open the question of how popular culture is socially and historically constituted. Third, and as a consequence of the second point, it fails to engage with the economic inequalities that govern "access" to popular culture. The "entrance price" created by the dominance of exchange relationships cannot be paid by all. The unequal distribution of "disposable income" (both in the wider society and within households) unevenly conditions access to the consumption of popular culture by class, gender, race, and age.

My second area of concern about cultural populism centers more specifically on the "cultural" and the processes of the creation of meaning. I argued earlier that a central theme was the idea of the polysemic quality of the sign—its availability to carry multiple meanings. Populism has stressed this volatility of meaning and has used it to define the theoretical "space" within which diverse audience "readings" of the same text are seen as possible. The corollary to such an insistence on the diversity of meanings that can be generated at the point of consumption is that the meanings inscribed in production are seen as less than monolithic or fixed. The "original" meanings (or those created in cultural production) are decentered, displaced by the meanings generated in the practices of consumption. This celebration of the volatility of meaning seems to me to be overstated. By decentering the question of cultural production, it leaves out of account the power of cultural industries to limit the range of meanings/ideologies that are in public circulation.

Equally, it underestimates the effectivity of the production or "preferred" or "dominant" meanings within the range of possible meanings of a particular practice, object, or sign. Although cultural production may not involve the power to fix a unidimensional or invariant meaning absolutely, it does involve the power to attempt closure and to narrow the range of possible readings or uses. This suggests that audience "readings" take place within a field of cultural struggle, which might be crudely characterized as reading "with or against the grain" of the preferred meanings inscribed in production. While I do not argue against the possibility that alternative meanings may be constructed in the social practices of consumption, I do see these as having a secondary quality: they are readings/uses of texts or objects already produced with meanings inscribed in them. They are "readings of" cultural products rather than cultural production: they are dependent rather than originating. The creation of readings of *Dallas* is dependent on, and secondary to, the production of *Dallas*.

Further, the construction of a "subversive" or "critical" reading is not a matter just of a position of "social difference" (as suggested by Kaplan) but of having cultural resources that can be mobilized to support and sustain such alternatives. By itself, "difference" is merely a positional precondition for alternative practices. To be realized as an active principle, such difference needs to be associated with a culture of difference: the availability of meanings that can be put to work in the active construction of alternatives "against the grain" of dominant meanings. To talk, as Kaplan does, of social differentiation as the basis of alternatives is to collapse the space between social position and cultural formation and, implicitly, to present a new essentialism that equates social position with cultural practice. In practice, what emerges is a speculative—rather than a grounded—defense of "resistance." Because it is gestural rather than material, it lapses into the "heroic" celebration of resistance of which the Ewens are so critical.

One further point needs to be made about "difference" and "resistance." While the fact of resistance (in terms of the continuation of social distancing, alternative meanings, and so on) demands our attention in the study of popular culture, it is not necessarily a cause for political celebration. Most studies of cultures of resistance also reveal their partial, uneven, and contradictory character—and the limits of their political horizons.[16] Subcultural resistances also need to be viewed as ways of "living subordination." Such a view is an important counterweight to the tendency of cultural pessimism to stress the passive incorporation of subordinated groups, but it is also important not to overestimate resistances by treating them as if they are self-evidently counterhegemonic.[17]

HEGEMONY AND THE POPULAR

Finally, I want to draw together the implications of my comments for a view of popular culture which treats it as a field of cultural power and struggle, and which might allow political analyses that do not lapse into the oscillation between pessimism and populism (and their different forms of political immobilization). I do not claim that any of what I have to say is particularly new, simply that confronted by an unattractive choice between pessimism and populism, I think the arguments are worth restating.[18]

Any analysis of contemporary popular culture must come to terms with the massive economic dominance of the cultural industries. The bulk of popular cultural texts, objects, and activities is produced, supplied, and delivered by these agencies, even though there remain areas of private and semicommercial cultural practice. On the one hand, that dominance poses issues about the concentration of cultural power; on the other, it makes popular cultural practice predominantly a practice of consumption. As Judith Williamson has argued:

> The conscious, chosen meaning in most people's lives comes much more from what they consume than what they produce. Clothes, interiors, furniture, records, knick-knacks, all the things that we buy involve decisions and the exercise of our own judgment, choice, "taste." Obviously, we don't choose what is available for us to choose between in the first place. Consuming seems to offer a certain scope for creativity, rather like a toy where all the parts are pre-chosen but the combinations are multiple....
>
> Ownership is at present the only form of control legitimized in our culture.[19]

The significance of Williamson's argument is not that it equates the economic domination of popular culture with a passive and incorporated "people" but that it registers how that economic (and ideological) dominance limits the spaces and forms available for alternative or oppositional cultural practice.

A similar argument needs to be made about the contradictory character of popular culture, which would recognize it as a field of conflict rather than representing it either as a monolithic reproduction of dominant ideology or as an unstructured array of endlessly volatile meanings. Against the former, the constant revitalizing of popular culture by the appropriation of subordinate cultural practices, meanings, and forms needs to be recognized. But this "appropriation of the vernacular" is conditional, involving struggles to conform and conventionalize subordinate meanings. And quite often it looks like the selective appropriation of the "bad sense" of "common sense" (its racism and its sexism, for example) rather than of its progressive elements. In these ways, we need to recognize the ways in which popular culture, although it may be a field of conflict, is tendentially "structured in dominance," tending toward the reproduction of domination.

None of this is intended to deny the continuing existence of forms of cultural practice involving critical distance, subversion, resistance, and opposition. But it is to insist on two qualifications to that view. On the one hand, the structural conditions of popular culture need to be recognized. On the other, the social and cultural conditions of "resistance" need to be considered. As I argued earlier, Kaplan's identification of social differentiation registers not the *existence* of resistance but its precondition.

The resources for realizing such possibilities are harder to identify. For example, the concept of the "knowing" consumer/creator of social meanings contains two problems. One concerns what it is that this "knowing" consumer knows. A thorough expertise in the codes, conventions, and forms of popular culture (and thus the ability to "play" with them) is rather different from the knowledge and ability to transform them.[20] The Ewens provide this reminder about the accomplishments of mass culture: "Its successes have been founded in the ability to define the realm of popular literacy, the terms of that literacy."[21]The difficulty in analyzing the political implications of alternative and subversive "readings" is recognizing the points at which they subvert the terms of that "popular literacy."

The idea of a "knowing" audience for popular culture also involves questions about what the political effects of "critical distance" from its products might be. Cultural populism has been right to argue against the notion of the people as cultural dupes, but the alternative is not necessarily a population of cultural activists conducting a cultural guerilla war. Mundanely, the critical distance from the institutions of popular culture and their products registers itself as skepticism: "it's only entertainment"; "nobody takes it seriously"; "well, they would say that, wouldn't they?" Skeptical distance may be a foundation for oppositional and subversive practices but is by itself an inert force, a state of "passive dissent." It is a dissent that can lead nowhere unless it is connected to systematic sets of alternative meanings, oppositional practices of control, and subversive vocabularies of "popular literacy." To read *and* practice "against the grain" requires access to cultural resources that can transform passive dissent into an active move in new directions. That is both the political problem and the prospect of popular culture.

NOTES

1. These arguments are developed at considerably greater length in John Clarke and Chas Critcher, *The Devil Makes Work: Leisure in Capitalist Britain* (Urbana: University of Illinois Press, 1985).

2. These issues have been the primary (though not exclusive) focus of work at the Centre for Contemporary Cultural Studies at the University of Birmingham, England.

3. E.g., Roy Rosenzweig, *Eight Hours for What We Will: Workers and Leisure in an Industrial City, 1870–1920* (New York: Cambridge University Press, 1983); Kathy Peiss, *Cheap Amusements: Working Women and Leisure in Turn-of-the-Century New York* (Philadelphia: Temple University Press, 1986); and Clarke and Critcher, *The Devil Makes Work.*

4. Edward P. Thompson, *The Making of the English Working Class* (London: Gollancz, 1963), 12.

5. Harry Braverman, *Labor and Monopoly Capital* (New York: Monthly Review Press, 1974), chap. 13.

6. What follows draws heavily on Clarke and Critcher, *The Devil Makes Work*, esp. chap. 4.

7. Stuart and Elizabeth Ewen, *Channels of Desire: Mass Images and the Shaping of American Consciousness* (New York: McGraw-Hill, 1982), 57–58 (original emphasis).

8. Ibid., 75 (original emphasis).

9. Ibid., 42 (original emphasis).

10. See Stuart Hall and Tony Jefferson, eds., *Resistance through Ritual: Youth Subcultures in Post War Britain* (London: Hutchinson, 1976); Dick Hebdige, *Subculture: The Meaning of Style* (London: Methuen, 1979).

11. Iain Chambers, *Popular Culture: The Metropolitan Experience* (London: Methuen, 1986), 185.

12. Cora Kaplan, "The Cultural Crossover," *New Socialist* 43 (November 1986): 39.

13. Chambers, *Popular Culture*, 185.

14. Stuart Hall, "Notes on Deconstructing the Popular," in Raphael Samuel, ed., *People's History and Socialist Theory* (London: Routledge & Kegan Paul, 1981), 233. The idea of cultural "ventriloquism," has been pursued in a number of works: e.g., A. C. H. Smith et al., *Paper Voices: The Popular Press and Social Change* (London: Chatto & Windus, 1975); and Christopher Wilson, "The Rhetoric of Consumption," in Richard W. Fox and T. J. Jackson Lears, eds., *The Culture of Consumption: Critical Essays in American History, 1880–1980* (New York: Pantheon, 1983), 39–64.

15. Ewen and Ewen, *Channels of Desire*, 281.

16. Hall and Jefferson, *Resistance through Ritual;* Paul Willis, *Learning to Labor: How Working Class Kids Get Working Class Jobs* (Westmead, Eng.: Saxon House, 1977).

17. Critics of the youth subcultural studies have argued rightly that the sorts of resistance with which the studies are concerned contain their own oppressive dynamics, such as racism and sexism.

18. These comments draw heavily on Antonio Gramsci's discussions of "hegemony" and "common sense," and the best discussion of these issues remains Hall, "Notes on Deconstructing the Popular."

19. Judith Williamson, *Consuming Passions* (London: Marion Boyars, 1983), 230–31.

20. Condensed here are a variety of difficulties about what should be opposed in popular culture: e.g., the move from a focus on ideological content to one on narrative and generic conventions (a politics of representation) created arguments about anticonventionalism as the basis of "progressive texts," such that *Miami Vice* can be celebrated for its narrative minimalism or *Moonlighting* for its self-conscious manipulation of generic convention.

21. Ewen and Ewen, *Channels of Desire,* 281.

PART II
COMMERCIAL ORIGINS

3 PACIFYING AMERICAN THEATRICAL AUDIENCES, 1820–1900

Bruce A. McConachie

American theatergoers rioted against the English actor Edmund Kean in 1825. In 1822, Kean had insulted American patriotism by refusing to perform for a small audience in Boston; a year later in England, he was sued successfully by a cuckolded husband, which added to the actor's infamy in the eyes of American spectators. When Kean appeared at the Park Theatre in New York in 1825 to begin his third tour of the United States, the audience refused to allow him to perform. Men in side-boxes shouted obscenities; some threw fruit and denounced the seducer; others outside the theater lobbed rocks through the windows. After struggling vainly to be heard above the din, Kean finally abandoned the stage and sneaked out the back door. The next day he published an apology in the papers. Despite his contrition, a Boston mob treated him no better, forcing him to cancel his performance there and damaging the Federal Street Theatre.[1]

No such public disturbance greeted the performance of Mrs. Leslie Carter at the Herald Square Theatre in New York seventy years later, despite widespread knowledge of her marital infidelities. The Carters' divorce had made national news in 1889, the *New York*

Times branding it "the most indecent and revolting divorce trial ever heard in the Chicago courts." With no other resource than her infamy, Mrs. Leslie Carter turned to the stage. Producer-director David Belasco, hoping to cash in on her notoriety, agreed to coach her. He wrote *The Heart of Maryland* for his redheaded star, ably mixing melodramatic thrills with sexual titillation in a Civil War potboiler. When the show opened in 1895, the critics' response was cool, but audiences flocked to see the scandalous divorcee in a role that combined conventional feminine passivity with suggestive sexual allure. Belasco ran *The Heart of Maryland,* starring Mrs. Leslie Carter, for four months in New York and took it on the road for two years, finally capitalizing on the play's success with a London production in 1898.[2]

In 1825, New York audiences had demonstrated their feelings against an adulterer by rioting; in 1895, they greeted a branded adulteress with enthusiastic applause. Significantly, both situations involved conventional audience responses supported by contemporary public opinion and well within accepted social norms: 1820s audiences were accorded a publicly sanctioned right to riot to protest against an actor's immorality; 1890s spectators assumed that the proper response to a star's adultery was discreet silence mixed with voyeuristic delight. The American public's valuation of marital fidelity had changed somewhat from the 1820s to the 1890s. Yet, despite the liberalization of divorce laws, most Americans throughout the nineteenth century censured women far more than men for adulterous behavior. Compared with the response to Kean, however, spectator reaction to Carter was a non-event. What had changed most was the experience of playgoing, specifically the accepted relationship in the theater between actors and audiences.

To discover why this change occurred, we must focus on alterations in the "rhetoric" of playgoing, alterations in the implicit social and aesthetic contract relating actors to audiences during theatrical performances. The necessary starting point is the traditional theater of the early nineteenth century, when local elites publicly dominated this rhetorical interplay for their own benefit. Only gradually did the star system shift the balance of power from spectator to star control, leaving audience members to praise charismatic performers rather than manipulate actors considered to be their inferiors. In the final phase of this ongoing tension, producer-directors like Belasco capitalized on the public's consumerist orientation toward theatergoing by fusing audience attraction to stars with spectator desire for more realistic illusion. Undergirding these changes was a transformation in social relations, including those between actors and spectators, from vertical and traditional to horizontal and modern. In the 1820s, the normal relationship of local performers and theater managers to local elites was one of craftsman to patron. By 1900, national merchandisers were selling the best theatrical products to a national, homogenized audience, and the relationship of producers and performers to their spectators had become that of capitalist to consumer, mystified by the dazzle of "show biz" and the aura of the stars. Not only had control shifted from the audience to the merchandisers, but the very nature of the theatergoing experience had changed. Rather than enjoying a public ritual in which they played a significant role as co-makers of the event, modern spectators withdrew from the social dynamics of traditional playgoing to consume theatrical products in the privacy of their fantasies.

PATRONS AND CRAFTSMEN

During the first third of the nineteenth century, local elites controlled the actor-audience relationship in American theaters much as they had done in the English-speaking playhouses of the eighteenth century. Theater managers deferred to upper-class tastes in the choice of plays and players, the architecture of the playhouse, and the price of seats. They did so because local elites dominated all the major institutions of the early nineteenth-century city. Philip Hone, one-time mayor of New York and a regular theatergoer himself, underlined elite social control in a speech celebrating the opening of the first Bowery Theatre in 1826: "It is therefore incumbent upon those whose standing in society enables them to control the opinions and direct the judgement of others to encourage, by their countenance and support, a well-regulated theatre."[3] The public dominated the actor-audience relationship through the 1820s. And since the needs and desires of upper-class urbanites were viewed by most city dwellers as coterminous with the public good, audience domination generally meant paternalistic control by the elite.

The upper classes owned all the major theaters in Boston, New York, and Philadelphia in the 1820s and attended them more regularly than did members of other classes. When the Park Theatre in New York burned down in 1820, for example, it was quickly rebuilt and leased back to its previous renters by John Jacob Astor and John K. Beekman, two of the richest men in the city. Elite males might attend the playhouse two to four times a week (their wives and daughters much less frequently) during a season that stretched from early fall to late spring in the Northeast. Generally, they sat with their friends in the fashionable boxes ringing the auditorium above the pit and below the gallery, an arrangement that continued the architectural conventions of the eighteenth century. The predominance of elite attendance may be seen in the fact that box seats outnumbered pit and gallery seating (the conventional preserves of the middle and working classes) in all the theaters built in the 1820s. The Chestnut Street Theatre in Philadelphia, for instance, accommodated more than 2,000 spectators, but of that number only 300 could sit in the gallery and 400 in the pit, leaving about 1,300 in the boxes. In financial terms, the predominance of the boxes was even greater. At 1822 prices, the Chestnut Street gallery had a potential nightly yield of $150, the pit $300, and the boxes $1,300—almost triple the combined revenue of the other two.[4] Although the elite exercised little direct control over the daily operation of urban theaters, they could rest assured that theatrical managers would seek their approbation before deviating from traditional practices. Without it, managers risked a riot, financial failure, or both.

Upon entering the theater in the 1820s, upper-class males might discuss business with a friend or make arrangements with a prostitute. It was not unusual for male spectators to spend almost as much time chatting with acquaintances as enjoying the performance. To accommodate their sociability, owners built large lobbies, spacious saloons, and semiprivate balconies. The Chatham Garden Theatre in New York, for example, boasted "a spacious balcony" where "the sentiments of friendship may be interchanged or any topic discussed, without molestations or interruptions."[5] As this promotional report implies, such spaces might also serve as meeting places to arrange assignations. Prostitutes, frequently given seats at a reduced price by managers eager to please their customers, regularly inhabited the third tier of side-boxes in virtually all playhouses until the 1840s. This not only lead churchmen to condemn the theater but made it impossible for respectable women to attend the plays unless accompanied by their fathers or husbands. Theatergoing in the 1820s remained predominantly a male activity.

No doubt elite males attended the theater primarily for their own enjoyment, but they also sought to display their status and to exercise direct social control. Throughout the antebellum period it was customary to leave houselights on during the performance, partly to increase spectator visibility of the stage, but mostly to allow the audience to see one another. Indeed, the technology of gas illumination—first tried at the Chestnut in 1816 and in general use in major theaters by the 1830s—made houselights during the show increasingly obsolete from a purely aesthetic point of view. A newspaper report on the opening of the second Bowery theater in 1828, for instance, made much of the social advantages of gas lighting. "On entering the box circle," gushed the enthusiastic reporter, "the spectator is dazzled with the blaze of light that suddenly bursts upon him." Further, the back walls of the Bowery boxes were "painted of the apple-blossom colour, as being most favorable to display the spectators to advantage."[6] In effect, the boxes became mini-stages designed to frame their fashionable spectators within small proscenia—stages the elite might use to attract the attention of others when they chose to do so.

In grabbing audience attention for themselves, upper-class males thought nothing of interrupting the actors, who were generally classed as artisans in the social hierarchy. Patrician control of the flow of the performance had changed little since 1810 when, as a fashionable New York magazine reported, the entire Park audience, "as was to be expected, was riotous and noisy, but excepting the throwing of a fork at Mrs. Oldmixon when singing the bravura song, was not guilty of any striking indecorum."[7] When the elite were not ignoring or mocking the actors, they might lead the house in driving them off the stage with booing and catcalls or, more frequently, in applauding their efforts and demanding the repetition of a particularly enjoyable speech or song. The so-called gallery gods, mostly laborers and servants sitting in the balcony, were generally even more vociferous in their praise or condemnation. But their responses usually stayed within the boundaries of acceptable public behavior—boundaries legitimated by elite authority. Similar to Renaissance princes, Restoration noblemen, and eighteenth-century patriarchs before them, upper-class Americans in the 1820s controlled "their" actors, treating them with the same easy familiarity they accorded their countinghouse apprentices.

And most actors had every incentive to encourage this unequal relationship. As members of local stock companies, they knew that the best way of ensuring the company's continuance or climbing its hierarchy was to win the favor of the fashionable. Besides, they depended on elite support to supplement their meager salaries on "benefit night," the once-yearly performance set aside for each stock company member when the actor could choose a leading role and pocket the evening's profits. Popular actors might make half as much from their benefit as from an entire season's regular pay. Thus the stock company's dependence upon local favor, of which the system of "benefits" was only the most obvious example, gave firm institutional support to the patron-craftsman relation between elite spectator and stock actor.

American theatergoers in the 1820s justified their relationship on paternalistic grounds. Men of character and wealth, it was believed, had a public responsibility to exercise their power for the benefit of all. Drawing little distinction between public and private institutions, most U.S. urbanites, the elite included, saw the theater as a public gathering place rather than as a private business organized for individual recreation. Historian Peter Buckley notes that the theater was "public" in a second sense as well: box, pit, and gallery were viewed as a "corporate body which represented the totality of class relations and the structures of power" in a city. Although the homology between the classes of the urban body politic and the distribution of audience members was never wholly accurate, belief in its symbolic reality allowed upper-class theatergoers to exercise their prerogatives in the name of "the public."[8] Not only did this further empower the elite to regulate the rhythm of the performance and the behavior of the audience; it also justified inciting a riot. After all, if "the public" was outraged, why should it not express its indignation and demand justice in a "public" forum?

Even in the Kean riots and similar disturbances, the mob, the elite, and the civil authorities stayed within generally accepted boundaries of traditional rioting behavior. Rioters planned their actions beforehand, determining the placement of their leaders inside and outside the theater and passing the word that women should stay away that evening. By common consent, the rioters limited their fury to the destruction of property, and a cadre of upper-class males not part of the mob usually took the responsibility of restraining the overeager from doing excessive damage. In the protest against Edmund Kean, for example, theater managers did not call in the constabulary until after the mob began breaking windows and pit benches, even though all knew that a riot had been planned. And when Constable Hays finally read the "riot act" from the Park Theatre stage, the mob, having succeeded in chasing the English star away, quickly ceased its disturbance. In short, the public mostly limited its vengeance to elite-approved targets, rarely threatening upper-class hegemony. Implicit elite control of these riots had more to do with traditional habits of deference than with upper-class manipulation of the agents of "law and order."[9]

The decade of the 1820s, however, was the last in which the American elite could be relatively sure of controlling a mob in the theater. By the middle 1830s, when one New York newspaper counted fifty-two riots in a five-year period, most urban American mobs had moved out from under the restraints of upper-class paternalism. By the time of the Astor Place Riot in 1849—which began in an envious dispute between the English actor William Macready and the American star Edwin Forrest—mob violence had become an expression of class conflict. The actors' rivalry flared out of control when Forrest's Bowery followers used Macready's scheduled performance at the Astor Place Opera House to avenge the wrongs suffered by their hero at the hands of English and American "aristocrats." Fearing more than the usual property damage, the mayor called out the militia, which shot into the crowd, killing twenty-two and wounding scores more. As one newspaper reported, "Macready was a subordinate personage and he was to be put down less on his own account than to spite his aristocratic supporters. The question became not only a national, but a social one. It was the rich against the poor—the aristocracy against the people."[10] The theatergoing "public," once generally content under elite paternalism, had become fragmented.

Changes in rioting behavior signaled other social developments during the Jacksonian years, all of which undercut traditional upper-class control of the theatrical interplay between actors and spectators. In the burgeoning cities of the Northeast, working-class spectators began attending their own playhouses, which by the 1840s had gained a reputation among the elite as sinkholes of low melodrama and anti-aristocratic sentiment. During the same decade, purveyors of "museum theater"—small playhouses attached to rooms displaying natural phenomena and fanciful hoaxes—were attracting moralistic spectators of both sexes to their shows. Even the elite were abandoning their favorite public theaters of the 1820s—the Park, Chestnut, and Tremont Street playhouses—and turning to "opera houses," where dress codes and social customs excluded almost all but the upper class.[11] The Astor Place riot, in fact, occurred at a theater primarily designed to house grand opera and its elite supporters. Working-class playhouses, museum theaters, and opera houses were no longer "public" in the sense of embodying in their audiences a representative cross-section of the town. The decline of elite control and the rise of specialized theaters marked the end of a genuinely "public" playhouse.

SPECTATORS AND STARS

The rise of the star system during the Jacksonian era further undercut elite prerogatives in American playhouses and permanently altered the traditional relation of spectator to actor. This new way of doing business dominated theatrical production and reception from the 1830s through the 1870s. Shifting American theater away from local and toward national organization, the star system substituted greater role specialization for what had been essentially a handicraft mode of production. It also forced changes in traditional managerial policies by providing a new path for theatrical success beyond the stock system. In the process, the star system swept away audience control of theatrical communication.

Like their counterparts in England, the best theaters in the United States had been local and regional institutions, tied to their cities by poor roads as much as by real estate investments and local popularity. But though stock companies could not easily move from town to town during the first half of the century, individual performers faced fewer difficulties, especially after the transportation revolution provided them with new roads, canal boats, and finally railway carriages. When more rapid travel allowed a popular player to perform with a local stock company for a week or so and then move on to the next town, the star's freelance status undermined the older system. As theater historian Alfred Bernheim explained, "Playing limited engagements of from one night to two or three months a year, at worst, the star was better able to keep up the interest of the audience than could the stock actor who might be seen once a week or more in a season of forty weeks, and perhaps for many seasons."[12]

While the transportation revolution made itinerant stardom possible, increasing audience need for charismatic heroes made the new system popular. As Victorian social philosopher Thomas Carlyle understood, the rapid pace of nineteenth-century change made hero worship a psychic necessity for many. "That wc all of us reverence and must ever reverence great men" was for Carlyle "the one fixed point in modern revolutionary history, otherwise as if bottomless and shoreless." Or, as historian of Romanticism Morse Peckham concludes, the star performer—whether poet, musician, or actor—became for his audience a fundamental "source of unimagined splendor, order, power and beauty." Hero worship virtually reversed the patron-craftsman relationship: from their followers' point of view, theatrical stars had exceptional, heroic powers that commanded spectators' deepest devotion. In the eighteenth century and before, actors such as David Garrick could gain great prestige with their auditors, but they were not "stars" in the modern sense because their craftsman status limited their ability to control their performance. Nineteenth-century stars, on the other hand, like their counterparts in military and political life, could hush their audiences with a single gesture.[13]

Such control did not pass to the new stars all at once, of course. As audiences grew more entranced by their idols, however, conventions such as an actor's repetition of popular speeches became less a matter of audience demand than a star's act of noblesse oblige. Gradually, audience response to star performers shifted from admiration of the actor's ability to interpret and present a dramatic character to worshipful wonder at the sublime personality of the star himself. By 1870, actress Olive Logan noted that "Americans care much more for the actors than for the merits of the play itself. This predilection is constantly accompanied by a regard less to a perfect ensemble than to the excellence of the 'star' of the evening."[14]

The first American actor to achieve stardom was Edwin Forrest. Packed houses and standing ovations were the rule for his performances, especially between 1835 and 1855 when he was at the height of his powers. One theater manager wrote in amazement of Forrest's effect on spectators: "Witness the furor of audiences subjected to his control, the simultaneous shouts of applause which follow his great efforts, see the almost wild enthusiasm he kindles in the breasts of his auditors and who will deny that Mr. Forrest has got the heart, nay 'the very heart of hearts,' of the masses." Forrest's charisma affected the public offstage as well as on. Actor Lawrence Barrett remembered when "the presence of Forrest upon Broadway attracted marked attention from friend and foe and led to a free exchange of opinions upon his appearance, expressions of admiration or condemnation being as vigorously offered as if in the theatre itself." Forrest's larger-than-life public image led people to name objects of power and danger after him: steamboats, race horses, fire engines, and locomotives. Audiences had respected Garrick; they worshiped Forrest.[15]

Forrest was one of several American stars whose charismatic appeal transformed the nature of antebellum audience response. Junius Brutus Booth, the father of Edwin and John Wilkes, won public acclaim for his fiery vehemence as Richard III, Macbeth, and Othello. Of equal power on the stage was Charlotte Cushman. Her Meg Merrilles, for instance, "half woman, half demon," terrified and thrilled audiences with her "savage animal reality of passion" and her "weird fascination with crime, redeemed by fitful flashes of womanly feeling." Several comic actors also achieved star status, among them James W. Wallack, who, said one observer, "filled the scene with pictorial vitality and dazzled the observer by the opulence of his enjoyment."[16] Like Forrest, Booth and Cushman and Wallack delivered aesthetic shock treatment, and their audiences, in gratitude, termed their performances "sublime"—the ultimate accolade for the high-voltage star.

Three significant new conventions institutionalized the altered actor-audience relationship: the curtain speech, the floral tribute, and the play contest. Kean had initiated curtain speeches in the United States during his tours in the early 1820s. Before that, a manager might appear before the audience at the end of a performance, usually to seek the approbation of the house, but by the 1830s Forrest and other stars had followed Kean's lead, and audiences began to look forward to this chance to "meet" the star out of character. The floral tribute, usually reserved for female stars, gained popularity during the same decade. An 1837 New York newspaper spoke of "male theatre goers who are wont, under the influence of admiration and late dinners, to shower upon the object of their enthusiasm whole boxes of artificial roses and daffy-down-dillies."[17] Occasionally, money and jewelry accompanied the flowers.

The curtain speech and the floral tribute were essentially rites of hero worship bonding audiences to stars, but some critics of the new conventions missed their significance. "What has the audience to do with the actor except to witness, to approve, or to condemn his performance," noted an irate editor, "As things are now," he continued, the star "is compelled to drop the character he is portraying and come, in his private person, before the audience and be be-cheered and be-bouquetted ad nauseam." From a traditional point of view, the editor was right to complain. The star's appearance at the end of the show "in his private person" to accept public thanks was the essence of the new system. Carlyle praised "sincerity" as the main attribute of the hero. Heroes were not to wear masks, not to engage in character-playing before their public, but to appear simply and magnificently as themselves.[18] Curtain speeches and floral tributes partly satisfied audience hunger to see the stars as they "really" were.

The need for "sincerity" in hero worship also lay behind the stars' quest for new plays. Traditional playwrights had written for stock companies, rarely for individual actors. The early stars used the heroes of Shakespeare and others to build their careers, but several sought heroic roles closer to their public personas. Urged on by a rapturous public, the stars were also eager to limit the number and kind of roles they performed, specializing their productions much more than stock companies had traditionally been able to do. Soon after Macready started the practice in England, Forrest held the first play contest in America in 1828, offering a financial prize for the best drama suited to his abilities. His initial contest netted him *Metamora,* the most popular play of his career. Eight subsequent contests yielded *The Gladiator* and *Jack Cade.* Like dramas written for other stars, each of these successful vehicles was "a sort of monodrama, or play with one absorbing character," as one critic complained.[19] Yet they allowed Forrest to fuse the muscular patriotism of his own convictions with the melodramatic rhetoric and action of the hero, thus giving his ecstatic auditors numerous opportunities to cheer the star's public image and his performance at the same time. The audience's desire for "sincerity" in their stars led, in Forrest's case, to self-glorification.

Self-promotion, of course, was endemic to the system. Entrepreneurs of their own careers, the stars pushed stock actors into minor roles, subjugated playwrights to their demands, and grabbed as much money and fame as they could wrest from weakened managers. Forrest, for example, usually demanded and received a clear half of the night's receipts, leaving the manager to pay salaries and expenses with the remainder as best he could. Late nineteenth-century actor Otis Skinner recalled that "caste distinctions were observed" whenever a star rehearsed with a stock company, and "if the leading man or woman noticed the utility people at all, it was with condescension."[20] Skinner was exaggerating, but stars were recognized by all as an identifiable class within the theater profession. Indeed, like their counterparts among energetic artisans in the mid-nineteenth century, most stars thrust themselves into the new middle class by climbing up the bodies of their peers. Self-aggrandizement was the primary path to stardom.

By the mid-1850s, entrepreneurs of the star system had established regional touring circuits that involved most of the major theaters in the United States east of the Mississippi. Among the most ambitious of these businessmen was E. A. Marshall, one of the few to profit immensely from the system who was not himself a star. Extending his control from his base at the enormous Broadway Theatre in New York (seating capacity 4,500), Marshall monopolized the tours of several minor European and American stars by arranging a circuit that comprised his own theaters in Boston, Philadelphia, Baltimore, and Washington plus allied theaters in Cincinnati, Louisville, St. Louis, and New Orleans. Knowing that most Americans came to watch stars rather than stock companies, Marshall was the first manager to initiate essentially "all star" seasons, employing only a skeletal stock company at each theater to support starring engagements. Unlike later merchandisers of theatrical entertainment, however, Marshall's control over his product was far from complete. "Big names" like Forrest and Cushman could arrange to work outside Marshall's circuit or bargain with him for favorable terms.[21] Economically, the star system was a part of the wide-open market capitalism of the antebellum era, too fluid to be controlled for long, much less fully monopolized.

The star system did significantly raise the percentage of American playgoers. Between 1825 and 1835, the first decade that star appearances outnumbered stock performances in the major cities of the Northeast, the number of theaters in Boston, New York, and Philadelphia grew from four to ten. By 1850 these centers of theatrical activity could boast twenty-four playhouses, an increase over twenty-five years out of all proportion to their population growth. Other historical dynamics also played a part—the development of working-class theaters, the greater attendance of women, the easing of Protestant prejudices against playgoing—but audience desire to enjoy the stars was probably the single greatest motivating factor behind the rapid rise. Indeed, during the New York theatrical season of 1854–55, star performances outnumbered stock by roughly 5 to 3.[22]

The advent of "combination" companies—a star plus a full company of actors—after the Civil War gave a further boost to the star system, at least initially. By then, the network of rail transportation was extensive enough for entire productions to tour the country. Stars preferred combination performing because it eliminated perfunctory rehearsals with each local stock company and assured them of a handpicked supporting cast at each stop on their tour. By 1881 there were 138 combinations on the road; by 1894, 234. As might be expected, combination production decimated local stock companies. Fifty companies had operated nationwide in 1871; by 1878 only eight remained.[23] Stock production of popular-priced shows picked up in the 1890s in response to the rising ticket prices of touring combinations, but stock never regained its place as the primary system for delivering dramatic entertainment to American audiences. National stars had triumphed over local managers.

In effect, the stars had triumphed over public control of theatrical interplay as well, since spectator domination had rested on the service function of the local stock company. Upper-class control of the performance was the first to ebb away in most theaters, although the elite did retain some of their traditional prerogatives at the opera house. Audiences in working-class theaters, where managers relied more heavily on stock productions, probably retained control the longest.[24] But legitimate theater across the United States was already a middle-class institution by the 1870s, and middle-class auditors worshiped the stars.

The tight rein these luminaries held on the performance situation did not lead directly to audience passivity, of course. Indeed, in the early years of the system the stars probably increased spectator participation by giving audiences more to cheer about. But public participation is not the same as public control. Gradually, audiences came to count on the stars to indicate those moments in the performance when applause was appropriate. In effect, the leading actors' arena of control during the show moved over the footlights to encompass the entire auditorium, allowing them to structure the norms of audience behavior. Not surprisingly, no major riots against stars occurred after 1849.

Initially, theatrical stargazing had left audiences increasingly powerless but still noisy; the norms of American Victorian behavior in the theater used this powerlessness to clamp down on spectators' emotional outbursts. As more Americans adopted these norms after 1850, displays of emotion in the playhouse gradually withered into decorous laughter and polite applause. Museum playhouses, the first to attract moralistic Protestants (including respectable females) in great numbers, introduced Victorian sensibilities into the actor-audience relationship in the late 1840s. Moses Kimball and P.T. Barnum banned liquor and prostitutes from their museum theaters in Boston and New York and established comfortable "orchestra" seating in place of the traditional pit benches. As a further attraction to female spectators, they initiated matinee performances, featured chaste entertainment such as temperance plays, and furnished their playhouses and museums like sumptuous parlors. Barnum, for example, boasted that his new 1850 "lecture room" was "surpassed in its elegance, taste, refinement, delicacy and superb finish by no royal saloon in the world." His and Kimball's combination of materialism and sentimentality had its desired effect. "Thousands, who from motives of delicacy, cannot bring themselves to attend theatrical representations in a theatre," stated one commentator, "find it easy enough to reconcile a museum, and its vaudevilles and plays, to their consciences."[25] The presence of numerous respectable women in the audience plus an increase in sentimental fare on the stage restrained hitherto boisterous spectators. Newspaper reporters noted that fashionable dandies and hearty workers alike might be seen weeping at museum performances of *Uncle Tom's Cabin* in the early 1850s.

Barnum's and Kimball's success spawned numerous imitations and influenced theatrical policies and architecture at regular playhouses for decades. By the mid-1850s most of the major towns in the Northeast (and several minor ones such as Troy, New York) boasted "lecture halls" in museums of their own. In addition, managers at most theaters replaced pit benches with cushioned chairs in the "orchestra." Several theaters banned liquor and prostitutes, often substituting a "family circle" for the third tier of boxes previously occupied by the ladies of the night. These Victorian trends made rapid strides after the Civil War, culminating in Augustin Daly's Fifth Avenue Theatre in 1875, the height of restrained respectability in acting company, decor, and audience. Daly policed his acting troupe, fining them for lateness and social indiscretions, to ensure the public image of his theater. His playhouse featured large, open balconies rather than the semiprivate boxes of old, and a wide aisle down the center of the orchestra permitted the fashionably late to display their gowns. Of his audience, Daly boasted:

> The purification of the temple of drama has been so thoroughly effected that the worthiest people find it worthy of their affectionate regard. From the topmost gallery down, respectability reigns. The "third tier" and the pit of thirty years ago, with their bars and their loungers, have disappeared. There is no attraction for the vicious. The constant patrons of the drama belong to the class of people who are strictest in the performance of every duty, moral and social.[26]

One of these spectator duties was the restraint of emotional behavior. To curb it, Daly did all he could to attract respectable women to his playhouse, scheduling more matinees than usual and featuring fashionable social comedies.

Writing in the 1880s, comic star Joseph Jefferson remembered when "hissing and jeering" greeted a mistake he had made on stage in the 1840s, early in his career, whereas "the well-dressed, decorous audience of today, when an accident occurs, sit quietly, bearing it with patience and consideration." For the sake of this passive audience, Jefferson urged that the contemporary performer be doubly conscientious:

> Should a picture in an art gallery be carelessly painted we can pass on to another, or if a book fails to please us we can put it down. An escape from this kind of dullness is easily made, but in a theater the auditor is imprisoned. If the acting be indifferent, he must endure it, at least for a time. He cannot withdraw, making himself conspicuous; so he remains, hoping that there may be some improvement as the play proceeds, or perhaps from consideration for the company he is in. It is this helpless condition that renders careless acting so offensive.[27]

For a spectator of fifty years before to believe that playgoing might put him in a "helpless condition" would have been unthinkable. As Jefferson's remarks suggest, the private manners of the genteel parlor had overtaken the public behavior of traditional theatergoing. Formerly dominant American audiences now waited for stars to cue their response, a response further constrained by the dictates of Victorian decorum.

CONSUMERS AND PROFESSIONALS

Jefferson's well-behaved middle-class audience was restless, however. Especially after 1880, the strictures of Victorian culture sent them to their theaters in search of ever more authentic and intense experiences than their everyday lives could provide. At the same time, theatrical production was becoming more realistic as stars turned increasingly away from presentational heroics and toward representational personality. These two trends—audience desire to be jolted by "reality" and realistic illusionism on the stage—reinforced each other and together hastened the arrival of two new institutional roles that were part of the theater by 1900: the producer-director, who fused the thrill of star entertainment and "slice of life" realism on the stage; and the theatrical merchandiser, who distributed the dramatic products to a national audience. Both, in their own ways, contributed to the pacification of the American theatergoer.

The gradual emergence of institutional roles that facilitated the production and marketing of stage realism was part of the general shift from a producer to a consumer culture for middle- and upper-class Americans. The early Victorian values of self-control, industry, and moral development were giving way to the newer notion of self-fulfillment through social performance in late nineteenth-century bourgeois culture. Energizing this shift was the quest for "real life," the "characteristic psychic project" of upper-middle-class life, according to historian T. J. Jackson Lears. Not only did this quest alter the theater; it drove the American bourgeoisie to begin settlement houses, to read adventure stories, to pursue the "strenuous life" in sports activities and imperialistic conquests, and—perhaps above all—to seek identity and success through the consumption of goods and experiences. Personality, the selection and performance of "correct" behavior traits, was replacing character, an inner strength and morality whose conscious performance risked the label of hypocrisy. Further, personality could be purchased—or so advertisers, world's fairs, and a plethora of advice books were persuading middle-class Americans.[28]

With social success becoming largely a matter of consumption and role playing, little wonder that spectators at the theater began to regard stars as models of successful and happy personalities. The stars, for their part, encouraged this identification by selecting plays and characters closer to the social lives of their audiences and (actresses especially) by endorsing products sold to middle- and upper-class Americans. More important, actors were modifying their overall style, bringing it more into line with the increasing realism of sets, costumes, and lights. Early star performing had presented character traits and emotions through rhetorical flourishes and pantomimic poses easily recognized by the audience as typical of heroic action. In contrast, "personality" stars in the 1890s generally represented atypical traits and emotions presumed by their audience to be somewhat unique to the stars themselves. William Gillette, celebrated for his realistic enactment of Sherlock Holmes, drew the audience into the psychology of his characters through deliberate underplaying and nervous intensity. "He seems to be doing nothing but he is doing many things," said one critic, "making a hundred subdued movements of his frame or head or face to reflect every change in the situation." Historian Benjamin McArthur concludes that "where traditional acting was culture- or community-centered, natural acting became individual-centered. The dramatic focus shifted to distinctions of personality. The audience viewed players less as types and more as actual people with distinguishing personalities."[29]

"Personality stars" such as Gillette could go only so far in providing the illusion of "real life" for their spectators, however. Despite their supervision of the other actors and the designs for their shows, stars could not both act their roles and pull all the aspects of a production together into an effective whole. Most stars hired stage managers to help them with this task, but as long as the stars retained ultimate control, complete coordination of all production effects was impossible. Not until producer-directors gained some power over the stars could New York theaters begin to offer the kinds of realistic productions increasingly in demand. Augustin Daly, for example, whose career spanned the 1860s through the 1890s, in his early years fought incessantly with stars over artistic and financial control. By the 1890s, Daly and other producer-directors had established their legitimate authority in the New York theater.[30] Though still vastly outnumbered by star producers and their combination companies, the producer-directors had won a reputation for the effectiveness of their realistic productions. More than to other factors, the rise of the stage director was due to the increasing eagerness of Victorian audiences to experience "real life" in the theater and the ability of the producer-directors to provide just that illusion.

Turn-of-the-century New Yorkers celebrated David Belasco as the foremost realist among this new breed. Belasco increased the power of the producer-director over his mostly upper-class audiences by his manipulation of the theatrical environment. His 1902 and 1907 playhouses ably demonstrated his ability to fuse consumer desires with stage realism. Both were intimate, opulent theaters, seating less than a thousand spectators and furnished with Tiffany lamps, rich carpets, tapestries, and silk-upholstered seats. "I am anxious to make my patrons feel at home when they honor me by coming," he told them in a curtain speech on opening night in 1902, "and so I have tried to make your surroundings in front of the curtain those of a comfortable, homelike drawing room." In both theaters electric lights "were so arranged that the light from them was diffused upon the stage and player without the spectators, even those in the upper stage boxes, being able to perceive whence it came," according to one commentator. Wrapped in darkness by the dimmed houselights of his comfortable theaters, audiences were encouraged by Belasco to surrender the last vestiges of their public control over production and to feed their private fantasies on his masterful illusions.[31]

At the center of Belasco's illusions for *The Heart of Maryland* was Mrs. Leslie Carter. Her curvaceous figure, shocking red hair, and more shocking reputation must have stirred the fantasies of the men and, in different ways, many of the women in 1895. Carter could not have been a star a decade earlier; in the mid-1880s the American public would still have shunned her as a lascivious divorcee. Belasco correctly sensed that cultural mores were changing, however. In their desire to be jolted and thrilled by "real life," the late-Victorian audience had left itself vulnerable, perhaps only half-consciously, to the manipulative strategies of sexual titillation on the stage. By the early 1890s, female beauty had become a significant factor in star appeal. Charlotte Cushman, in midcentury, had been large-featured and plain, but in 1893, proclaimed *Cosmopolitan*, "so great is the might of a fair face that the happy owner conquers managers, triumphs over critics, and wins the golden favor of the public." Further, "personality" stars were no longer expected to lead morally spotless lives. Articles in the *Dramatic Mirror* in 1888, for instance, dwelt on the "Bohemian" habits of New York actors, suggesting a link between their sometimes illicit sexual behavior and their success at leading rich and vital lives. Personality stars, in other words, were becoming all the more appealing to their audiences as they found ways around the formal restraints of Victorian culture. Belasco, a Bohemian himself, seems to have understood that the presence of Mrs. Carter opened up untold opportunities for voyeuristic, peephole theater, provided that realism and respectability masked his manipulation of sexual desire. Accordingly, he built additional vehicles for his emotional star—*Zaza* and *DuBarry* among them—centering on her sensual allure.[32]

Belasco further extended his control over his spectators through the realism of his sets, lighting, and other effects. A newspaper reviewer for his production of *The First Born* (1897), set in San Francisco's Chinatown, noted: "The senses of sight, hearing and smell are violently appealed to for the sake of creating an illusion; for the perfume of Chinese punk fills the theatre and the music is as Chinese as possible." A similar Bohemian exoticism combined with voluptuous materialism in Belasco's production of *DuBarry* in 1901. Although this spectacle eventually condemned the escapades of the infamous pre-Revolutionary courtesan, audiences were treated to several provocative scenes along the way. DuBarry's boudoir, for instance, displayed walls "covered with frescoes in the opulent, voluptuous manner of Boucher and Fragonard," stated one critic. "Mirrors reflect her comeliness. Cupids everywhere, on pedestals, holding up sconces, drawing back the canopy of the great gilded bed, attest the business of her life." Equally compelling and exotic were Belasco's staging of *Madame Butterfly* (1900) and *The Darling of the Gods* (1902), both set in Japan.[33]

Critics generally appreciated the startling effects Belasco achieved by controlling all aspects of his productions, but several denied him the status of a genuine realist. "Realism is truth to the facts of life. . . . It is because his interest rests on surface detail and his insight is limited to superficial reality that David Belasco is not a true realist," noted Walter Pritchard Eaton. Eaton was a better judge of the theater than of his culture, however. It was, indeed, Belasco's lavish attention to the "surface details" that partly accounted for the success of his productions. What for Eaton were illusions of "superficial reality" were for Belasco's spectators frequently thrilling jolts of authentic experience, performed by "personality" stars but couched within a comfortable respectability to cushion the delicate tastes of female auditors. "The great thing, the essential thing, for a producer is to create illusion and effect," claimed this director of theatrical consumables. David Belasco knew his audience.[34]

By 1900, Belascoism had set standards of realistic theatrical production in New York that most other producer–directors aspired to achieve. But a larger audience of American theatrical consumers, just as hungry as New Yorkers for Belasco's mix of thrills, illusion, and respectability, crowded playhouses beyond the Hudson River. How could the cumbersome realism of true-to-life sets and complicated lighting techniques reach the American heartland?

The answer, of course, lay in extending and specializing the "combination" system, the national circuit of theaters featuring stars and their supporting casts. Begun by stars interested in performing with their own well-rehearsed companies, combination playing gradually devolved into single-show tours, popular with most stars because of their smaller expense and with American audiences who increasingly identified the stars with their most successful roles. Joseph Jefferson, for example, began touring *Rip Van Winkle* exclusively, despite his versatility in several parts. James O'Neill (father of Eugene) made a career in the 1880s and 1890s of *The Count of Monte Cristo*. By the mid-1890s several stars had significantly improved the realism of their touring productions. William Gillette's *Sherlock Holmes*, for instance, needed three railroad boxcars to transport scenery, costumes, and props.[35]

But just as stars faced challenges in adopting stage realism, they also found it increasingly difficult to arrange their tours without help from others. As local stock companies folded during the 1870s, control of their playhouses passed from theater managers to businessmen interested in real estate and theatrical booking. To increase their profits, some of these merchandisers of dramatic entertainment grouped their theaters into regional circuits and encouraged the stars to arrange their combination tours through themselves or their agents. By 1890 two merchandising agencies dominated the market, Erlanger and Klaw in New York and its environs, and Frohman and Hayman west of the Mississippi. In 1896 these two agencies joined forces with Nixon and Zimmerman in the Philadelphia–D.C. area to form the Theatrical Syndicate.

Like other monopolistic pools at the turn of the century, the syndicate moved quickly to corner the market. The partners agreed to book combination productions exclusively in the theaters they controlled and to refuse permission to perform in any of their houses if productions played elsewhere. Since the syndicate controlled several of the best playhouses in the land plus many of the critical "one night stand" theaters along major rail lines, most stars had little choice but to comply. Syndicate leaders also coerced independent theater owners to join their monopoly. They had begun with only thirty-three theaters under their direct control in 1896; by 1904, critics estimated that the syndicate shaped the booking policies of more than five hundred playhouses throughout the country.[36]

The new system, however efficient and profitable, completed the transformation of American spectators into consumers. As long as the stars and their combination companies had controlled their own circuits, middle-class audiences had retained the option of making their feelings known directly to the people in charge of the show (even though their willingness to exercise this option had been waning since the 1860s). Now, with merchandisers in New York exercising the real power, the spectators' only remaining choice was whether or not to purchase the theatrical product. In effect, the syndicate had transformed middle-class, legitimate theater into a vertically integrated merchandising system, manufacturing or controlling stage productions in New York and distributing them to a national audience. The rhetorical strategies of Belasco-style realism—in conjunction, of course, with the effects of several late-Victorian institutions—socialized most middle- and upper-class Americans to accept syndicate power as the necessary price for the efficient delivery of consumable entertainment.

Although rivals to the syndicate later broke their monopolistic hold, local influence over professional theatrical fare of high quality did not return to the United States until regional companies began proliferating in the 1960s. Audience control of the performance event, undercut when spectators began worshiping stars, has never returned. Since the 1820s, stargazing, the fragmentation of a public audience, the influence of Victorian decorum, the success of consumer-oriented stage realism, and the control of theatrical production and distribution by national merchandisers have rendered American audiences increasingly passive—a passivity generally reinforced in the twentieth century by movies and television.

Yet there are some signs that such passivity may be giving way to more active involvement. Since 1960, American audiences have been more responsive to productions "in the round," Brechtian political theater, improvisation, and participatory theater—all modes of performing that depend upon a relationship with the audience different from that of realistic illusionism. On the other hand, despite the proliferation of local theater troupes, audiences are reluctant to exercise much direct control over a performance or over a season of shows. Of all of the trends weakening audience influence in the nineteenth century, theatrical consumerism—the tendency to define a performance as a product to be purchased and privately enjoyed—still remains the overriding obstacle to more active audience involvement.[37]

NOTES

1. For an extensive treatment of the Kean riots, see Peter G. Buckley, "To The Opera House: Culture and Society in New York City, 1820–1860" (Ph.D. diss., SUNY at Stony Brook, 1984), 168–80.

2. See Craig Timberlake, *The Life and Works of David Belasco, the Bishop of Broadway* (New York: Library Publishers, 1954), 139–90.

3. *New-York Mirror*, 24 January 1826, p. 382.

4. Chestnut Street Theatre playbills, in Harvard Theatre Collection, Harvard University, Cambridge, Mass.

5. Quoted from William C. Young, ed., *Documents of American Theatre History: Famous American Playhouses, 1716–1899* (Chicago: American Library Association, 1973), 74.

6. *New-York Mirror*, 23 August 1828, p. 49.

7. *Rambler's Magazine and New York Theatrical Register* 2 (2 February, 1810): 26.

8. See Buckley, "To the Opera House," 120–25, which cites definition 10 of "public" in the *Oxford English Dictionary* and discusses its implications.

9. See George Rudé, *The Crowd in History: A Study of Popular Disturbances in France and England, 1730–1848* (New York: Wiley, 1964), 237–57; and Paul A. Gilje, "The Baltimore Riots of 1812 and the Breakdown of the Anglo-American Mob Tradition," *Journal of Social History* 13 (Summer 1980): 547–64.

10. Anon., *Account of the Terrific and Fatal Riot at the New York Astor Place Opera House* (New York: H. M. Ranney, 1849), 19. See also my " 'Theatre of the Mob': Apocalyptic Melodrama and Preindustrial Riots in Antebellum New York," in Bruce McConachie and Daniel Friedman, eds., *Theatre for Working-Class Audiences in the United States, 1830–1980* (Westport, Conn.: Greenwood, 1985), 17–46.

11. See my "Opera-Going in New York, 1825–50: Creating an Elite Social Ritual," *American Music* 6 (Summer 1988): 181–92.

12. Alfred Bernheim, *The Business of the Theatre: An Economic History of the American Theatre, 1750–1932* (1932; rpt. New York: Benjamin Blom, 1964), 27.

13. Thomas Carlyle quoted in Walter J. Reed, *Meditations on the Hero: A Study of the Romantic Hero in Nineteenth-Century Fiction* (New Haven, Conn.: Yale University Press, 1974), 1; Morse Peckham, "The Dilemma of a Century: The Four Stages of Romanticism," in *The Triumph of Romanticism* (1964; rpt. Columbia, S.C.: University of South Carolina Press, 1970), 43. See also Max Weber, *The Theory of Social and Economic Organization*, trans. A. M. Henderson and Talcott Parsons (New York: Oxford University Press, 1947), 358–64.

14. Olive Logan quoted in Benjamin McArthur, *Actors and American Culture, 1880–1920* (Philadelphia: Temple University Press, 1984), 11.

15. Noah Ludlow, *Dramatic Life as I Found It* (St. Louis, Mo.: G. I. Jones, 1880), 691; Lawrence Barrett, *Edwin Forrest*, American Actor Series (Boston: Osgood, 1881), 44–45.

16. Actor George Vandenhoff on Cushman, quoted in Barnard Hewitt, *Theatre U.S.A., 1668–1957* (New York: McGraw-Hill, 1959), 127; critic William Winter on Wallack, quoted in William C. Young, ed., *Famous Actors and Actresses of the American Stage*, 2 vols. (New York: Bowker, 1975), 2:1114.

17. *Spirit of the Times*, 15 April 1837, p. 65.

18. For Thomas Carlyle's views on hero worship, see his *Heroes, Hero-Worship, and the Heroic in History* (1841; rpt. New York: Scribner, 1900).

19. Quoted by David Grimsted, *Melodrama Unveiled: American Theater and Culture, 1800–1850* (Chicago: University of Chicago Press, 1968), 148.

20. Otis Skinner, *Footlights and Spotlights: Recollections of My Life on the Stage* (1923; rpt. Westport, Conn.: Greenwood Press, 1972), 58.

21. See an 1881 obituary on Marshall in *New-Yorker Clipper*, included in Joseph Ireland's "Extra-Illustrated Records of the New York Stage," vol. 2 (pt. 13): 35, Harvard Theatre Collection, Harvard University, Cambridge, Mass.

22. This ratio was derived by totaling all stock and star performances in legitimate theaters (excluding minstrel shows, operas, and foreign-language productions) noted by George C. D. Odell, *Annals of the New York Stage*, 15 vols. (New York: Columbia University Press, 1927–49), for the 1854–55 New York City season. Included were performances at the Broadway, Burton's, Wallack's, the Bowery, the National, Niblo's, the Metropolitan, and Barnum's theaters between 1 September 1854, and 31 August 1855. Of 1,240 performances, those featuring a star totaled 771; those relying on a stock company, 469. Because Odell (6:341–98) does not give a complete account of stars and daily performances, these totals are probably in error; however, more accurate figures would not likely alter the general ratio of 5 to 3. My thanks to Deborah Taylor for compiling these figures.

23. McArthur, *Actors and American Culture*, 10, 8.

24. See Francis Couvares, "The Plebeian Moment: Theatre and Working-Class Life in Late Nineteenth-Century Pittsburgh," in McConachie and Friedman, *Theatre for Working-Class Audiences*, 47–60.

25. American Museum playbill in Ireland, "Extra-Illustrated Records," 2 (pt. 13): 163; comment quoted by Mary C. Henderson, *The City and the Theatre: New York Playhouses from Bowling Green to Times Square* (Clifton, N.J.: James T. White, 1973), 80. I agree in general with Grimsted, (*Melodrama Unveiled*, 75) and Lawrence Levine ("William Shakespeare and the American People: A Study in Cultural Transformation," *American Historical Review* 89 [February 1984]: 62) that the "theatre no longer functioned as a cultural form that embodied all classes within a shared public space" after 1850. Levine, however, following Richard Sennett in *The Fall of Public Man: On the Social Psychology of Capitalism* (New York: Random House, 1976), overemphasizes the extent to which values articulated in the theater before 1850 were genuinely shared by all classes in the audience, and he tends to equate spectator participation with spectator domination of the performance situation.

26. Augustin Daly, "The American Dramatist," *North American Review* 142 (May 1886): 491. On Daly's policies, see Marvin Felheim, *The Theatre of Augustin Daly* (Cambridge, Mass.: Harvard University Press, 1956), 11–46.

27. *The Autobiography of Joseph Jefferson*, ed. Alan S. Downer, (1890; rpt. Cambridge, Mass.: Belknap Press, 1964), 42, 318–19.

28. T. J. Jackson Lears, "From Salvation to Self-Realization: Advertising and the Roots of Consumer Culture, 1880–1930," in Richard W. Fox and T. J. Jackson Lears, eds., *The Culture of Consumption: Critical Essays in American History, 1880–1980* (New York: Pantheon, 1983), 10. See also the rest of Lears's article, and Lewis Erenberg, *Steppin' Out: New York Nightlife and the Transformation of American Culture, 1890–1930* (Westport, Conn.:

Greenwood Press, 1981), 5–110. On the "culture of character/personality," see Warren Susman, " 'Personality' and the Making of Twentieth Century Culture," in John Higham and Paul Conkin, eds., *New Directions in American Intellectual History* (Baltimore, Md.: Johns Hopkins University Press, 1979), 212–25.

29. Norman Hapgood, *The Stage in America, 1897–1900* (New York: Macmillan, 1901), 70; McArthur, *Actors and American Culture*, 186.

30. See Felheim, *Theatre of Augustin Daly*, 15–21, 28–33, 192–93.

31. David Belasco quoted in William Winter, *The Life of David Belasco*, 2 vols. (1925; rpt. New York: Benjamin Blom, 1972), 2:61; Young, *Documents of American Theatre History*, 2:13–14.

32. Joseph Reed and William Walsh, "Beauties of the American Stage," *Cosmopolitan* 14 (January 1893): 294. "Bohemian" actors are discussed in McArthur, *Actors and American Culture*, 160–67.

33. The critics are quoted in Lise-Lone Marker, *David Belasco: Naturalism in the American Theatre* (Princeton, N.J.: Princeton University Press, 1975), 63–64; and A. Nicholas Vardac, *Stage to Screen: Theatrical Method from Garrick to Griffith* (Cambridge, Mass.: Harvard University Press, 1949), 116.

34. Walter Prichard Eaton, *The American Stage of Today* (Boston: Small, Maynard, 1908), 207, 208–9; David Belasco, *The Theatre through Its Stage Door* (New York: Harper, 1919), 167. My critique of Belasco's illusionary emotionalism draws on Bertolt Brecht's excoriation of "dramatic" theater in contrast to the aims of his own "epic art." Brecht charged that realistic plays, by arousing in the spectator only empathy and sympathy for the events on the stage, provided "a sensual satisfaction" that dulled the "capacity for [political] action." He termed such cathartic self-indulgence "culinary," suggesting that bourgeois audiences enjoyed thrilling emotions much as they devoured banquet dinners. See "The Modern Theatre Is Epic Theatre," in *Brecht on Theatre*, ed. and trans. John Willett (New York: Hill & Wang, 1964), 39, 37.

35. Harlowe R. Hoyt, *Town Hall Tonight* (Englewood Cliffs, N.J.: Prentice-Hall, 1955), 87.

36. For the rise of the Theatrical Syndicate, see Bernheim, *Business of the Theatre*, 34–59; and Jack Poggi, *Theater in America: The Impact of Economic Forces, 1870–1967* (Ithaca, N.Y.: Cornell University Press, 1968), 3–27.

37. I discovered after completing this essay that my conclusions accord quite closely with three of the four "deep-rooted historical tendencies which give contemporary leisure relations their specific organizational forms," as noted by sociologist of leisure Chris Rojek in *Capitalism and Leisure Theory* (New York: Metheun, 1985): (1) individuation, "the processes which demarcate the individual as a specific person who is publicly recognized as separate and distinct from others" (pp. 19–20); (2) commercialization; and (3) pacification, dampening "the extremes of powerful and passionate outbursts ... by built-in restraints maintained by social control"

(p. 22). The fourth tendency Rojek lists is privatization, which renders the home "the major site of leisure experience in advanced capitalist society" (p. 19). Theatrical production could never become completely private, of course—live theater is not TV—but it is interesting to note that Belasco's illusionism took the privatization of theater about as far as it could go. Contemporary dinner theaters continue the trend.

"ADOPTED BY ALL THE LEADING CLUBS": SPORTING GOODS AND THE SHAPING OF LEISURE, 1800–1900

Stephen Hardy

In the fall of 1873, Yale and Princeton met in the first game of their long football rivalry. The players had no uniforms or equipment as we think of them now. They played a soccerlike game under rules agreed on just one month earlier. But only four colleges shared these rules. On most campuses football was an informal, unorganized, intramural pastime, and the Yale-Princeton match was still a casual affair—so casual, in fact, that no one had brought a football, and the game was delayed an hour and a half until one could be found.[1]

Twenty years later, teams throughout the country were playing a distinctly American game of football under a standard code of rules, with standard formations and tactics. They also had plenty of footballs and special football uniforms, made in America and clearly products of a prospering sporting goods industry—a network of

Acknowledgments: I am grateful to the following for assistance: Ann Chaney, Jose Alvarez, and Mary Daniels in Manuscripts and Archives, Baker Library, Harvard University; Fran Caplan, Caroll Eckroat, Robert Lockard, Margot Turner at Robert Morris College; and Melvin Adelman, Steven Gunn, Steven Riess, Ronald Smith, Nancy Struna, Dean Sullivan. I also thank the Dun & Bradstreet Corp. for permission to quote from the R. G. Dun & Co. Collection.

manufacturers, distributors, and retailers that had meshed in the late 1860s as baseball became the national pastime. By 1899 Henry Chadwick, the immigrant "father" of baseball, could write that "our Yankee manufacturers now control the supply of sport goods the world over."[2]

Chadwick neglected to say that sporting goods firms played a much larger role: they did not simply supply goods to meet existing demand; in baseball, football, and other sports they helped expand and shape the demand for special game forms. Further, through their involvement with such nascent governing bodies as the National League, the Intercollegiate Football Association, and the United States National Lawn Tennis Association, sporting goods firms helped turn informal activities into commodities of fun and spectacle. This collaboration set the foundation for an even larger sports industry: an interlocking network of the rules committees, trade associations, manufacturers, and professional groups that have heavily influenced both the range and styles of sports in America.[3]

Sociologists refer to this process as "institutionalization." Richard Gruneau, Alan Ingham, and John Loy have emphasized its importance to the world of sport by posing the question, "How does *a* way of playing become *the* way of playing?" Think of football. Of the many styles of play available in 1873, why did one style conquer America to become an institution, taken for granted on New Year's Day and Super Bowl Sunday? To seek the answer is to uncover the bones of rival leagues and rival game forms strewn across a vast cultural battlefield.[4]

Such struggles have several outcomes. Not only do certain game forms dominate interest, but certain clusters of organizations begin to control the practices surrounding those games. The National Football League, the National Collegiate Athletic Association, the United States Golf Association, and the United States Tennis Association are examples of dominant groups that manage dominant game forms. They supervise the playing and the players; moreover, they exercise extraordinary influence on the career plans of young Americans who base educational and life-style choices on regulations governing eligibility and competition.

John Clarke and Chas Critcher note that a similar process has occurred over the last two centuries throughout much of the leisure domain: though informal pastimes remained a central part of most people's life styles, "the major forms of organized leisure were outside the control of those who enjoyed them"; and though controlling bodies could not ignore their consumers—whether in football, model building, music, or dance—"the essential relationship was that of provider and customer."[5]

These "new providers" determined much of the leisure revolution that turned informal pastimes into commodities. But their importance goes well beyond the issue of commercializing football or music or art. They raise an issue about the nature of leisure itself. Leisure is typically thought of as self-determined, creative, and fulfilling. But if an industry of "providers" selects the goods, facilities, and services we use in our leisure, then is it still leisure? This question is philosophical. The question of institutionalization and control, however, is historical.[6]

Scholars considering the institutionalization of American sport have correctly focused on the growth of bureaucracies—voluntary associations, corporate businesses, state agencies—and the struggles among them. At the same time, research has looked at the ideological debates and legal battles among sporting elites: the Amateur Athletic Union versus the NCAA, the National League versus the Brotherhood, Yale's Walter Camp versus Harvard's Charles W. Eliot. Historians have vividly described most of the key antagonists and their competing ideas about what sport should mean, but formal opinion offers only limited explanation of why some activities and their sponsors caught the fancy or devotion of a wide range of consumers. Another source of explanation lies in the physical materials that consumers used to participate in leisure. Equipment and uniforms provide important clues about how sports developed. Indeed, an examination of sporting goods takes us out of the realms of high ideology into the store windows, onto the streets, and all over the playgrounds of history, where sports were lived experience and not just written expressions.[7]

Of course, sporting goods are not value free. Like all goods, they are physical expressions of ideology, and that is precisely their importance. As anthropologist Mary Douglas argues, goods are the markers of culture itself. Consumers of goods share names, legends, histories, and behavior patterns that correspond with special products and brands of products: in all segments of life, "the stream of consumable goods leaves a sediment that builds up the structure of culture like coral islands."[8] Balls, bats, spikes, hats, sticks, gloves have built up the structure of America's sporting culture, and they continue to do so. In fact, a recent estimate revealed that such goods make up almost one-third of the "gross national sports product." Ticket sales and television nurture our sports fantasies; consumable goods shape our sporting practices.[9]

This chapter considers the historical influence of sporting goods on America's sporting culture, particularly during the nineteenth century, when many of the forms developed that we take for granted today. After describing the growth of sporting goods firms and markets, I look at how the industry and its products aligned with other "providers" to institutionalize certain types and styles of games. My focus is on those sports that take the form of rulebound, competitive play such as baseball and football, but it is important to note the influence of fishing and hunting during the early nineteenth century. These traditional field sports provided the basis for the earliest periodicals devoted to promoting outdoor activities; they were the source of the initial markets for specialized sporting equipment; and it was frequently the journalists and merchants of field sports who became product champions for the "new" varieties of games that emerged during the middle third of the century.[10]

SPORTS MARKET FOUNDATIONS, 1800–1860

American colonists brought traditional sports to the new world as part of their cultural baggage. These activities were integral to life styles that could be patrician or plebeian, segregated or communal, urban or rural. Rules, records, and reputations were basically *local* accords, although eighteenth-century elites did begin to nurture and formalize wider understandings about behavior and attitudes appropriate to such activities as horse racing. Even so, in 1800 there were few published works on sport and leisure. By the mid-nineteenth century, however, ingenious journalists and entrepreneurs had circulated persuasive arguments about the value of fishing, hunting, horse racing, rowing, and other activities assisting Americans to confront the disruption and uncertainty of an emerging urban and industrial order.[11] Their publications—*American Farmer, American Turf Register, Spirit of the Times,* and assorted books and monographs—contributed to a slow expansion of local to regional to national accords about sports and leisure. They represent the beginnings of an industry of providers, even though the production of sporting goods appears to have lagged behind the production of formal ideology. Through the first half of the century, consumers who could *read about* sports in speciality publications tended to *play* sports with goods furnished through homecrafting, merchant importers, or local artisans. Not until the mid-century would they enjoy the products of large-scale, integrated manufacture from American specialty firms.

Homecrafting was the most traditional form of production, for which many nineteenth-century books provided instructions, suggesting the authors' awareness of the limited production of ready-made goods. Early handbooks for boys often contained such instructions. William Clarke's *Boy's Own Book* (1834) and the *Boy's Treasury* (1847) both explained, for example, how to make a baseball by cutting India rubber bottles into coils that could be wound round a cork, then covered with a tight winding of wool yarn and a hand-stitched leather cover. In similar fashion, *The Boy's Own Book*—an often praised "bible" for middle-class youth—noted that footballs should be made of "light materials—a blown bladder, cased with leather, is the best." It also advised that the easiest method of making fishing line lay in the use of a "little machine which may be bought at most of the shops where also you purchase your lines, if you think fit." *The American Anglers Book* (1865), aimed at an older audience, contained a chapter on rodmaking that listed the equipment a nineteenth-century do-it-yourselfer would need—bench, vise, knife, jack plane and fore plane, files, paper—and included a picture of a steel template of notches and gauged holes of various diameters. One can imagine that many anglers found the instructions simpler on paper than in practice.[12]

Homecrafting continued as a popular and necessary art throughout the century, though the mention of "shops" indicates that wealthier sportsmen might opt to buy custom or ready-made equipment. In a sample of Maryland estate inventories, Nancy Struna found that the ratios of sporting goods to total inventories rose from under 6 percent in 1770 to over 26 percent in 1810. While the lists do not distinguish homemade from finished goods, they probably do reflect a movement toward the latter, as well as wider sporting interests among wealthy and middling well-to-do Marylanders.[13]

Struna wisely concludes that "no consumer revolution occurred" during that period. Nonetheless, even before the Revolutionary War, urban merchants offered stocks of imported goods, mostly from England. One James Rivington advertised shuttlecocks, cricket balls, and tennis rackets in New York. Jeremiah Allen imported bamboo, dogwood, and hazel fishing rods to Boston. Rivington and Brown offered Philadelphians an assortment of sporting goods that included quail nets and cock spurs. English goods would continue to enjoy periods of popularity that coincided with the importation of new activities from Albion's workshop of sport.[14]

Until the mid-nineteenth century, however, most finished sporting goods on both sides of the Atlantic came from the shops of small craftsmen. Struna found that there were numerous such artisans by the late 1700s: Hardress Waller of Norfolk, for example, sold his finished ivory billiard balls for ten shillings a pair. While such equipment was typically a small item among larger areas of craft, such as leather- or woodworking, the evidence does suggest some slight movement toward specialization before the Civil War, particularly for field sports. Two of the oldest specialty firms were located in Philadelphia. George W. Tryon, a gunsmith, bought out his mentor in 1811 and began to develop a special niche with sportsmen. In 1836 son Edward persuaded him to expand the business by importing fishing tackle from England. Under the name of Edward K. Tryon, the firm would become a major wholesaler of sporting goods east of the Mississippi. Tryon nevertheless had competition: in 1826 gunmaker John Krider opened his "Sportsman's Depot" and also began retailing angling apparatus. While he advertised the finest in imported goods for hunting and fishing, he also complained of unnamed "scribblers" of American field sports who spent too much time glorifying British goods. He suspected that these early sports journalists were "paid by London gunmakers to puff their work on this side of the Atlantic." No doubt they were, as the competition became stiffer. The first useful American fishing guide, which appeared in 1845, claimed that American-made rods had overtaken their British counterparts in volume and quality. The compiler was a New York tackle dealer who operated "The Angler's Depot."[15]

Such dealers slowly multiplied during these years. William T. Porter's *Spirit of the Times* ran advertisements for several New York establishments. One was "Hinton's Military and Sportsmen's Warehouse and Manufactory," where one could buy "on reasonable terms" a variety of muskets, pistols, cartridge boxes, trout rods "of all descriptions," single and multiplying reels, sinkers, hooks, files of all types, and even boxing gloves. William Read & Son carried similar goods in Boston, as did Samuel Bradler's store at the "Sign of the Angler." By the 1840s the *Spirit* had notices for cricket bats and stumps, such as those manufactured by Philadelphia's William Bradshaw, reflecting an expanding notion of "sport."[16]

The trend toward specialization represented by these firms was slow to evolve before the Civil War, but one can find clear evidence of public awareness that a separate industry was emerging, one that supplied goods and services for consumption during leisure time.[17] Leisure was a small but special niche for the sharp entrepreneur such as Jonas Chickering, who rationalized the production of pianos in his Boston factory during the 1830s. Perhaps the best example of the markets and the fortunes to be made in sports lies in the career of Michael Phelan, arguably America's first prominent sports hustler. Phelan, an Irish immigrant, began in the 1840s as a "marker" in a New York billiards saloon. After a sojourn to the California gold country, he returned to New York in the early 1850s to make and sell his own billiards equipment. In 1857 a local credit agent could find little in his reputation or his means to warrant a good rating and characterized him in 1860 as a "fast man, betting on horse races or anything that turns up." Yet it was also obvious that the firm of Phelan and Collender was doing a "large business." Phelan's promotions through playing tours and books all paid off. By 1866 his personal worth was estimated to be at least $250,000.[18]

One of Phelan's major competitors was the Cincinnati firm of Swiss immigrant John Brunswick. A carriagemaker by training, Brunswick built his first billiard table in 1845, viewing it as a challenge in woodworking as much as a source of profit. His craftmanship found an eager market, however, and within two years orders were arriving from cities as distant as New Orleans and Chicago. By the time of the Civil War the "J. M. Brunswick & Brother" company was operating a large factory that employed seventy-five hands and produced $200,000 worth of tables.[19]

Phelan and Brunswick were extraordinary successes in a young sporting goods industry. Although field sports and horse racing (thoroughbred and harness) enjoyed widespread popularity in the antebellum years, there was no real national market for brand-name goods related to those activities. Similarly, while rowing, cricket, and baseball were gaining participants and spectators, their equipment production had not yet developed beyond the limited artisan stage. The 1860 *Census of Manufactures* reflects the marketplace: federal enumerators recognized discrete categories for billiard cues, billiard and bagatelle tables, pianos, playing cards, toys, and games; there is no mention of cricket or baseball equipment. In the next two decades, however, sporting goods would become a separate segment of manufacture.[20]

MARKET RECOGNITION, 1860–1880

The next twenty years saw the clear emergence of a sporting goods industry. The conditions—social, economic, and cultural—were ripe for it, despite or perhaps because of the Civil War. The expansion of rail lines, improvements in printing, and advances in production technology combined with anxieties about social dissolution, exhaustion, and degeneracy to provide a most opportune moment for marketing products linked to wholesome recreation. But even fertile ground requires husbandry and cultivation. This was especially true for such "new" sports as baseball, croquet, football, tennis, and bicycling, which most Americans viewed as exotic and frivolous indulgences.[21] It was one thing to write an article or book promoting the value of a new activity; it was quite another to risk capital and credit in the production or sale of sports equipment. Nevertheless, venturesome souls did gamble on opportunity. During this period two types of entrepreneurs emerged, both in manufacturing and in retail. The first were those who diversified into the "new" sports, either from field sports or from a non-sports product. The second, often athletes or former athletes, opened businesses solely devoted to sports. Their combined activities meant that Americans could for the first time enjoy a steady and increasing supply of finished sporting goods.

Baseball offers the clearest example. As early as the 1850s its promoters had proclaimed it the "National Pastime," and growth in participation had been impressive, but there is little evidence of a baseball goods industry until after the Civil War. The 1870 census was the first to list "baseball goods" as a discrete category of manufacture, and even then it showed a paltry five companies—three in New York and two in Massachusetts—employing a total of only 118 workers, with an aggregate capital value of $24,500 and product value of $72,605. This is in sharp contrast to a frequently cited claim in the *Baseball Player's Chronicle* of 17 June 1867 that every city had a "regular bat and ball manufactory . . . turning out bats by the thousands and balls by the hundreds."[22]

The discrepancy may be explained in part by the *Chronicle's* boosterism and in part by the still-casual nature of the census itself. It is more likely, however, that many a "bat and ball manufactory" was a sidelight enterprise in a larger firm. The credit ledgers of R. G. Dun & Co. show, for instance, that Charles W. Jencks & Brothers in Providence produced paper boxes, particularly those used in the packaging of perfumes. As early as 1875 and into the next decade, however, the firm also operated the "American Base Ball Co." In similar fashion, the Philadelphia firm of J. D. Shibe & Co. was listed as a manufacturer of "fancy leather goods," but in 1882 its credit report notes that it had "been in the manufacture of base balls for a long time." By 1883 about sixty hands were devoted to the baseball side of the business, and a year later the firm's account lists it as a baseball manufacturer—appropriate recognition of its conversion into the expanding industry. Apparently, brother Benjamin Shibe had thought the family too slow in adjusting to the market: three years earlier he had taken his $400 interest and joined the Reach Sporting Goods firm.[23]

The R. G. Dun credit ledgers do not indicate exactly when these firms first diversified to include baseball products, but their doing so appear to represent the sort of gradual activity that baseball promoters recognized and census enumerators missed. As late as 1895 the *Sporting News* reported that the production of uniforms was not far removed from the days of "putting it out" to undisclosed manufacture. Many entrepreneurs were slow to convert to all-sports production. Hillerich and Bradsby, now famous for their baseball bats, began in 1859 as a small wood-turning shop in Louisville, where J. Frederich Hillerich crafted such products as bedposts, handrails, balusters, tenpins, and bowling balls. When his son "Bud" encouraged him in 1884 to expand into the production of baseball bats, the conservative father resisted, seeing greater market potential in the current rage for swinging butter churn booms, and little profit in a "mere game." Only slowly did Bud's persistence succeed in converting the firm.[24]

Other entrepreneurs were more eager. Often athletes themselves, with a feel for the market's potential, they typically began in retail operations, which required less initial capital investment. Their established reputations as athletes doubtless aided their young businesses, but it was aggressive promotion of sport and careful integration into manufacture that enabled some to become giants in the field. Al Reach, celebrated subject of an 1863 bidding war between several supposedly "amateur" baseball teams, wound up in Philadelphia; by 1869 he had opened a retail outlet there for cigars and other goods, including baseball equipment. In 1874 his stock's estimated value was $3,000 to $4,000. Throughout the next decade he expanded his line of sporting goods, probably first selling the "Reach" name brand by farming out manufacture to existing companies such as the Shibe brothers, who made baseballs as a sideline. Benjamin Shibe's defection to Reach may have been the catalyst for expansion; in any case, by the late 1880s Reach had integrated into manufacture and had agents around the country selling his brand.[25]

Another professional ballplayer who turned to the new market was George Wright, who opened his Boston store in 1871 while he was still playing for the local Red Stockings. His salary was the store's only capital in the early years, but in 1879 Wright brought a wealthy partner, H. A. Ditson, into the firm. Despite generous credit the partners were cautious and in 1881 carried a stock worth only about $5,000, yet two years later they were "monopolizing the bulk of the trade" in Boston. Recognizing the value of celebrity status, Wright began to market goods under the name brand Wright and Ditson. For a number of years his fellow star John F. Morrill served as the firm's general manager.[26]

The greatest exemplar of the gamesman turned goodsman was Albert G. Spalding, who started later but would within two decades outstrip and silently acquire both Reach and Wright. In March 1876, however, A. G. and his brother J. Walter opened a modest Chicago retail store, which they claimed to credit agents was capitalized at about $2,500. Spalding's cash sales policy, his prominence and salary as a ballplayer, and his Rockford, Illinois, property clearly bolstered his credit, but it was his shrewdness in marketing and backward integration that ensured rapid growth. Within two years the Spaldings' stock of goods had more than tripled, to about $12,000 in value. Late in 1878 the Spaldings and their wealthy brother-in-law William J. Brown purchased half the stock of Wilkins Manufacturing Co., a firm in Hastings, Michigan, that was already making bats, skates, fishing gear, and croquet equipment. For the first time in America a sporting goods house began on a large scale to sell goods of its own make.[27]

Reach, Wright, and Spalding were noteworthy successes in the sporting goods industry. Hundreds of others had an eye on this marketplace, especially at the retail level: hardware stores, department stores, and the old field sports "depots" diversified their lines to include goods for baseball, croquet, and other sports. A similar expansion occurred in manufacturing. The census of 1880 counted eighty-six firms in the newly defined category of "sporting goods" manufacture—almost double the number found in 1870 for baseball, croquet, and field sports equipment combined (guns were a separate category). And despite the severe economic woes of the 1870s, aggregate capital in sporting goods manufacture had more than doubled, to $1,444,750—the largest rate of increase until the twentieth century if one excludes the bicycle industry.[28]

Still, this figure was less than one-fifth the capital value of, for example, the fancy paper box industry, and some credit agents were skeptical about the prospects for sporting goods. Dun's Brooklyn agent noted in 1875 that the new firm of Heege and Kiffee faced a cloudy market; chances for success "in their locality" appeared "somewhat doubtful," since the demand for "this class of goods" was "very limited." As late as 1882 a Boston agent thought it unlikely that there was business enough for Wright and Ditson to make money.[29] The credit agents were wisely cautious, for in the 1870s entrepreneurs were probably hurtling ahead of market demand.

COMPETITION IN THE MARKETPLACE, 1880–1900

If the 1870s were a period of market recognition, with entrepreneurs becoming aware that sports could provide more than an artisan-level trade, the 1880s saw a mass of capitalists on the make. Product markets became arenas of competition among manufacturers and retailers easily as intense as the rivalries emerging on the diamond or the gridiron. Improved economic conditions doubtless had an encouraging effect. So did the nation's stronger embrace of physical activity. The calls had been issued by reformers for over forty years; the 1880s, however, brought peace, relative prosperity, and expanded public space to go along with a heightened consciousness of the benefits of sport and exercise. Equally important, increased numbers of sporting goods manufacturers and retailers expanded their efforts to attract consumers.

There were few barriers to entry in the 1880s, especially with infant sports like tennis and football. These replicated the cycle of initial dependence on imports and small-scale manufacture, with eventual movement toward large-scale manufacture. Wright and Ditson, Bancroft of Rhode Island, and D. W. Granbery of New York all prospered through their efforts in the promotion of tennis. Lester C. Dole's small New Haven store, opened in 1880, made a strong name for itself by supplying the prominent college football teams with "official" imported English rugby balls.[30]

Around the country, entrepreneurs moved into sporting goods production and distribution. In 1888 the Rawlings Brothers opened in St. Louis, promising a "full-line emporium" of all goods, although they also claimed a specialty in baseball uniforms and gloves. Rawlings had strong competition in St. Louis from C. & W. McClean, which diversified into the new lines from the production and sale of field sports equipment. Stronger still was the Meachan Arms Company, which moved beyond guns and powder into baseballs and bicycles. In Philadelphia the Tryon brothers expanded their line of sporting goods. In Covington, Kentucky, Philip Goldsmith was moving out of toy production and into sports, having recognized that cheap baseballs were his hottest product. Through mergers, his firm eventually grew into the giant MacGregor Company.[31]

Firms scrambled for market share. Al Reach sought control through rationalized production, greater volume, and wider price ranges. Under the direction of Benjamin Shibe, the Reach plant in Philadelphia set standards for quality and consistency. While cheap balls could be made by covering a compressed pulp of poor yarn and rubber, the better balls required careful attention to winding layers of yarn around a small rubber center. The outer cover of leather was always handstitched. High-grade balls remained a labor-intensive product, although machines developed in the 1890s automated the winding process. In 1899 the Reach plant had machines said to wind upward of 18,000 balls a day, but only four years earlier the *Sporting News* estimated that over a thousand workers toiled inside the building preparing the balls for the final covers, which were stitched on by hundreds of women doing sweatshop labor at home. Writer A. H. Spink marveled at the range of balls the plant could produce, from the $1.50 Association Ball to the nickel ball used all over the country's back fields and side streets. The style names were dazzling: Deadball, Bounding Rock Ball, Out of Sight Ball, Cock of the Walk Ball. Spink was further amazed that Reach could produce a good leather glove selling for as little as twenty-five cents. Even the top-of-the-line Buckskin fielder's glove was priced at only $3.00.[32]

Because such quantities of sporting goods could bring "clutter" to the marketplace, manufacturers responded by promoting brand recognition. One of their shrewdest practices was the publication of "guidebooks." Of course, introductions to sports activities were nothing new. Treatises on field sports date back at least to Xenophon; Dame Juliana Berners and Sir Izaak Walton carried a long tradition into the modern age. And as noted earlier, there were many "boy's books" and adult guides to sports of all kinds, often providing details about the construction of equipment. What proliferated in the late 1800s, though, were guidebooks published by sporting goods manufacturers who promoted activities in the hope of creating customers for *their brands* of finished products.[33]

Baseball is a good example. As David Voigt has showed, the earliest guidebooks—*Beadles Dime Base Ball Player* (begun 1860) and *Dewitt's Base Ball Guide* (begun 1868)—came from firms outside of baseball. This began to change in 1876, when Spalding got exclusive rights to publish the "official" book of the National League—and at the same time slyly began to produce a separate *Spalding's Official Baseball Guide,* the word "official" clearly intended to convince the consumer that he was purchasing the league book. Ethics aside, the Spalding guide was probably a better purchase; at ten cents it included not only the league rules and constitution but also records, descriptions of the past season's play, instructions, and history. The reader was also introduced to Spalding products. Peter Levine has carefully documented Spalding's efforts to expand both the guide's circulation and its advertising.[34]

Spalding was not alone. In 1883, Reach began publishing his own guide, which was "official" to the American Association and later to the American League. Then George Wright joined the fray, publishing the "official" guide of the Union Association in 1884. In all cases the guides appeared in March and April, their promotional campaigns helping to elicit the annual spring renewal of baseball euphoria.

A major promotion medium was the *Sporting News*. Advertising in the *News* meant advertising largely for market share, since one could assume that readers of this specialty magazine were already hooked on sports in general and baseball in particular. The *News* began publication in 1886 and quickly rivaled the *Clipper* and *Sporting Life* for preeminence in the field of sports papers. Within a year it claimed a circulation approaching 60,000. In 1890 it began a Chicago edition to supplement its home edition in St. Louis. The growing list of advertisers from around the country makes it a useful source for analyzing competition within the industry.[35]

Manufacturers had a compelling interest in advertising. Wherever or however the consumer might purchase an article of sporting goods—through the mail or at a hardware store, general store, department store, or sportsman's "depot"—the manufacturer wanted him to buy a specific brand. Spalding, Reach, Rawlings, Meacham, and McClean continually presented their names to the readers of the *News*, especially in the spring, when athletes and their managers would be in the market for new uniforms and equipment. Smaller firms, too—Keefe and Becannon of New York, Chicago's John Wilkinson and Jenny and Graham—tried to capitalize on the baseball wars of the period. Rawlings ran full-page ads offering large discounts for bulk orders. These seemed to overwhelm the announcements of competitors like H. H. Kiffe of Brooklyn, who promised "no discounts to anyone."[36]

Manufacturers also fought to promote brand recognition by acquiring the rights to supply a top league with the "official" ball. In the late 1870s Spalding wrested this advantage from L. H. Mahn of Boston by agreeing to *pay* the National League a dollar a dozen for the privilege of supplying *free* balls. Reach soon had a similar deal with the American Association; Wright and Ditson became the official ball for the Union Association; and Keefe and Becannon claimed to manufacture the "real" thing for the Brotherhood League.[37]

The struggle did not stop at the major league level, since consumers might be tied emotionally to a local minor or amateur league. By 1884 Spalding had gained recognition from the Northwestern League, the American College Baseball Association, the Louisiana Amateur Baseball Association, and the Iron and Oil

Association. Nor did he lose any time in grabbing a share of the expanding football market. Though an 1890 ad noted that the firm was sole agent for the British "Lillywhite Regulation Football," three years later the ball of notice was the Spalding "Official Intercollegiate Foot Ball," which had been "adopted for the second year by the Intercollegiate Association and must be used in Match Games."[38]

Manufacturers were so liberal in their proclamations of "official" status that one must be ever suspicious; the hapless consumer was confronted with "league" balls produced by virtually every baseball manufacturer. Rawlings, which offered a minimum nine-inning guarantee for its top-of-the-line baseball, claimed that it was not only any ball's equal but was made by the same factory that had produced the National League balls for years.[39]

Actual adoption by a recognized league was certainly worth the effort, however, and a related means of product distinction was an ad carrying a personal endorsement: from a satisfied customer ("Every ball player's batting average who uses [these bats] should increase at least fifty percent") or, better yet, a player or manager. In 1889 the young Rawlings Company published an endorsement from "Der Boss," Chris Von der Ahe, who noted his satisfaction and his promise to purchase more Rawlings goods for his St. Louis team.[40] Sometimes the endorser's name could become a generic term. In January 1890 Reach advertised its new "Reach Mit [*sic*] Glove," as "manufactured under the personal supervision of Mr. Harry Decker, catcher of the Philadelphia Baseball Club." Just five months later the Paul Buckley Glove Company of Chicago included "Deckers" among their glove styles, without further reference to the well-known player.[41]

Endorsements presented other problems of timing as well, as Reach discovered. When boxing gloves and Queensbury rules gave boxing a veneer of respectability, especially after 1892 when James Corbett defeated John L. Sullivan in the first gloved heavyweight championship, Reach moved quickly to run ads for his brand-name gloves, which he claimed had been used by the famous pugilists. A year later he began selling "Corbett (Trade-Mark) Boxing Gloves." Unfortunately for Reach, in March 1897 a large endorsement by Gentleman Jim appeared in the same issue of the *Sporting News* that described how Bob Fitzsimmons had pummeled the champion and taken the title. Corbett's promise to "win in a walk and Reach Fitz with Reach Gloves" must have drawn snickers from readers.[42]

While every firm was seeking increased market share, Spalding was perhaps the most aggressive and most successful. By 1892 the company had silently acquired Reach, Wright and Ditson, Peck and

Snyder, the St. Lawrence River Skiff, Canoe & Steam Launch Co., and George Barnard & Co., even though for years the subsidiaries continued to offer their own name brands.[43] Spalding was not the only expansionist, however; in 1898 Rawlings acquired the vast manufacturing plant of the Meacham Arms Company, a move that vaulted the firm toward the top of the competition.[44]

Indeed, it is a distortion to think of Spalding as a "monopolist." He might have aspired to monopoly, but no manufacturer controlled channels of distribution that well. Spalding complained bitterly about jobbers and mail-order houses that discounted goods, and in 1899 he began selling directly to retailers on a "one-price" basis. But he could not keep Montgomery Ward or Sears from succeeding in just that strategy.[45] At the "high" end of equipment lines, his products faced competition from such specialists as the Ted Kennedy glove company of Peoria and the Waldo Claflin shoe company in Philadelphia. Moreover, major teams such as the Harvard football club often preferred to place their orders with smaller local firms, where they could exert greater control on design.[46]

Except for the bicycle trade, there were few barriers to entry into sporting goods. The market was expanding, manufacturing was not capital intensive, and distribution was dominated by independent wholesalers and retailers who took on the brands that would sell. By 1900 the census listed 144 sporting goods manufacturers (excluding bicycles and billiards), a 67 percent increase from 1880; aggregate product value had more than doubled to $3,633,396. Given the continued existence of "sidelight" manufacturing, these figures are clearly conservative. Retail outlets expanded as well. In 1899, Spalding and Bros. claimed to have 20,000 accounts on their books. This number—which doubtless included hardware stores, department stores, old sporting goods depots, and younger specialty stores—suggests the extent of a distribution system that also involved direct mail and extended from the posh houses of Fifth Avenue to Bowery pawn shops that did a brisk trade in boxing gloves.[47]

EXPANDING THE MARKET FOR FINISHED GOODS AND GAMES

Sporting goods, then, found a competitive marketplace. Manufacturers like Spalding enjoyed a strong presence, but there was plenty of room for more. There was also enough room and enough cooperation to allow trade associations of manufacturers and dealers to develop in the early 1900s. Publishers had already sensed enough industry identity to establish trade journals: the *Sporting Goods Gazette* began in 1888; eleven years later Charles C. Spink started the *Sporting Goods Dealer,* which continues to this day.

This combination of competitiveness and special identity was reflected in an 1889 advertisement from R. E. Dimick, a St. Louis retailer. Dimick highlighted the prominent name brands he carried—Wright and Ditson tennis goods, Abbey & Imbries fishing tackle, Gray's body protectors. Reach's bats—all testimony to consumer awareness. At the same time, however, he emphasized that "we are not in the gun business and for that reason we only cater to the wants of the athletes and gymnasts."[48] Dimick, I suspect, did not mean to say that guns could not be part of a sport but only that his business was specialized. He wanted to position himself in the distinct area of commerce that I have called the sport industry.

Like Dimick, Albert Spalding was eager to promote the *special* nature of his products. In one series of ads that ran in the spring of 1893, the copy each week offered folksy commentary on the benefits of various Spalding baseball products: balls, bats, chest protectors, shoes. A description of Spalding bats began with a story about the pathetic "crank" who couldn't even hit a ball until his team captain insisted that he throw away the "'Jonah' Bat that was made for him by a wheelwright up in the country," but with a new Spalding bat, he was soon leading the team. Then there was the hapless runner, staggering between bases in clodhoppers habitually purchased "from some inexperienced cobbler," who might be able to fit the lad but "not with Base Ball shoes."[49] This was the fundamental message of all manufacturers: sporting goods were specialized products, not to be entrusted to the hands of old-style general craftsmen.

Even as they competed with each other, sporting goods entrepreneurs worked to expand the market for all. They were hardly content to leave promotional efforts in the hands of liberal theologians and urban reformers. One method was to sponsor sports contests, as boatbuilders and gunmakers had done for years. In the 1850s Michael Phelan had carried the art to new heights on behalf of billiards, and in 1869 George B. Ellard, who owned a "Baseball Depot" in Cincinnati, was active in the formation of the professional Red Stockings. A. G. Spalding too sought to expand the market for his goods by investing in such promotions. Best known was the "world tour" of 1888–89, in which his Chicago ball club played a series of exhibitions against an "all-star" team in venues as far away as Australia, Ceylon, Egypt, Italy, France, England, Scotland, and Ireland. He also sponsored amateur baseball tournaments in England, the Philippines, and Canada.

Though bold enough to seek a global market, Spalding knew that the foundation for profits lay at home, where he championed sports of all kinds. He donated "Play Ball" trophies to school leagues around the country. Following a successful association with the Paris Olympics of 1900, his firm designed the stadium, organized the athletics competition, and provided equipment for the St. Louis Games of 1904. Although he never failed to nurture sales of his own brands, these promotions were aimed at increasing general activity.[50]

Golf is another sport that the Spalding company promoted in America; it was the first to begin large-scale American manufacture of golf clubs (1894) and golf balls (1898). More important, in 1899 Spalding financed a national tour by Harry Vardon, one of the sport's premier players.[51]

No such tour would have been possible, of course, without the prior existence of a circuit of golf courses around the country. It would have been out of the question as late as 1890, when George Wright imported his first order of golf equipment from England. The game was then virtually unknown in America; the St. Andrews "course" in Yonkers, New York, was only two years old and hardly a landmark. Hence, displaying the logic of an experienced promoter, Wright wrote to the Boston Parks Commissioners requesting a permit for the "privilege to play in Franklin Park the game of Golf." Since the commissioners were known to be protective of the park's tranquillity, Wright assured them that the exhibition "would not draw a crowd, as the interest in the game is only with the players, there is nothing to the playing of the game to cause a noise, or injure the shribery [*sic*] in the park." On the strength of Wright's reputation and assurances the commissioners granted the request, and Boston had its first public display of the game that rapidly became the hallmark of the country club set. Wright's continued promotion led to the establishment of public links in Franklin Park; more important, the development by 1899 of twenty-nine courses around Boston meant increased sales of golf equipment.[52]

While George Wright was promoting the game of golf, J. M. Raymond of Boston was trying to resurrect interest in roller-skating, which had been in vogue in the 1860s. The Raymond Skate Company was a firm with a sputtering history. Organized in 1884 with a capital stock of $10,000, it manufactured the "Raymond" skate, which enjoyed brisk sales initially. By 1886, however, demand had lagged. Four years later Raymond reopened the "Olympian Skating Club" in the Mechanics Building, and the *Sporting Goods Gazette* credited this move with reviving "the once popular craze of roller skating in this city."[53]

Like Wright and Spalding, Raymond and others realized that the purveyor of goods had to be a promoter of activity. As Albert Pope wrote in 1895, bicycle manufacturers knew "at the outset" in the 1870s that they must "educate the people to the advantage of this invigorating sport"; hence, "with this end in view, the best literature that was to be had on the subject was gratuitously distributed." This was true in all sports. When George David announced the opening of his new store in Worcester, Massachusetts, he added that he wanted to sell sports as well as equipment. He promised that his store would have a gathering spot where "the sporting papers of the country would be kept on file." When the Rawlings Brothers moved to larger quarters in St. Louis, they featured a "wigwam" where sportsmen could congregate and "swap hunting and fishing stories to their hearts content." The provision of meeting rooms, the dissemination of information and instruction, the sponsorship of leagues and contests all became part and parcel of the selling function.[54]

In short, sporting goods manufacturers and dealers did not simply fatten off some vast instinctive demand. As Arjun Appadurai argues generally, demand is neither a "mechanical" response to production nor a "bottomless natural appetite." Nineteenth-century sporting goods firms knew they could not rely on a fickle public which, as Thomas Wentworth Higginson realized, was always hungering for novelty, ever "dissatisfied with last winter's skates, with the old boat, and with the family pony." Too many velocipedes, tennis rackets, and roller skates lay in barns and cellars collecting dust, rust, and mold—testimony to fleeting profits.[55]

Few serious entrepreneurs wait around for demand. They create customers. In order to do so, sporting goods firms became the front line of promoters and educators during the great sports surge of the late nineteenth century. Retailers especially were face-to-face instructors, teaching not only the use of equipment but the value of physical activity. Reformers could pen all sorts of rationales for the benefits of active sports in opposing their favorite menace, "commercial amusements," but dealers saw the enemy up close. If they didn't act, they went out of business. As one dealer wrote in the early twentieth century: "If you don't do something to encourage sports, the nickelodeons are going to win hands down." He suggested the promotion of youth leagues.[56]

As they competed, then, dealers and manufacturers expanded demand with aggressive marketing. Their tactics included ingenious mixes of the four P's associated with modern marketing: product, price, place, and promotion. Designs became safer and easier to use.

There were inexpensive models of most equipment (inexpensive Japanese sports items started arriving in the early twentieth century). Furthermore, the industry's sense of product always emphasized information about the craft and lore of the sport. Always in the forefront, Spalding developed a series of volumes in the 1880s called the Library of American Sports, and his American Sports Publishing Company soon churned out three hundred publications explaining the nuances of different sports, extolling their virtues, and hawking Spalding products.[57]

Smart retailers in turn advertised and sold these and other guides. "We make a specialty of Sporting Books of every description," announced R. E. Dimick of St. Louis. "They are very good to have when settling disputes." For the homebody or the hot-stove leaguer, sports knowledge was increasingly available through a system of distribution that linked goods with game forms. Albert Applin has argued that much of the remarkable spread of basketball in the 1890s may well have been related to the circulation power of Spalding's *Official Basketball Guide,* which immediately gave the young game exposure in thousands of outlets like Dimick's and, along with the YMCA's promotion, resulted in what was arguably the fastest national diffusion of any sport before or since.[58]

REALIZING AN INDUSTRY AND INSTITUTIONALIZING SPORT

The marketing efforts of sporting goods firms clearly expanded opportunity and interest in active play among a wide range of Americans; Spalding, Reach, Wright, Dimick, Rawlings, and the rest had a serious interest in democratizing leisure activities. But democratizing should entail more than just the opportunity to participate; it should include an opportunity to determine the nature of participation—and here the industry tended to part company with democracy. Success in the marketplace depended on packaging and selling *preformed* games and goods. Manufacturers and dealers had an interest in innovation, but they had a greater stake in the stable growth of widely understood products. To achieve it, they established ties with other specialists who had similar interests, particularly coaches, players, journalists, and the administrators of leagues and associations. They all shared a vision: to be providers of particular forms of activity, which they would sell to the public. Their alliances resulted in mutual legitimacy and market influence, the foundations of a larger sport industry. Every successful partnership *inside* the industry, however, established firmer boundaries on the range and styles of sports offered to consumers on the *outside.* This was how *some* games became *the* games.[59]

Just as Spalding aggressively promoted standardized goods made by rationalized production, so also did he and his colleagues champion scientific action, crafted by expert coaches, trainers, and managers. What counted most, though, was the circulation of inexpensive, standardized *packages* of expert knowledge that linked sporting goods to game forms. Guidebooks were a perfect medium; so were such specialty booklets as Henry Chadwick's *Technical Terms of Baseball,* published by Spalding in 1897. Another Spalding product, "Professor" William Elmer's *Boxing,* promised in 1903 that "any boy with the aid of this book can become an expert boxer." Catalogues offered ready-made instruction and ready-made goods through the mail. The 1886 Peck & Snyder *Price List of Out & Indoor Sports and Pastimes* offered "Goodyear's Pocket Gymnasium" and "Prof. D. L. Dowd's Home Exerciser," each with accompanying texts written by experts.[60]

Aligning with *scattered* experts and scientists of sport and exercise, however, would not ensure the more stable or *institutionalized* markets that sporting goods firms desired. An expert's endorsement might give a product *legitimacy* but would not necessarily provide *authority* or legitimate domination in the marketplace. Authority depended on what Paul Starr has called effective "gatekeeping," or strategic positioning between technology, expertise, and consumers. Starr has masterfully outlined the gatekeeping of the new medical profession: in the late nineteenth century physicians successfully positioned themselves so that consumers increasingly had to work through them to enjoy the benefits of medical expertise and technology. The concept is valuable also to an understanding of the way sports evolved.[61]

I have shown how Reach and others sought market share by gaining or claiming a product's status as the "official" ball of this or that league. Likewise, when Peck & Snyder introduced its new tennis ball in 1886, the firm happily announced that it had been "adopted by the United States National Lawn Tennis Association and by the Intercollegiate Association, as the Regulation Ball to be used in all match games." There was a similar message on lacrosse balls; since there was no American governing body in lacrosse, however, it could only state that Peck & Snyder published the rules of the Montreal Lacrosse Club and that this ball had been "adopted by all the leading clubs." Spalding aggressively pursued such sanctions, seemingly from every association in existence, claiming more exclusivity than he actually had—though his influence with the National League, the Intercollegiate Football Association, and the Amateur Athletic Union is obvious.[62]

Endorsements and official sanctions were important credentials for any piece of equipment, but authority worked in two directions. Just as an endorsement helped the tangible goods in the marketplace, so too did "official" goods provide legitimacy and authority to the distant endorsers. Walter Camp understood this very well. His *Book of College Sports* cautioned: "It is best that [football] players should never use anything but the regulation ball" and duly noted that two brands met the standard: the British "J. Lillywhite" and the American "Spalding." At the same time, he added that a regulation ball "should bear the stamp, 'Adopted by the Intercollegiate Foot-ball Association.'" Every Spalding ball repaid Camp's endorsement with interest, for every person who bought an official IFA ball paid homage to Camp's version of the game. A similar process occurred in all competitive sports—for example, track and field, women's basketball, and field hockey, where leagues and governing associations emerged to standardize and regulate competition.[63]

Historians have recognized the importance and power of these organizations but have not examined *how* they achieved control. It appears that much of their authority stemmed from their symbiotic affiliations with sporting goods firms. Tangible goods, then, built up the structure of authority like "coral islands."

I do not mean to suggest that a few moguls had a plan to steal sports from "the people." The relationship between sporting goods and governing bodies shows that in fact the providers were often at odds. While equipment helped to legitimate control by leagues and associations, product innovations could challenge and stretch the boundaries of rules and styles of play. Football is a case in point. In 1902 Rawlings ran advertisements for a new line of football equipment, designed by the company's product genius, William P. Whitley. Aptly named "Whitley's Football Armor," the line included a jacket "reinforced with cane ribs which, when struck, equally distributes the force of the blow, thus preventing injury to the player." Ironically, amid a growing controversy over football violence and governance, protective uniforms doubtless *increased* the levels of aggressive play.[64]

A similar boomerang apparently occurred in ice hockey, where protective equipment developed in tandem with the slashing, hard-checking "Ottawa" style of play. Elliott Gorn notes that the same thing happened in boxing: manufacturers such as Reach and Shibe claimed that their gloves would "preclude the possibility of injury or disfigurement," whereas in fact, gloves allow the slugger to be even more brutal in his attack because he has less fear of hand injury. Leagues and governing bodies, then, may sometimes embrace equipment that ultimately makes their sports less controllable.[65]

Sporting goods can challenge in other ways. As manufacturers worked to "democratize" game forms, they developed equipment that simplified the activity. The safety bicycle was one example. So was Coburn Haskell's rubber-thread-wound golf ball, which turned more golfers into long hitters and caused wholesale changes in course design. Such pressures have led to many jousts between manufacturers and rulemakers; they continue today over specifications on ball dimples, club grooves, graphite bats, and oversized racquets, to name only a few.[66]

Even as they pressed the boundaries of established rules, however, manufacturers did not radically challenge institutionalized sport. If anything, the occasional squabbles have further cemented the gatekeeping status of governing bodies, coaches, and other new experts. Just as the public increasingly bought ready-made equipment designed by product experts like William Whitley, so too they bought ready-made rules and ready-made styles of play crafted by governing bodies and expert coaches or players. As Donald Mrozek has argued, advertisements for training equipment—blocking sleds, tackling dummies, rowing machines—were liberally sprinkled with references to science. No wonder the public worshiped professional coaches and champion athletes: they were masters of a *new* science. Their knowledge of equipment and technique gave them what Burton Bledstein has called "special power over worldly experience."[67]

Their authority came from their working *within* the structures of the emerging sport industry. They offered what the public seemed to want: mastery, efficiency, and victory within the rules they had helped to write. Yet many critics protested the consequences for sports in the schools and colleges. Their feelings are summarized in a scathing 1929 report on American College Sports, published by the Carnegie Foundation for the Advancement of Teaching:

> If athletics are to be "educational," the player must be taught to do his own thinking. In every branch of athletics the strategy of the game should not be beyond the capacity of the alertly-minded undergraduate. As matters now stand, no branch owes even a vestige of its strategy to the undergraduates engaged. Such matters are the affair of the coach.[68]

Such an outburst, which typified the profession of physical education, revealed serious marketing myopia. Physical educators and sports reformers were well intended but out of touch. They wrote articles about educational sports, but they could not understand, as Hal Lawson notes, "that not all knowledge is of equal value in the eyes of society's members." Coaches offered what players, college presidents, boosters, and fans wanted: mastery and victory in *preformed* packages.[69]

Moreover, reformers failed to see that school and college sports could not be isolated from the wider marketplace of goods and game forms, flowing in vast circulation among manufacturers, retailers, professional leagues, and their associated experts. If equipment, techniques, and styles of play emanated from *other* providers, they could not be transformed merely by hope. Only women educators realized this, developed their *own* styles of play, and until the last two decades enjoyed a special sphere of authority.[70] Successful reformers, then, had to become active providers of preformed play.

Indeed, this is a peculiar and recurring irony in the history of sport. Reformers do not democratize. For instance, at the turn of the century when some reformers became "play specialists," they developed "play curriculums" and scientific equipment, thus nurturing their own profession of recreation, which sought legitimacy and authority for programming the leisure time of children and adults in playgrounds and community centers around the country. Even the current reformers—proponents of "new games" that are supposedly educational, creative, cooperative, and nondebilitating—market packages of "Earthballs," "stretch-ropes," and "bataca boffers" along with instruction booklets, thus themselves becoming the experts of a new science of creative play.[71]

Has this industry of providers strangled sport as play? Is sport now part of some mass culture of leisure sold along with radios, records, and videotapes to an inert and pliant public? I don't believe so. Players at all levels create their own styles of play, their own rules, and their own meanings. Players and spectators are always at once both producers and consumers of sports and games. In their dual role they may press out the boundaries of structure. What actually occurs on the fields, on the playgrounds, and in the stands may differ from what the providers intended.[72]

Nevertheless, the spread of standardized goods does reflect and support the spread of standardized behaviors and values. Providers do make buying or adopting packaged goods and games easier than "free play." Control in the marketplace does make a difference. A relative handful of rules committees do control the game forms played by most Americans, and relatively few manufacturers do supply the goods used at all levels. For almost a hundred years this network of expert coaches, journalists, administrators, manufacturers, and dealers has largely shaped the boundaries of American sport.

Unfortunately, today's periodic laments about sports—accusations of commercialism, violence, alienation—are typically directed at individual teams, leagues, and associations. These are myopic views. Control and influence are much more complex. Philosophers and critics who seek to change the nature of sport in America must first understand its complex history from the inside out.

NOTES

1. Alexander M. Weyand, *American Football: Its History and Development* (New York: D. Appleton and Co., 1926), 4.

2. Henry Chadwick, "Past and Present," *Sporting Goods Dealer* 1 (October 1899): 8.

3. For more detail on the sports industry, see my "Entrepreneurs, Organizations, and the Sport Marketplace: Subjects in Search of Historians," *Journal of Sport History* 13 (Spring 1986): 14–33.

4. For more on institutionalization, see Richard Gruneau, *Class, Sports, and Social Development* (Amherst: University of Massachusetts Press, 1984); Alan Ingham and John Loy, "The Social System of Sport: A Humanistic Perspective," *Quest* 19 (1973): 3–23; Richard Butsch, "The Commodification of Leisure: The Case of the Model Airplane Hobby and Industry," *Qualitative Sociology* (Fall 1984): 217–35; and Raymond Williams, *Sociology of Culture* (New York: Schocken, 1982).

5. John Clarke and Chas Critcher, *The Devil Makes Work: Leisure in Capitalist Britain* (Urbana: University of Illinois Press, 1985), 70.

6. For useful introductions to the literature on leisure, see John R. Kelly, *Leisure* (Englewood Cliffs, N.J.: Prentice-Hall 1982); and Kelly, *Freedom to Be: A New Sociology of Leisure* (New York: Macmillan 1987). See related theoretical comments in Robert Heilbroner, *The Nature and Logic of Capitalism* (New York: W. W. Norton, 1985), p. 60; David Held, *Introduction to Critical Theory: Horkheimer to Habermas* (Berkeley: University of California Press, 1980), p. 77–80; Chris Rojek, *Capitalism and Leisure Theory* (London: Tavistock Publications, 1985); Robert Lane, "The Regulation of Experience: Leisure in a Market Society," *Social Science Information* 17, no. 2 (1978): 147–84.

7. Two valuable studies that focus on ideological struggles are Melvin Adelman, *A Sporting Time: New York City and the Rise of Modern Athletics, 1820–1870* (Urbana: University of Illinois Press, 1986); and Donald Mrozek, *Sport and American Mentality, 1880–1910* (Knoxville: University of Tennessee Press, 1984). The classic work on the material side of sport history is John R. Betts, "The Technological Revolution and the Rise of Sport, 1850–1900," *Mississippi Valley Historical Review* 40 (September 1953): 231–56. See also Betts, *America's Sporting Heritage* (Reading, Mass.: Addison-Wesley, 1974); and Peter Levine, *A. G. Spalding and the Rise of*

Baseball: The Promise of American Sport (New York: Oxford University Press, 1985). I have profited greatly from Levine's splendid biography. The major histories of baseball also provide material on sporting goods manufacture: see David Voigt, *American Baseball: From Gentleman's Sport to the Commissioner System* (Norman, Okla.; Oklahoma University Press, 1966); and Harold Seymour, *Baseball: The Golden Years* (New York: Oxford University Press, 1960).

8. Mary Douglas and Baron Isherwood, *The World of Goods: Toward an Anthropology of Consumption* (London: Allen Lane, 1979), 75. See also Arjun Appadurai, ed., *The Social Life of Things: Commodities in Cultural Perspective* (Cambridge: Cambridge University Press, 1986); Cary Carson, "Doing History with Material Culture," in Ian M. G. Quimby, ed., *Material Culture and the Study of American Life* (New York: W. W. Norton, 1978), 41–64. Janet Harris has examined the ideology of material goods in "Pride and Fever: Two University Sport Promotion Themes," in Frank Manning, ed., *The World of Play* (West Point, N.Y.: Leisure Press 1983), 25–33.

9. Richard Sandomir, "GNSP: The Gross National Sports Product," *Sports Inc.*, 16 November 1987, pp. 14–18.

10. For a good introduction to the early sports literature, see Jack W. Berryman, "The Tenuous Attempts of Americans to 'Catch up with John Bull': Specialty Magazines and Sporting Journalism, 1800–1835," *Canadian Journal of History of Sport and Physical Education* 10 (May 1979): 40–61.

11. For these arguments, see Jennie Holliman, *American Sports, 1785–1835* (Durham, N.C.: Seeman Press 1931), 178–92. Adelman, *A Sporting Time*, also uncovers regular essays in local newspapers. On colonial sport, see Nancy Struna, "The Formalization of Sport and the Formation of an Elite," *Journal of Sport History* 13 (Winter 1986): 212–34. For an excellent study of working-class sentiments in one sport, see Elliott J. Gorn, *The Manly Art: Bare-Knuckle Prize Fighting in America* (Ithaca, N.Y.: Cornell University Press, 1986). The advanced state of British sport is well described in Allen Guttmann, *Sports Spectators* (New York: Columbia University Press, 1986); and Richard Mandell, *Sport: A Cultural History* (New York: Columbia University Press 1986).

12. William Clarke, *Boy's Own Book Extended: A Complete Encyclopedia of All Athletic, Scientific, Recreative Outdoor and Indoor Exercises and Diversions* (New York: James Miller, 1864), 17, 164; Robin Carver, *The Book of Sports* (Boston: Lilly, Wait, Colman, and Holden, 1834); Samuel Williams, *Boys' Treasury* (Philadelphia: Lea & Blanchard, 1847), cited in Betts, *America's Sporting Heritage*, p. 45. On homemade baseball equipment, see Seymour, *Baseball*, 7–8; for fishing rods, see Thaddeus Norris, *The American Angler's Book* (Philadelphia: E. H. Butler and Co., 1865), 441–49.

13. Nancy Struna, "Sport and the Awareness of Leisure," in Cary Carson, Ronald Hoffman, and Peter J. Albert, eds., *Of Consuming Interests: Style of Life in the Eighteenth Century* (Charlottesville, Va.; University of Virginia Press, forthcoming). The seminal work on the "consumer revolution" is Neil McKendrick, John Brewer, and J. H. Plumb, *The Birth of a Consumer Society: The Commercialization of Eighteenth Century England*

(Bloomington, Ind.: Indiana University Press, 1982). On the move toward "finished goods," see Stuart Bruchey, *The Roots of American Economic Growth, 1607–1861* (New York: Harper & Row, 1965), 26–31.

14. Struna, "Sport and Awareness"; Holliman, *American Sports,* 7; Esther Singleton, *Social New York under the Georges* (New York: D. Appleton and Co., 1902), 265; Betts, *America's Sporting Heritage,* 45.

15. Struna, "Sport and Awareness"; Edward K. Tryon Co., *The History of the Oldest Sporting Goods House in America, 1811–1936* (Philadelphia: by the Company, 1936); John Krider, *Krider's Sporting Anecdotes* (1853; rpt. New York: Arno Press, 1966), 57–58. For early American equipment, see Elisha Lewis, *The American Sportsman* (Philadelphia: Lippincott, Grainbo and Co., 1855), 363, 411–18; John J. Brown, *The American Angler's Guide* (New York: Burgess and Stringer, 1845), cited in Charles E. Goodspeed, *Angling in America* (Boston: Houghton Mifflin, 1939), 159–60.

16. *Spirit of the Times,* 26 May, 7 July, 21 July, 22 September, 1832; 9 May 1835; 8 March 1845; 3 and 10 May 1845; 21 March 1846; 16 February 1856. "William Read & Son," Massachusetts 69: 448 (26 July 1850), R. G. Dun & Co. Collection, Baker Library, Harvard Graduate School of Business Administration (hereafter cited as Dun Collection). See also James H. Madison, "The Credit Reports of R. G. Dun & Co. as Historical Sources," *Historical Methods Newsletter* 8 (September 1975): 128–31.

17. For suggestions on the relation between this specialization and class structure, see Stuart Blumin, "Black Coats to White Collars," in Stuart Bruchey, ed., *Small Business in American Life* (New York: Columbia University Press, 1980), 100–21.

18. *Spirit of the Times,* 28 June 1856; New York 267: 438 (28 January 1857, March 1860, 15 June 1866), Dun Collection; Adelman, *A Sporting Time,* 220–29; Gary J. Kornblath, "The Craftsman as Industrialist: Jonas Chickering and the Transformation of American Piano Making," *Business History Review* 59 (Autumn 1985): 349–69.

19. Rick Kogan, *Brunswick: The Story of an American Company from 1845–1985* (Skokie, Ill.: by the Corporation, 1985), 10–15.

20. Bureau of the Census, *Manufactures of the United States in 1860, Eighth Census* (Washington, D.C.: Government Printing Office, 1865), 733. Gun brands such as Colt had national markets, but it is impossible to distinguish their "sports" from their "general" utility in consumer thinking. Luna Lambert, "The American Skating Mania," *Journal of American Culture* 1, no. 4 (1978): 683–99, claims that the 1860 census listed ice skates as a separate category of hardware; unfortunately, she gives no clear documentation, and I have found no such listing.

21. The economic and technological background may be found in Thomas Cochran, *Business in American Life* (New York: McGraw-Hill, 1972); Nathan Rosenberg, *Technology and American Economic Growth* (New York: Harper & Row, 1972); Alfred D. Chandler, Jr., *The Visible Hand: The Managerial Revolution in American Business* (Cambridge, Mass.: Harvard University Press, 1977); David Hounshell, *From the American*

System to Mass Production, 1800–1932: The Development of Manufacturing Technology in the United States (Baltimore, Md.: Johns Hopkins University Press, 1984). The cultural tensions are linked clearly to sports in Mrozek, *Sport and American Mentality*, and Gorn, *The Manly Art*. For the experience in one city, see my *How Boston Played: Sport Recreation and Community, 1865–1915* (Boston: Northeastern University Press, 1982).

22. Bureau of the Census, *Statistics of the Wealth and Industry of the United States, Ninth Census*, vol. 3 (Washington, D.C.: Government Printing Office, 1872), 349–51, 551, 559; *Ball Player's Chronicle*, 27 June 1867, cited in John R. Betts, "Organized Sport in Industrial America" (Ph.D. diss., Columbia University, 1951), 161.

23. Rhode Island 10: 206 (January 1875); Pennsylvania 148: 164 (January 1881) and 148:450 (February 1884), Dun Collection.

24. "Hillerich & Bradsby Co., Incorporated" (unpublished, undated release, in author's possession); *Sporting News*, March 30, 1895.

25. Pennsylvania 4: 442, (7 March 1874, 20 May 1880, 8 September and 10 December 1881); 4: 859 (28 July 1886), Dun Collection.

26. Massachusetts 88: 82 (28 April 1881, 3 August 1882, 24 September 1883), Dun Collection; *Sporting News*, 26 August 1937.

27. The best account of the Spalding firm is in Levine, *A. G. Spalding*, 71–94. See also Illinois 42: 122 (17 April 1876, 12 March 1878, 13 December 1878), Dun Collection. Spalding's estimate of initial capital varies from Spalding family and company lore that mother Harriet provided the "entire" capital of $800. Given A. G.'s frugality and salary as a player, it is likely that the $2,500 figure accurately includes his own contribution; given his love of morality plays, it is likely that he fostered the legend of maternal assistance. Information on the Wilkins merger is in Michigan 5: 207 (5 December 1878), Dun Collection.

28. Bureau of the Census, *Wealth and Industry, Ninth Census*, 394 ff.; Bureau of the Census, *Report on the Manufacturers of the United States, Tenth Census* (Washington, D.C.: Government Printing Office, 1883), 9–14.

29. Massachusetts 88: 442 (26 January 1882); New York 134:57 (8 October 1875), Dun Collection.

30. Lester Dole & Co., *1884 Trade Catalogue*, in Baker Library, Harvard; D. W. Granbery & Co., *Wholesale Catalogue and Price List, 1885*, in Baker Library, Harvard; "Oldest U.S. Firms," *Sporting Goods Dealer*, February 1983, p. 110; Connecticut 41:407 (5 April 1880, 23 October 1885), Dun Collection.

31. On Rawlings, see *Sporting News*, 31 December 1887; 7 January 1888. On McClean and Meacham, see Missouri 38:122, 191, 424 (7 July 1863, January 1879, 15 October 1880) and 42:289, 354, 379 (December 1871; 22 October 1878; 6 December 1878, 28 January 1880, 9 March 1882), Dun Collection. For Tryon's move into new sports, see Pennsylvania 132:736 (10 April 1888), Dun Collection. For similar diversifications in manufacture and retail, see *Sporting Goods Gazette* 5 (April 1892): 7; Massachusetts 100: 497, 524, 569 (5 November 1884, May 1886, 24 November 1888), Dun Collection.

On Goldsmith, see Hugo Autz, "Three Generations of Progress," *Sporting Goods Dealer*, August 1946, pp. 103–6; Kentucky 19 (30 January 1880), Dun Collection; *Sporting News*, 1 April 1899.

32. *Sporting News*, 23 February 1895. See also stories on baseballs in the issues for 7 November 1891, 12 November 1892, 13 December 1902; and *Sporting Goods Dealer*, October 1899, pp. 4–6.

33. Richard Butsch found publishers playing a lead role also in the hobby airplane industry; see his "Commodification of Leisure."

34. *Dewitt's Baseball Guide* (New York, 1869–80); Levine, *A. G. Spalding*, 75–76; Voigt, *American Baseball*, 91.

35. See, e.g., the issues of 30 March and 20 April 1889, 1 January 1890, 2 April 1892, 1 April 1893. In 1889 and 1890 the *News* was at war with Spalding and so praised Reach's guide while pointing out numerous errors in Spalding's. Ironically, Reach and Spalding were possibly silent partners by this time. See Levine, *A. G. Spalding*, 82. The circulation figure is from *Sporting News*, 4 February 1887; the Chicago edition was announced 15 March 1890.

36. *Sporting News*, 30 March 1889; 1 and 8 February, 15 March 1890; 21 February, 4 and 11 April 1891.

37. See Levine, *A. G. Spalding*, 77–78; Arthur Bartlett, *Baseball and Mr. Spalding: The History and Romance of Baseball* (New York: Farrar, Straus and Young, 1951), 102–3, 157; *Sporting News*, 1 February 1890. In 1879, *Dewitt's Base Ball Guide* (p. 75) still recognized the Mahn ball as the official National League ball.

38. *Sporting News*, 18 October 1890, 23 July 1893; Levine, *A. G. Spalding*, 77.

39. *Sporting News*, 30 June 1900, 16 November 1901, 8 February 1902, 7 and 14 March 1903.

40. *Sporting News*, 5 May 1887; 2 February 1899. Early ads by Hillerich and Bradsby for the "Louisville Slugger" included an endorsement by Hanlon of Baltimore (e.g., 4 May 1895).

41. *Sporting News*, 18 January, 31 May 1890.

42. *Sporting News*, 6 January 1900, 24 September 1892, 7 October 1893, 20 March 1897. The following week, the advertisement for "Corbett" gloves contained only general copy about quality and workmanship.

43. Bartlett, *Baseball and Mr. Spalding*, 147, 231; Voigt, *American Baseball*, 1:217–18; Levine, *A. G. Spalding*, 80.

44. *Sporting News*, 22 January 1898.

45. See Voigt, *American Baseball*, 217, for the "monopolist" sentiment; Montgomery Ward & Co., *Catalogue and Buyers Guide*, No. 55, Spring & Summer 1894, at Baker Library, Harvard Graduate School of Business; *1897 Sears Roebuck Catalogue*, ed. Fred L. Israel (rpt. New York: Chelsea House, 1968), 562–619.

46. *Sporting News*, 16 June 1900, 27 April 1901. I am indebted to Ronald Smith for pointing out the information on the Harvard orders.

47. *Sporting Goods Gazette*, April 1892, p. 28; *Sporting News*, 5 March 1887, 1 July 1899; Levine, *A. G. Spalding*, 83; Bureau of the Census, *Census*

of Manufacturers, Twelfth Census, 1900, vol. 7 (Washington, D.C.: Government Printing Office, 1902), 20–55.

48. *Sporting News,* 23 February 1889.

49. *Sporting News,* 13 and 27 May 1893.

50. Levine has documented these promotions in *A. G. Spalding,* 88–89, 97–121. On Phelan, see Adelman, *A Sporting Time,* 221–29. On George P. Ellard, see Voigt, *American Baseball,* 25.

51. Levine, *A. G. Spalding,* 81, 89; Armond Van Pelt, "Spalding's 75th Anniversary," *Sporting Goods Dealer,* February 1951, pp. 112–14.

52. Minutes of the Board of Parks Commissioners (Department of Parks and Recreation, Boston City Hall), 5 December 1890, 23 October 1892, 18 April 1898; Harold Kaese, "George Wright," *Dictionary of American Biography* (New York: Charles Scribners' Sons 1958), 11:737. For more on sports in the parks, see Hardy, *How Boston Played.*

53. Massachusetts 90:232 (4 December 1884, 17 April 1886) Dun Collection; *Sporting Goods Gazette* 3 (December 1890): 30.

54. Albert A. Pope, "The Bicycle Industry," in Chauncey, M. De Pew, ed., *One Hundred Years of American Commerce* (New York: D. O. Haynes and Co., 1895), 551. On Rawlings and Davis, see *Sporting Goods Gazette* 3 (December 1890): 7, 32. For a list of "tried and true" promotional activities, see Hugo Autz, *Establishing and Operating a Sporting Goods Store,* Industrial Small Business Series no. 54 (Washington, D.C.: U.S. Department of Commerce, 1946), 35–38.

55. Appadurai, *Social Life of Things,* 40; Thomas Wentworth Higginson, "Gymnastics," in his *Outdoor Papers* (Boston: Houghton Mifflin, 1871), 158.

56. Quoted in special "1000th Issue" supplement of *Sporting Goods Dealer,* February 1983, p. 86.

57. Ibid.; Levine, *A. G. Spalding,* 82. On the deep historical roots of so-called modern marketing, see Ronald A. Fullerton, "How Modern Is Modern Marketing? Marketing's Evolution and the Myth of the 'Production Era,'" *Journal of Marketing* 52 (January 1988): 108–25.

58. Albert Applin, "From Muscular Christianity to the Marketplace: The History of Men's and Boys' Basketball in the United States, 1891–1957" (Ph.D. diss., University of Massachusetts, 1982), 55; *Sporting News,* 23 February 1889.

59. On the social and economic basis of these centripetal tendencies, see Williams, *Sociology of Culture,* 97–118.

60. *19th Century Games & Sporting Goods: Peck & Snyder, 1886* (Princeton, N.J.: Pyke Press, 1971); *Sporting News,* 26 December 1896, 12 June 1897, 23 January 1903. Mrozek provides rich description and insight into the new sport and exercise "experts" in *Sport and American Mentality,* 67–102. See also Burton J. Bledstein, *The Culture of Professionalism: The Middle Class and the Development of Higher Education* (New York: W. W. Norton, 1976), 81–83.

61. Paul Starr, *The Social Transformation of American Medicine* (New York: Basic Books, 1982), 15, 223. On notions of authority and legitimacy,

see also Thomas Haskell, ed., *Authority of Experts* (Bloomington, Ind.: Indiana University Press, 1984); and Max Weber, *Economy and Society*, ed. Gunther Roth and Claus Wittich (Berkeley, Calif.: University of California Press, 1978), 1:31–38, 212–301.

62. *Peck & Snyder, 1886;* Levine, *A. G. Spalding*, 77; Applin, "Muscular Christianity," 54; James B. Connolly, "The Capitalization of Amateur Athletics," *Metropolitan Magazine*, July 1910, pp. 443–54. The Walter Camp Papers, Yale University Library, include correspondence from the Victor Sporting Goods Company to the Rules Committee complaining about Spalding's tactics. I am grateful to Steven Gunn for pointing this out.

63. *Walter Camp's Book of College Sports* (New York: Century Co., 1895), 114 (again, I am indebted to Steven Gunn). For track and field, see James E. Sullivan, ed., *An Athletic Primer* (New York: American Sports Publishing Co., 1907); for basketball, Senda Berenson, *Basketball for Women* (New York: American Sports Publishing Co., 1903). The basketball guidebook includes an ad for Appleby field hockey sticks. On Sullivan's role in fusing sporting goods with governing bodies, see Stephen Hardy, "The Sportgeist and Historical Structures," in Donald Kyle and Gary Stark, eds., *Essays on Sport History and Sport Mythology* (College Station, Tex.: Texas A&M Press, forthcoming).

64. *Sporting News*, 22 September 1902. Ironically, too, the firms pressed Camp for a more "open" and less violent game. See Guy Lewis, "The American Intercollegiate Football Spectacle, 1869–1917" (Ph.D. diss., University of Maryland, 1965), 79; and Roberta J. Park, "Physiologists, Physicians, and Physical Educators: Nineteenth Century Biology and Exercise," *Journal of Sport History* 14 (Spring 1987): 31.

65. *Sporting News*, 30 January, 5 September 1897; Gorn, *The Manly Art*, 297; Lyle Hallowell, "The Political Economy of Violence and Control: A Sociological History of Professional Ice Hockey" (Ph.D. diss., University of Minnesota, 1981), 131.

66. On democratization, see Michael Schudson, *Advertising, the Uneasy Persuasion: Its Dubious Impact on American Society* (New York: Basic Books, 1984), 181–82. On the Haskell golf ball, see William Baker, *Sports in the Western World* (Totowa N.J.: Rowman & Allenheld, 1982), 188. On current issues, see Lisa Goulian, "The Graphite Bat," *Sports Inc.*, 16 November 1987, p. 92; Chuck Stogel, "Profile—Frank Hannigan," *Sports Inc.*, 25 January 1988, pp. 24–26; *Sporting Goods Dealer*, January 1987.

67. Mrozek, *Sport and American Mentality*, 86–91; Bledstein, *Culture of Professionalism*, 90.

68. Howard Savage et al., *American College Athletics*, Bulletin no. 23 (New York: Carnegie Foundation for the Advancement of Teaching, 1929), 176.

69. Hal A. Lawson, "Knowledge for Work in The Physical Education Profession," *Sociology of Sport Journal* 2 (1985): 20. For more on physical education and the marketplace, see Park, "Physiologists, Physicians, and Physical Educators"; Paula Lupcho, "The Professionalization of American Physical Education, 1885–1930" (Ph.D. diss., University of California, Berke-

ley, 1986); Janet Harris, "Social Contexts, Scholarly Inquiry, and Physical Education," *Quest* 39 (1987): 282–94; Mrozek, *Sport and American Mentality*, 97–102.

70. See Joan Hult. "The Governance of Athletics for Girls and Women: Leadership by Women Physical Educators, 1899–1949," *Research Quarterly for Exercise and Sport*, Centennial Issue, April 1985, 64–77.

71. See *Catalogue of the Snitz Manufacturing Co.* (East Troy, Wis., 1988), 39, 116. On the play movement, see Stephen Hardy and Alan Ingham, "Games, Structures, and Agency: Historians on the American Play Movement," *Journal of Social History* 17 (Winter 1983): 285–301.

72. For thoughtful analysis of the balance between agency and structure in sport, leisure, and consumption, see Gruneau, *Class, Sports, and Social Development;* Roy Rosenzweig, *Eight Hours for What We Will: Workers and Leisure in an Industrial City, 1870–1920* (New York: Cambridge University Press, 1983); Daniel Horowitz, *The Morality of Spending: Attitudes toward the Consumer Society in America, 1875–1940* (Baltimore, Md.: Johns Hopkins University Press, 1985).

PART III
COMMERCIALIZATION TAKES SHAPE

5

COMMERCIAL LEISURE AND THE "WOMAN QUESTION"

Kathy Peiss

The capitalist penetration and mediation of leisure in the last hundred years—the emergence of leisure as a purchasable commodity or service—has had significant implications for the daily lives of women and men. Activities once organized on a local, neighborhood, or voluntary basis have been transformed by a process characterized by capital concentration, consolidation, and rationalization, by the introduction of new technologies, and by the elaboration of ideologies justifying commodified leisure forms. One of the most significant aspects of this process has involved the creation and socialization of consumers. In their drive to expand profitmaking opportunities in leisure, entrepreneurs have looked toward the development and expansion of the consumer market for amusement and entertainment.

In the late nineteenth and early twentieth centuries, the development of this market proved to be not only an economic

Acknowledgments: Thanks to Richard Butsch and the anonymous reviewer for their helpful suggestions.

problem for entrepreneurs but a cultural one. In order to create consumers of their entertainment, they found it necessary to negotiate social divisions that permeated American society and shaped the character and consumption of commercial leisure. Handling gender was one of the challenges that leisure enterprises had to resolve to ensure the growth of commercial entertainment and recreation. Patriarchal social relations rendered problematic the notion of women as consumers of leisure; given the sexual division of labor and women's economic dependency, they could not be viewed as autonomous individuals in the marketplace. Hence, entrepreneurs faced a version of the "woman question" so prominently debated in the same period. Could women be enticed into commercial forms of recreation? Under what conditions? What forms of leisure activity could include women as well as men?

Although some leisure businesses targeted households, changing the practice of leisure within the domestic sphere with such goods as stereopticons and player pianos, the dominant direction of commercialization involved the use of public, nondomestic space. Addressing the "woman question" involved not only overcoming ideological and material barriers to women's social activity in the public sphere but also the redefinition of masculinity in that sphere. Inviting women into activities that had been socially constructed as masculine posed enormous problems. Leisure entrepreneurs solved them in several ways: by manipulating and delimiting public space, by domesticating the male audience, and by consciously identifying their amusements with cultural messages congenial to women. The scripts they presented, however, were not simply affirmations of a single cultural style; rather, they entailed a complex mediation of evolving cultural definitions of appropriate and desirable female behavior. In addressing women as a potential market, leisure entrepreneurs had to read the complexities and fluctuations of the cultural construction of gender.

In the nineteenth century the cultural opposition between women, the privatized family, and "femininity" on the one hand and a masculine public order on the other had gained legitimacy in a society undergoing bewildering industrial and urban transformation. Cultural definitions of masculinity were bound up not only with the realms of politics, civic duties, and labor but also with commercially provided social activities. Indeed these arenas of activity were intertwined, with leisure spaces facilitating men's involvement in other aspects of public life. Although some mixed-sex forms of entertainment, such as the legitimate stage and beer gardens, were popular, the most widespread forms of commercial leisure throughout the nineteenth century were dominated by men and expressive of a male culture.[1]

Saloon owners, for example, encouraged men of various classes to understand social drinking as a ritual that not only provided a respite from their work and family lives but also offered economic services, psychological support, and sociability. Working-class bars often served as employment agencies, provided banking and credit services, and were the locus of union and political meetings; middle-class saloons were places to make professional contacts and lubricate business agreements. At the same time that such leisure activity reinforced men's public roles, it strengthened an ethos of masculinity through the use of language, the acceptability of rowdiness, the presence of gambling, and, at times, the availability of prostitutes.[2]

Notions of womanhood derived from the antebellum "cult of domesticity" retained their salience in the late nineteenth century's leisure patterns. While commercialized leisure was integrated into men's public life, the codification of women's domestic role, especially in the middle class, located their leisure primarily in the family, church, voluntary organizations, and neighborhood ties. For women, the household was identified as the location for rest and refreshment, the "haven in a heartless world" of male competition and potentially dangerous public spaces. Privatization and more stringent notions of sexual purity meant that middle-class women's respectability was tied to their conceptual exclusion from the familiarity and heterogeneity of public spaces, particularly contact with men of the "lower" and "dangerous" classes.[3]

This ideological construction had less salience in the lives of most working-class women. Concepts of public and private space were less rigid; the streets, for example, served as intermediary conduits for women's socializing, household labor, and consumption. Yet for most of these women, especially wives and mothers, the material conditions of their lives dictated their exclusion from commercial leisure. The sexual division of labor that assigned women to household duties, plus the asymmetrical distribution of financial resources, gave women few opportunities for participation in commercial leisure. For many, family income barely purchased necessities, while housework and child-rearing responsibilities consumed their hours. Relative to their husbands and brothers, working-class women had little spending money for amusements. For wives in particular, their moments of leisure were constructed around the home, church, and free pastimes, including holiday rituals, excursions to parks, and after-dinner promenades.[4]

Broad social and cultural changes in the nineteenth century, however, created the conditions under which many women might choose to participate in commercially provided entertainment. For middle-class women the ideology of domesticity and maternalism formed the basis for the flowering of public activities; this "women's movement" included club and church work, higher education, reform, and political activism. Indeed, by the late nineteenth century such public activity had become identified with an emergent feminine ideal, the "New Woman," which signaled greater personal autonomy and social participation, placing new categories of behavior under the rubric of female respectability. Some working-class women, usually single and in the labor force, also experimented with new social roles and activities. These women not only populated the noncommercial spaces of the streets but frequented the popular theater, beer gardens, dance halls, and commercial picnic grounds.[5]

At the same time, from as early as the mid-nineteenth century some leisure entrepreneurs sought actively to cultivate this potential female audience. Such showmen as P. T. Barnum and Moses Kimball enticed women into museum theaters in the 1840s and 1850s with a mix of respectable entertainment and refined surroundings (see Bruce McConachie, Chapter 3 in this volume). The so-called legitimate theater had by the 1860s ousted prostitutes from the "guilty third tier" and banned male drinking in the pit in an effort to attract middle-class family groups; reducing the informality and rowdiness of theater audiences, it was felt, would appeal to heightened notions of female respectability. But even though public leisure space per se and some forms of commercial entertainment were not barred to women, entering certain commercial leisure places continued to trouble many women in the late nineteenth century: places whose forms of entertainment had had their origins in male commercial culture, the world of the saloon, music hall, dance house, and arcade.[6]

Breaking with that tradition to gain female patronage proved a complex task for amusement entrepreneurs, who sought to foster an aura of respectability appropriate to female sensibilities without emasculating the entertainment. First, they tried to delimit and stratify leisure spaces to reduce the heterogeneity of the audience and the possibilities of unwelcome interaction. This effort had both a class and gender dimension and proved to be a necessary strategy for businesses seeking a middle-class audience. Physical barriers were used, for example, to enclose the Coney Island amusement parks that emerged at the turn of the century. Enclosures with a single entrance allowed owners not only to control admission but to differentiate the parks, with their claims of "clean, wholesome fun," from the rowdier areas of Coney Island whose saloons, music halls, and salacious sideshows respectable women would want to avoid. The control of heterogeneous and potentially promiscuous leisure space occurred at a more minute level of organization as well. The spatial arrangement of the tables, dance floor, and stage in cabarets, Lewis Erenberg has shown, placed barriers between friends and strangers, audiences and performers, and particularly limited the contacts between unacquainted women and men. In the early twentieth century, table-hopping and talking across tables, for example, were outlawed at a number of night spots, and entertainers were not permitted to mingle with the patrons.[7]

Implicit in the effort to reorganize space was a concern among leisure entrepreneurs with the domestication of the male audience, particularly in entertainments seeking middle-class patronage. The attack on male culture involved several key elements: limiting the availability of alcohol in commercial amusements; barring prostitutes, demimondaines, and other women of questionable repute from those spaces; and cleaning up the language and behavior of both entertainers and audience, especially ribaldry, rowdiness, and the use of slang and obscenities.

Though this drive to limit male culture was not new, it broadened with the rapid expansion of commercial leisure in the late nineteenth century, proceeding not only in a few higher-status entertainments but also in a wide range of working-class and middle-class amusements. The process can be seen most clearly in such popular theatrical entertainments as variety and vaudeville. The origins of vaudeville have been traced to two forms of variety: dime museums, which offered variety performances as well as "freak" shows, attracted a respectable audience of working-class people and rural visitors to the city; concert saloons embodied a male culture devoted to drinking, noisy sociability, and racy entertainment. In the 1850s and 1860s some saloon owners began to convert their back rooms and cellars into small concert halls and hire specialty acts to amuse their patrons and encourage drinking. Gradually, the comic skits, sentimental songs, acrobatics, minstrelsy, and dance routines became as important as the drinking. "Waiter girls," scantily clad female performers, and prostitutes added to the salacious connotations of the shows. Both the entertainment and the audience marked this form of variety as a space of male sexual and social privilege; it would have repulsed most Victorian women.[8]

Prescient entrepreneurs, however, began to create a new language of entertainment in variety that would be acceptable to women. In the 1860s, showman Tony Pastor, ambitious to expand his audience, began to make theatrical entertainment, rather than barroom drinking, the *raison d'être* of his variety house. He ordered performers to refrain from vulgar songs and obscene skits that might offend the ladies. He could not get rid of the theater saloon, but he allowed drinking only during the intermission rather than throughout the show, to prevent men from becoming too drunken and rowdy. Moreover, he tried to entice women with reassurances of "family entertainment," matinees that would be convenient for mothers, prizes of coal, flour, and dress patterns, and free admission on "Ladies Invitation Night."[9]

Despite his efforts, variety never fully lost its disreputable aura; it remained a male, primarily working-class, form of entertainment. The transformation of variety into vaudeville, however, was a more successful effort to divorce commercial leisure from antecedents that would alienate women. For some promoters the larger scale of vaudeville, the national syndicates, and the star system meant heavier investments, necessitating an appeal to a large, mixed-sex, mixed-class audience. At the "big-time" level of vaudeville, managers insisted on refined language and drawing-room manners, leading some to call it the "Sunday School circuit." Neophyte writers were warned not to use improper themes, offensive slang, or double entendres in their vaudeville sketches. B. F. Keith sought to tame the men in his audience as well, with signs admonishing them to remove their hats, not stamp their feet, and generally remember that there were ladies present.[10]

Audiences for motion pictures, the most popular form of commercial entertainment among working-class people in the early twentieth century, developed quite differently from those for vaudeville, but some of the same issues of gender and respectability were important to the nascent movie industry. In the 1890s and early 1900s, some movies were viewed through peep-show devices in penny arcades, but by the turn of the century most were projected on screens in vaudeville houses, traveling shows, and amusement parks. Some of the short films shown in arcades to a largely male clientele must be considered sexually explicit for this time period—brief scenes of kissing, women undressing, voyeurism, and other sexual stage business—but most projected films made after 1903 were "respectable" comedies and melodramas acceptable to women, who viewed them at vaudeville shows. After 1905, when storefront nickelodeons and small theaters sprouted in cities and towns throughout the country, the movies became immediately popular with working-class and immigrant women. Storefront shows were frequented especially by wives and mothers who theretofore had had little exposure to commercial leisure. They defined the nickelodeon as a social center where they could get an inexpensive respite from housework, meet the neighbors, and distract their children. Moreover, the movies were a potential "substitute for the saloon" that might replace the threat that drink posed to the family's economic and psychological well-being. While the movie manufacturers and exhibitors did not *create* the demand for movies among women, they sought to encourage and expand upon the nickelodeons' immediate popularity among working-class women and began to build a middle-class audience.[11]

By attacking the drinking culture, prostitution, explicit sexuality, and male rowdiness that had traditionally characterized the commercial entertainment patronized by men, leisure businesses focused on some of the most potent symbols of gender conflict in American society. As sites of male sexual and social privilege, places of commercial leisure had drawn the fire of many women, who saw in them a challenge to family-centered values. Many women of both the middle and working classes were struggling as individuals to prevent their husbands and sons from attending saloons, music halls, and the like, where they spent wages needed by the family. Moreover, middle-class women who had organized movements for temperance and the eradication of the double standard sought the regulation of public commercial amusements, particularly the saloon trade but also music halls, dime museums and arcades, variety shows, and movies.[12]

Yet in taming the male audience, the purveyors of leisure did not simply invoke an earlier notion of womanhood characterized by purity, maternalism, and domesticity. Indeed, given their roots in male, working-class, and/or ethnic popular cultural traditions, many entrepreneurs delighted in poking fun at the middle-class mores they associated with women. Rather, they approached the "woman question" as *bricoleurs,* combining cultural elements to satisfy women's notions of respectability while still catering to the male audience. They built their concept of the female audience out of the constellation of cultural beliefs and social practices that inscribed the "New Woman." But since the term "New Woman" carried a range of meanings in the period from 1890 to 1920, entrepreneurs played upon the concept in a variety of ways.

Some leisure businesses conceptualized women as extending their household roles into public spaces, like many New Women of the day who justified their public activity as an extension of their domestic and maternal roles. Their involvement in urban reform, for example, could be called "Municipal Housekeeping," while activism on behalf of temperance, including demonstrations and prayer vigils at saloons, was legitimated in the name of "Home Protection." Using the same kind of mediation between "home" and "world," leisure businesses might define their offerings as "family entertainment."[13]

As we have seen, vaudeville managers and movie exhibitors sought to provide social spaces where women could take their children for a few hours in the afternoon, and where the entire family could spend an evening. The early trade journals of the motion picture industry, for example, explicitly directed manufacturers and exhibitors to reassure women that the movies were acceptable family entertainment, as a way of gaining a respectable audience. "Play to the Ladies," one writer advised, by not showing objectionable films. Slides projected between movies conveyed the message directly: "We are aiming to please the ladies," and "Bring the children."[14]

But all this was more than an effort to make commercial entertainment seem homelike. Appeals to women, particularly in the middle class, affirmed them as individuals who had public roles, however gender based. Women were shoppers in the market and participants in the spectacle of urban life; they had domestic and maternal obligations that led them into the public realm. Leisure entrepreneurs played on this notion of womanhood as they stage-managed women's entrance into commercial entertainment. Many of the large vaudeville palaces, for example, were located close to major shopping districts; in New York, as shopping moved uptown, so did the theaters, which ran ladies' matinees and "continuous performances." Like the department store, the quintessential urban space for women in the late nineteenth century, these vaudeville houses were palaces of consumption, amusement, and service. Keith and other owners carefully orchestrated the experience: solicitous ushers led the women into these temples of entertainment, implicitly promising comfort and safety within public space. The studied opulence of lobbies and interiors catered to women's sense of gentility and refinement; gilt fixtures, plush seats, artwork, and lounges contributed to an ambience far removed from the saloon culture of earlier commercial entertainments.[15]

Yet this version of the "New Woman," stressing women's respectability and safety in public space, was not the only constellation of images that leisure entrepreneurs drew upon. By 1900 many commercial amusements stressed another cultural message, that these were public spaces wherein women could experiment with new social roles. In the promotion of the dance craze in the early 1910s, for example, both middle-class cabaret owners and working-class dance hall managers enticed female patrons with promises of excitement, glamour, and sensuality.

The dance halls attracted young working women interested in meeting men and having a good time, and managers fostered an ambience that was far removed from the demands of the workplace and family. Although many working-class halls had their origins in the saloon trade, managers differentiated this mixed-sex arena of pleasure from the world of male culture by welcoming women attending alone or in groups, sponsoring fancy dress balls and masquerades, and mixing unusual cocktails to appeal to their female customers. Moreover, they looked the other way as their youthful patrons danced sensual dances, drank, and engaged in sexual banter. Age-segregated dance halls specifically catered to a subculture of young women and men who sought escape from traditional notions of respectability, whether these came from their immigrant working-class families or from the dominant middle-class culture.[16]

Middle-class cabarets, while more restrained, also evoked new models of womanhood for their patrons. As Erenberg has argued, the cabarets were social spaces where a segment of the middle class could experiment with a more expressive, sensual culture in glittering surroundings, with ragtime music punctuating the pleasures of consumption. Dancing celebrities like Irene Castle epitomized a "New Woman" who was sophisticated, free-spirited, athletic, and sensuous. With Vernon Castle, she symbolized the new "manners and morals" of the Progressive era, stressing intimacy and freer sexuality between women and men. As Lary May has shown, a similar cultural message can be read in many of the movies of the late 1910s, in the film performance and celebrity lives of such actors as Mary Pickford and Douglas Fairbanks.[17]

At the same time, overtures to respectability limited the expression of these new social roles, particularly in middle-class amusements. Women's experimentation with individuality was shaped by their situation as contingent consumers, as half of a heterosexual couple. Cabarets, for example, often banned unescorted persons in order to eradicate the association of commercial leisure with "loose" women and prostitution.[18] Leisure entrepreneurs must also have recognized women's economic dependence on men, their lack of the resources necessary to purchase leisure on their own. Indeed, the one option the leisure industry did *not* choose in fostering a female audience was a homosocial women's culture, a separate female commercial leisure space. Encouraging women and men to define leisure as a form of mixed-sex activity, it promoted both an emergent culture of heterosocial and heterosexual pleasure and an older ethos of familism in a new commercial, consumption-oriented context.

Clearly, leisure entrepreneurs were not an undifferentiated mass in their handling of "the woman question." Social divisions of age, race, ethnicity, and class segmented the market for leisure, and businesses carved out different pieces of it that required varying responses to the shifting relations of gender. The scale of the entertainment—whether it was aimed at a local, regional, or national audience—had its effect, as did the different degrees of political pressure brought to bear on the industry by reform groups, civic leaders, and others. The variations in the responses of commercial leisure businesses to the presence of women suggest the essentially contested and negotiated character of gender definitions. Leisure institutions played an intricate game of mediation in which the lines between cultural oppositions—female and male, domestic and public, respectability and disrepute, sexual purity and sensual playfulness—were shifting and indeed blurred. However varied and multidimensional this process, the intensifying commodification of leisure contributed significantly to the twentieth-century gender definitions that emerged in a "culture of consumption." In a period when the Victorian construction of gender was in flux, indeed had begun to break down in important ways, leisure entrepreneurs groped toward a redefinition of womanhood that linked respectability, sexual and social expressiveness, familism, and commodity consumption.

NOTES

1. On the construction of gender in leisure and daily social life, see Kathy Peiss, *Cheap Amusements: Working Women and Leisure in Turn-of-the-Century New York* (Philadelphia: Temple University Press, 1986); Christine Stansell, *City of Women: Sex and Class in New York, 1789–1860* (New York: Knopf, 1986). On masculinity, see, e.g., Peter Filene, *Him/Her/Self: Sex Roles in Modern America* (2nd ed.; Baltimore, Md.: Johns Hopkins University Press, 1986); E. Anthony Rotundo, "Body and Soul: Changing Ideals of American Middle-Class Manhood, 1770–1920," *Journal of Social History* 16 (Summer 1983): 23–38; Ava Baron, "Contested Terrain Revisited: Technology and Gender Definitions of Work in the Printing Industry, 1850–1920,"

in Barbara Wright et al., eds., *Women, Work, and Technology: Transformations* (Ann Arbor: University of Michigan Press, 1987), 58–83.

2. Roy Rosenzweig, *Eight Hours for What We Will: Workers and Leisure in an Industrial City, 1870–1920* (New York: Cambridge University Press, 1983); Jon M. Kingsdale, "The 'Poor Man's Club': Social Functions of the Urban Working Class Saloon," *American Quarterly* 25 (October 1973): 472–89; John Alt, "Beyond Class: The Decline of Labor and Leisure," *Telos* 28 (Summer 1976): 55–80. See also Francis Couvares, *The Remaking of Pittsburgh: Class and Culture in an Industrializing City, 1877–1919* (Albany, N.Y.: SUNY Press, 1984).

3. On the social definition of womanhood, see, e.g., Mary P. Ryan, *Cradle of the Middle Class: The Family in Oneida County, New York* (New York: Cambridge University Press, 1981); Nancy Cott, *The Bonds of Womanhood: 'Woman's Sphere' in New England, 1780–1835* (New Haven, Conn.: Yale University Press, 1977); Carroll Smith-Rosenberg, *Disorderly Conduct: Visions of Gender in Victorian America* (New York: Oxford University Press, 1985).

4. Peiss, *Cheap Amusements;* Stansell, *City of Women;* Judith Smith, *Family Connections: A History of Italian and Jewish Immigrant Lives in Providence, Rhode Island, 1900–1940* (Albany, N.Y.: SUNY Press, 1985); Laura Oren, "The Welfare of Laboring Families," in Mary Hartmann and Lois Banner, eds., *Clio's Consciousness Raised* (New York: Harper & Row, 1974); Elizabeth Ewen, *Immigrant Women in the Land of Dollars: Life and Culture on the Lower East Side, 1890–1925* (New York: Monthly Review Press, 1985); Lizabeth Cohen, "Embellishing a Life of Labor: An Interpretation of the Material Culture of American Working-Class Homes," *Journal of American Culture* 3 (Winter 1980): 752–75.

5. On the middle-class "New Woman," see Smith-Rosenberg, "New Woman as Androgyne," in *Disorderly Conduct;* Sheila Rothman, *Women's Proper Place: A History of Changing Ideals and Practices* (New York: Basic Books, 1978); Barbara Epstein, *The Politics of Domesticity: Women, Evangelism, and Temperance in Nineteenth-Century America* (Middletown, Conn.: Wesleyan University Press, 1981); Ruth Bordin, *Woman and Temperance: The Quest for Power and Liberty, 1873–1900* (Philadelphia: Temple University Press, 1981); Rosalind Rosenberg, *Beyond Separate Spheres: Intellectual Roots of Modern Feminism* (New Haven, Conn.: Yale University Press, 1982). On working-class women, see Peiss, *Cheap Amusements,* and Ewen, *Immigrant Women.*

6. Claudia D. Johnson, "That Guilty Third Tier: Prostitution in Nineteenth-Century American Theaters," in Geoffrey Blodgett and Daniel Walker Howe, eds., *Victorian America* (Philadelphia: University of Pennsylvania Press, 1976).

7. John Kasson, *Amusing the Million: Coney Island at the Turn of the Century* (New York: Hill and Wang, 1978); Lewis Erenberg, *Steppin' Out: New York Nightlife and the Transformation of American Culture, 1890–1930* (Westport, Conn.: Greenwood Press, 1981). See also Vice Inves-

tigator's Reports in the Committee of Fourteen Papers, Rare Books and Manuscripts Division, New York Public Library, Astor, Lenox and Tilden Foundations.

8. Parker R. Zellers, "The Cradle of Variety: The Concert Saloon," *Educational Theater Journal* 20 (December 1968): 578–86.

9. H. E. Cooper, "Variety, Vaudeville, and Virtue," *Dance Magazine* 7 (December 1926): 31–32, 64; scrapbook of Tony Pastor's Opera House, Theater Arts Collection, Lincoln Center Library of the Performing Arts, New York Public Library.

10. See Robert Snyder, Chapter 6 in this volume; Albert F. McLean, Jr., *American Vaudeville as Ritual* (Lexington, Ky.: University of Kentucky Press, 1965); Edward B. Marks (as told to A. J. Liebling), *They All Sang: From Tony Pastor to Rudy Vallee* (New York: Viking Press, 1934).

11. Russell Merritt, "Nickelodeon Theaters, 1905–1914: Building an Audience for the Movies," in Tino Balio, ed., *The American Film Industry* (Madison, Wis.: University of Wisconsin Press, 1976), 59–82; Garth S. Jowett, "The First Motion Picture Audiences," *Journal of Popular Film* 3 (1974): 39–54; S. C. Kingsley, "Penny Arcade and the Cheap Theater," *Charities and the Commons* 18 (8 June 1907): 295–97. For a more extensive discussion, see Peiss, *Cheap Amusements*, 145–62.

12. See, e.g., Lillian Betts, *The Leaven in a Great City* (New York: Dodd, Mead & Co., 1903), 258: Albert Kennedy, "The Saloon in Retrospect and Prospect," in Collateral Papers, Prohibition, Papers of Lillian Wald, Rare Books and Manuscripts Division, New York Public Library, Astor, Lenox, and Tilden Foundations. A wide range of middle-class women's organizations, including the WCTU, YWCA, and settlement houses, attacked commercial leisure; for an overview of the reform impetus, see Paul Boyer, *Urban Masses and Moral Order in America, 1820–1920* (Cambridge, Mass.: Harvard University Press, 1978).

13. On the mediation between domestic and public roles, see, e.g., Rothman, *Women's Proper Place*.

14. *Views and Films Index* 2 (11 May 1907): 3; *Views and Films Index* 3 (29 February 1908): 5; *Nickelodeon* 1 (February 1909): 33–34.

15. For a discussion of vaudeville houses and department stores, see Gunther Barth, *City People: The Rise of Modern City Culture in Nineteenth-Century America* (New York: Oxford University Press, 1980); and Robert Snyder's essay, Chapter 6. On women consumers in department stores, see William Leach, "Transformations in a Culture of Consumption: Women and Department Stores," *Journal of American History* 71 (September 1984): 319–42; Susan Porter Benson, *Counter Cultures: Saleswomen, Managers, and Customers in American Department Stores, 1890–1940* (Urbana, Ill.: University of Illinois Press, 1986).

16. Peiss, *Cheap Amusements*, 88–114.

17. Erenberg, *Steppin' Out*, 146–75; Lary May, *Screening Out the Past: The Birth of Mass Culture and the Motion Picture Industry* (New York: Oxford University Press, 1980), 96–146; Elizabeth Ewen, "City Lights: Immigrant Women and the Rise of the Movies," *Signs* 5, supp. (1980):

S45–65; Robert Sklar, *Movie-Made America: A Cultural History of American Movies* (New York: Vintage, 1975). See also Kay Sloan, "Sexual Warfare in the Silent Cinema: Comedies and Melodramas of Woman Suffrage," *American Quarterly* 33 (Fall 1981): 412–36.

18. Erenberg, *Steppin' Out*, 135–37. On the cultural ideal of companionship between the sexes, see Christina Simmons, "'Marriage in the Modern Manner': Sexual Radicalism and Reform in America, 1914–1941" (Ph.D. diss., Brown University, 1982), 105–49.

6

BIG TIME, SMALL TIME, ALL AROUND THE TOWN: NEW YORK VAUDEVILLE IN THE EARLY TWENTIETH CENTURY

Robert W. Snyder

Imagine an aerial photograph of the New York City vaudeville scene taken during its prime, around 1915: a picture of a cultural nerve system, with vibrant centers of activity located throughout the city and vigorous messages pulsating between them. The hub is at Times Square in Manhattan, site of the famous Palace Theater and the major booking offices. Secondary centers appear in the major business districts of other boroughs: 149th Street in the Bronx, home of the Royal and National theaters; the Fulton Street area of downtown Brooklyn, home of the Orpheum. Farther afield in the most localized business districts of the city, often in working-class or immigrant quarters, are neighborhood small-time theaters such as Loew's Avenue B on the Lower East Side of Manhattan, and Fox's Folly

Acknowledgments: This essay derives from a chapter of my book *The Voice of the City: Vaudeville and Popular Culture in New York* (New York: Oxford University Press, 1989) and is used here by permission. It was written with the support of a Smithsonian Institution predoctoral fellowship and presented at the Commercial Culture seminar of the New York Institute for the Humanities in February 1986. Many who were there that day offered worthwhile advice; the suggestions of William Taylor and Daniel Czitrom were particularly helpful.

Theatre in Williamsburg, Brooklyn. On the city's fringe at the seaside cluster summertime vaudeville houses that cater to resort and amusement park crowds: the Brighton Beach Music Hall in Brooklyn; the Terminal Music Hall in North Beach, Queens; Nunley's Casino in South Beach, Staten Island.

Such a photograph is imaginary, but the networks were real. Their history began in the 1880s and 1890s, when entrepreneurial showmen refashioned male-oriented, plebeian, licentious, alcoholic variety theater into vaudeville. The two were structurally identical: a series of individual acts strung together to form a complete bill. But vaudeville was variety cleaned up—at least in theory—to attract a broader and more profitable audience that included women and middle-class families. The creators of vaudeville attempted to bridge the enormous social differences that had splintered the more cohesive theater audience of the early nineteenth century.[1]

The vaudeville years—the 1880s to the 1920s—marked a critical period in the evolution of popular culture. Popular culture is defined by its broad audience and its accessibility to all segments of society, but at the turn of the century the conditions under which it was produced and enjoyed were changing. From colonial days to the middle nineteenth century, American popular culture had been deeply influenced by custom, tradition, and public festivity. It was usually rooted in a specific place—such as the Bowery of New York City, with its saloons and cheap theaters—where local likes and dislikes exercised a profound influence over the relationship between artists and audiences. But in the twentieth century, popular culture came to be defined by electronic mass media—film, radio, recordings, and television. A centrally controlled entertainment industry, disseminating standardized products from coast to coast, undermined the local bases of culture. Audiences, which had once so intensely interacted with performers, came to be consumers of electronic sounds and images, often in the privacy of their homes. The relationship between popular culture and place was transformed.

Vaudeville played a critical early role in this transformation. Touring vaudevillians took their acts to one theater after another, making it possible for people in the Bronx to see the same performances as people in Brooklyn. The artists were attentive to the differences between the theaters they played in, but when New Yorkers in disparate parts of the city saw the same performers, the cultural elements they held in common were enlarged. They were that much more ready for even more uniform products such as films, radio shows, and records.

The creation of vaudeville never erased the differences between New Yorkers, but the vaudeville house and the citywide vaudeville scene did become a huge arena for cultural exchange between the city's many peoples. Inside the vaudeville house, immigrants encountered a commercial ethnic culture rooted partly in the immigrant world and partly in Tin Pan Alley. Middle-class Victorians found their culture of restraint and self-discipline challenged by brash comedians, singers, and dancers from the Lower East Side. New Yorkers from far corners of the city came to participate in an expansive, dynamic metropolitan popular culture that transformed all involved.

Vaudeville was everywhere in New York City during the first two decades of the twentieth century because profit-seeking vaudeville entrepreneurs attempted to sell it everywhere. In their economic empire-building they created city- and nation-wide circuits of vaudeville theaters. Critics of the powerful Keith-Albee organization correctly likened it to an octopus, with a Times Square booking office brain and theater circuit tentacles.[2] Circuit-building was also part of New York's social and geographic evolution. Vaudeville houses followed the subway lines outward, relying on proximity to transit and shopping to draw patrons and becoming central to new business districts.

Yet even though vaudeville was everywhere in New York City, it was not monolithic. It did not bridge the city's different cultures by shoehorning diverse peoples into standardized, homogenized theaters. Showmen fit their entertainment wares into a complicated city, recognizing and often accommodating their audience's enormous diversity. There was a vaudeville house for practically every kind of New Yorker. Middle-class women out shopping could seek a refined Keith-Albee theater. Working-class Jewish immigrants on the Lower East Side found vaudeville at Loew's theaters on Delancey Street or Avenue B. Vaudeville reached people from different classes and ethnic groups because for each of them it appeared in familiar surroundings, smoothing their entry into a heterogeneous cultural network.

The distinctions between theaters were partly a function of the difference between big-time and small-time vaudeville. Big time meant two shows per day; small time, four or five shows a day or continuous performances. Big time featured star performers, whose high salaries compelled higher ticket prices. Small-time acts were paid less, allowing for lower ticket prices (entrepreneurs were compensated by the greater number of shows). Small-time vaudeville generally appealed to local neighborhoods, often those of working-class or immigrant New Yorkers. Big time, higher priced and located in major shopping and entertainment districts, sought city- or borough-wide audiences and consequently a broader mixture of ethnic groups and classes. Big time often aimed at the middle class but remained open to working-class patrons who could afford the higher ticket prices. Aesthetically, small time had a reputation for being rougher, with somewhat broader humor. Its performers were almost always people on their way up to the big time or down from it.[3]

The cultural dialogue that distinguished vaudeville was the sum of many conversations, conducted from the elite stages of midtown Manhattan to the small-time halls of Brooklyn. To hear and witness them, begin at Times Square, home of the famous Palace.

Times Square was not the only neighborhood to serve as the hub of New York vaudeville, but in the twentieth century it became the most important. Throughout Manhattan's history, the theater district—along with the commercial district—had moved steadily uptown, staying just ahead of the ever northward movement of the city's core. Theater owners built on the fringe of the city's central business district, apparently to take advantage of lower land prices.[4] The theaters were shadowed by two other trades: Tin Pan Alley, home of song writing and publishing, which relied on the theaters to disseminate its songs;[5] and the vice district, which after the 1850s moved uptown from the Bowery. By the 1870s and 1880s Manhattan's red-light district reclined along Sixth Avenue between 24th and 40th streets.[6]

From the 1880s into the early 1890s, vaudeville's center was on 14th Street near Union Square, where Tony Pastor established his theater in Tammany Hall. Then the hub moved north to 23rd Street, home of Koster and Bial's music hall and Proctor's 23rd Street music hall (its slogan for continuous vaudeville: "After breakfast go to Proctor's, after Proctor's go to bed"). Near both were the Keith offices at 26th Street and Broadway, off Madison Square.[7]

Showmen sought to draw crowds with the right combination of mass transit, busy streets and sidewalks, and distance from vice districts—a distance often mostly psychological. "Be careful to locate on the right side of the street," Edward Renton wrote in a guide to running the vaudeville theater, "for there are a right and a wrong side of every street, a popular and an unpopular side."[8] By the turn of the century, the right side of the street was nearing 42nd Street and Broadway, an intersection then known as Longacre Square.[9]

In November 1895, Oscar Hammerstein opened the mammoth

Olympia Theatre on Broadway between 44th and 45th streets, heralding Longacre Square's emergence as an entertainment center. At the Olympia a fifty-cent ticket bought admission to a pleasure palace incorporating a music hall, a theater, a concert hall, bowling alleys, a billiard hall, a rathskeller, lounges, smoking rooms, and a Turkish bath, all capped by a roof garden. The interior was decorated with stucco, sculptures, and designs in styles attributed to the French kings Louis XIV, XV, and XVI. The music hall, for example, was Louis XIV: a white and gold motif, with paneled ceilings decorated in floral designs, a massive chandelier hanging from a rosette surrounded by dancing cupids, and walls covered with ornamental medallions and panels. But behind this bold enterprise was Hammerstein's flawed business management: the Olympia failed to turn a profit. In 1898 the building was mortgaged to Klaw and Erlanger of the legitimate theatrical syndicate, who eventually sold it to vaudeville magnate Marcus Loew. But Hammerstein's decision to build where he did, and other entrepreneurs' willingness to follow him, showed that something was happening.[10]

The biggest boost for the area's theatrical fortunes came in 1904, when New York City opened its first subway line. The Interborough proceeded north from the Brooklyn Bridge along Manhattan's East Side, then headed west on 42nd Street before turning north at Broadway to continue uptown. When the *New York Times* opened a new office building at the spot where the subway turned north, the intersection acquired its new name: Times Square. Mass transit brought millions to the square, and in less than ten years it had become Manhattan's new entertainment center.[11]

Times Square used electric lighting and a concentration of attractions to create the fantastic environment described by Stephen Jenkins in 1911.

> Broadway from Thirty-fourth to Forty-seventh street has been for the last few years the locality where the gay life of the metropolis has been most readily seen. Here are congregated great hotels, famous restaurants, and theatres; and the brilliant illumination at night by countless electric lights has caused this section of the avenue to be called the "great white way"; and no stranger has seen New York who has not transversed it.
>
> When we cross Forty-second street we are in the very heart of the "great white way" ... and the owners and purchasers of property seem to be imbued with a perfect mania for tearing down and rebuilding.[12]

By 1913 the bright lights were illuminating vaudeville houses that included Hammerstein's Victoria at 42nd Street and Seventh Avenue, Loew's American at 42nd and Eighth, and the Palace at Broadway and 47th.[13]

Big-time theaters could be lavish: paved marble entrances, marble columns, statues, elaborately ornamented proscenium arches, and vibrant color schemes. The Palace had richly decorated box seats resting beneath sculpted wall ornaments, and its proscenium arch was outlined in bas-relief designs.[14] All this anticipated the movie palaces of the 1930s (though these theaters were often more intimate: the Palace had 1,736 seats, the quintessential 1930s movie palace, Loew's Paradise in the Bronx, had 3,884).[15]

There was a purpose to this opulence. As Renton noted, vaudeville house decor fed working-class dreams of luxury and middle-class ideas of status.

> It should never be forgotten that the theatre draws people from all sorts and conditions; in particular does the vaudeville house draw from both the classes and the masses. A theatre should represent to the less favored of its patrons, something finer and more desirable than their ordinary surroundings; and to the better class, it should never present itself as inferior to the environment to which such persons are accustomed.[16]

A balance of price, design, location, appeal, and inclusiveness was critical to a theater's success. The Palace, opening 24 March 1913, initially failed to attract many customers, possibly because its ticket prices ranged from twenty-five and fifty cents for gallery seats to two dollars for boxes. Other vaudeville houses nearby were less expensive: the average ticket to Hammerstein's Victoria cost one dollar, and a front-row seat could be had at Loew's American for twenty-five cents. Appearances by Ethel Barrymore in April and Sarah Bernhardt in May, however, attracted patrons and helped make the Palace the premier vaudeville theater in New York City.[17]

Times Square, like the theater districts that preceded it, featured many levels of vaudeville. There was a tension between building a mass audience and recognizing the city's multiple theatrical tastes. When the differences between patrons were too great to be reconciled under one roof, entrepreneurs acknowledged them by establishing different theaters. Consider Norman Hapgood's comparison in 1901 (the street he describes is almost certainly either 14th or 23rd street):

> There are two . . . houses on a certain street in New York, within a block of each other. A knowledge of the two would be enough to suggest the differences in the lives of various "artistes" in the same general world,

> both artistically and professionally. Sometimes the same person will appear at both places, but in the main the whole personnel is unlike, the superiority of the performances in tone and ability at one house corresponding to the superior quality of the patrons. The same contrast holds between the most respectable . . . and the ordinary music hall, which has its exhibitions in the evening and is supported as largely by "sporty" men as the other is by the steady bourgeoisie.[18]

This diversity persisted in Times Square, as *Variety* noted in 1914: "Hammerstein's and the Palace are only a stone's throw from one another and the atmosphere of both is absolutely different." The Palace was the embodiment of Keith and Albee refinements, their theater for "the silk stocking trade."[19] Hammerstein's Victoria recalled the Barnum Museum of the mid-nineteenth century. Willie Hammerstein ran the house for his father, Oscar, and his methods of attracting crowds in hot weather were vintage humbug. In the Victoria's lobby he placed a thermometer purporting to indicate the temperature inside. A blackboard behind it recorded seventy degrees on the hottest days and urged skeptics to look at the thermometer—which actually rested on an exposed cake of ice. Hammerstein also heated the elevator that carried customers to his theater's roof garden. When sweltering passengers reached the roof, they could only conclude that it really was cooler there.[20]

Newsmakers appeared regularly at the Victoria: participants in sex scandals, prizefighters, wrestlers, bicycle racers, runners, sharpshooters, and suffragists. Woman's Suffragette Week of 1915 was a box-office failure but a publicity bonanza, with suffragists delivering speeches inside and outside the building. Hammerstein presented Jack Johnson, the black heavyweight champion whose affairs with white women were as famous as his pugilism. When chorus girls Lillian Graham and Ethel Conrad were released on bail after shooting Graham's wealthy lover, W. E. D. Stokes, the Victoria put them onstage as "The Shooting Stars." They packed the house.[21]

The Victoria's shows also encouraged the rowdy audience participation that was frowned on in big-time Keith houses, preserving some of the ambiance of the old variety theater. The Cherry Sisters, billed as "America's Worst Act," performed behind a net; it protected them when the audience threw vegetables and eggs. A sketch called "Hanged" climaxed with the warden refusing to spring the trap because he opposed capital punishment. A volunteer was then called from the audience to do the job. "Hanged" evolved into "Electrocution," in which an audience member pulled a switch that sent sparks flying from a simulated electric chair.[22]

The Victoria closed in 1915, partly the victim of competition from the Palace.[23] But nearby Loew's American was still offering low-priced vaudeville, and former vaudeville stars were appearing in revues such as the Ziegfeld Follies; with these attractions and the legitimate theaters, the crowds that filled Times Square found something for everyone, from the "gallery god" who had reveled in throwing rotten tomatoes in the cheap, upper seats in the Victoria to the middle-class couple who cherished the swank style of the Palace and the office worker on a tight budget who appreciated the cheap tickets at Loew's.

Sometimes, recognizing and accommodating New York's various classes and cultures was a matter of geography. Theaters in secondary business districts—the Upper West Side of Manhattan, the South Bronx, downtown Brooklyn—also presented top shows at a more local level; their patrons could see touring big-time performers without going to Times Square. Vaudeville thus enlarged the cultural elements these otherwise disparate people held in common. Keith's Riverside at 96th Street and Broadway was more than fifty blocks from the Palace, but a reviewer could conclude that "Riverside clientele, coming from Broadway and the Drive, understand their big time vaudeville."[24] Such theaters drew from pools of viewers smaller than those of Times Square but larger than those of neighborhood small time. Proctor's Pleasure Palace, an elaborate continuous vaudeville house on 58th Street between Third and Lexington avenues,

> has many thousands of people to draw from, being the only pretentious place of amusement between Harlem and the lower portion of the city upon the east side. It is between two immense arteries of travel traversed by cable cars and the elevated railway, with ample cross-town communication. Magnificent hotels . . . and the marble palaces of the Fifth Avenue dwellers, are close at hand. Within a stone's throw are luxurious club-houses of the principal German societies. Upon the north and east is an enormous population that before had been compelled to seek its amusement at remoter resorts. There is much to attract all classes.[25]

Wherever they opened, theaters relied on the same factors: transportation, population, and proximity to a business district. The Sewell brothers, real estate brokers from Port Richmond, Staten Island, took all these into account in 1911 when they announced plans to build a 1,000-seat vaudeville and film house on the south side of Richmond Terrace, near the post office and "handy to the various trolley lines." The local newspaper noted that the location

> is one of the finest that can be found anywhere on the north shore of Staten Island for such a purpose. It is located right in the heart of Port Richmond, and what makes it so valuable as a site for a modern theatre is that it is easily reached by the Staten Island Rapid Transit trains, the Bull's Head, Concord, Silver Lake and shore line trolley cars, and the Bergen Point and Elizabethport ferries.[26]

In the Bronx, entrepreneurs followed new subway lines to prosperity. Until the late nineteenth century most of the Bronx was woods, meadow, and farmland dotted with small villages, and Bronx theater consisted of local halls that accommodated concerts, political rallies, traveling shows, and wedding receptions. All appear to have been local institutions, with no pretensions to a city-wide audience. Eventually, however, in a commercial district at 149th Street and Third Avenue that became known as "the Hub," the Bronx acquired two legitimate theaters: the Metropolis in 1904 and the Bronx Opera House in 1913.[27]

Population changes ushered in the Hub's vaudeville years. From 1900 to 1910 the Bronx grew from 200,500 residents to almost 431,000, the greatest rate of increase in any borough of New York City. This population boom and the real estate bonanza that accompanied it were caused partly by the extension of the IRT subway line. The tracks reached the South Bronx in 1904 and the northern regions of 242d Street and Broadway in 1908.[28]

As more middle- and working-class people moved into the Bronx, the upper classes fled the Hub—just as they had forsaken such areas as 14th Street in Manhattan. As a result, the Metropolis, already shaken by competition from the newer Bronx Opera House, was isolated from its old "society" audience. Metropolis management tried a variety of offerings, from dramatic stock to vaudeville, films, and Italian shows, but none brought lasting success. A fling at burlesque attracted the police, and the theater was closed in 1926; in 1929, the building was sold to Loew's for use as a scenic studio. The Bronx Opera House thrived longer, but in the 1920s it was converted into a movie theater.[29]

But the changes in population and transportation that shook the legitimate theaters meant opportunity for vaudeville entrepreneurs. The Hub, served by the Third Avenue elevated line and the Seventh Avenue and Lexington Avenue subway lines, was the major shopping district of the Bronx. With new residents streaming into the borough, the Hub became a lucrative site for vaudeville.[30]

Consequently, Keith and Loew houses opened all around the district. In 1909 Keith opened the Bronx Theater, seating 1,220 at Melrose Avenue and East 151st Street. Marcus Loew responded in 1910 by opening the 2,397-seat National two blocks away on Bergen Avenue. Keith countered in 1913 with the Royal, a big-time house of 2,070 seats, which continued to compete with Loew's National even after Keith abandoned the Bronx Theater in 1918.[31]

As rapid transit lines continued to move northward, new business and residential districts grew up and with them new theaters from sections such as Fordham Road and Tremont Avenue. Major circuits hurried to open vaudeville and combination vaudeville-film houses. From around 1910 to 1920 the Loew, Keith, and Fox interests built or acquired at least twelve Bronx theaters, each seating more than 1,000.[32] Many of these new stages were neighborhood, small-time houses. Unlike theaters in Times Square or downtown borough centers, they catered to people who lived within walking distance. It was in small time that immigrant and working-class New Yorkers encountered vaudeville on their home ground.

The theater operator most associated with New York small time was Marcus Loew. "The Loew circuit had theatres in every neighborhood in New York City and Brooklyn," vaudevillian Fred Allen noted. "The acts moved from neighborhood to neighborhood. At the Delancey Theater, on the Lower East Side, Mae West was the star of the bill. At the National Theater, in the Bronx, there was Harry Jolson, Al's brother; at the Columbia Theater in Brooklyn, there were Burns and Lorraine."[33] Loew's first houses, opening around 1905, were little more than nickelodeons that featured singers between reels. Over the next five years he acquired a succession of full-fledged theaters in Brooklyn, Manhattan, and the Bronx and put them into service featuring combination film and vaudeville bills.[34] These new-style theaters presented shows at an inexpensive price—five to twenty-five cents in 1914—at least three times a day. By 1918, Loew was operating thirty-two theaters in New York City and another eighty throughout the United States and Canada. A performer playing only Loew houses could tour for fifteen weeks in New York City alone, according to agent H. B. Marianelli.[35]

Loew showed that there was no contradiction between cheap tickets and profits. According to his basic principle, selling five ten-cent tickets is as profitable as selling one fifty-cent ticket, provided the cheaper seats are consistently turned over. In contrast to big-time Keith houses, which promised the stars, Loew made a point of offering less famous acts for a less expensive price,[36] although some Loew acts did make it to stardom. A 1914 article lauding his theaters called them places where "the man with the wage or small salary looks for an evening's pleasure," houses for "the filling of the poor man's hour with fun" and "helping the strugglers to forget their poverty." Even though Loew houses ranged from Times Square to local shopping districts, a guide to the 1913–14 vaudeville season listed three in the immigrant Lower East Side, more than any other vaudeville circuit.[37]

A 1914 magazine article recognized Loew's local appeal.

> When one of his emporiums of pleasure is opened in any city district, half of the families within twenty minutes' walk are counted on for one visit a week, three persons a visit should be the average. One fourth of the residents in the tributary circle must be inveigled into dropping dimes and quarters into the box office twice a week, for doesn't the complete bill change every Monday and Thursday? A Loew manager must make that change pay.[38]

The local orientation of small-time vaudeville was noticeable even when presented in a more lavish Keith style. A 1918 article on the opening of a new Keith house on Fordham Road in the Bronx described a fancy interior: roomy lobby, elevators, carpeted corridors, marble stairs, women's rooms furnished with ornate framed mirrors, men's rooms paneled in English walnut, and tables decorated with fresh cut flowers. But if the interior was big time, the intended audience was not. The reporter contrasted the theater's anticipated patrons and the "vast floating population" that filled the Palace: "This is strictly a neighborhood house; that is, it draws only on the residents of that immediate region. The same people come week after week. It gives a program of mixed vaudeville and pictures at a low price."[39]

The Fox vaudeville firm also ran small-time theaters all around New York. The Hyperion, which opened in Corona, Queens, in December 1910, offered vaudeville, films, dancing, and amateur nights for prices of five to fifteen cents.[40] *Variety* corroborated the local orientation of such theaters when it covered the opening of the Halsey in Brooklyn in 1912. The operator, M. H. Saxe, owned movie houses at Times Square and 116th Street in Manhattan, but "the Halsey," *Variety* asserted, "was built... to give the amusement-seeking people of the Saratoga Park neighborhood a chance to spend their rusty dimes without crossing the river."[41]

Neighborhood vaudeville houses were a part of everyday life, "like your local movie," said vaudeville fan Harold Applebaum, who lived near the Royal in the Bronx. An attachment to neighborhood vaudeville was apparently widespread among New Yorkers of his time. In the late 1910s and early 1920s, Applebaum preferred the Royal at the Hub over Keith's fancier Fordham Road theater. The Royal, he felt, was for "the lower element, the ritzier element was for Fordham," which was farther from his neighborhood and not "home" like the Royal.[42]

At small-time houses, contests and giveaways were complemented by promotions designed for neighborhood appeal. In June 1915, Loew's Avenue B Theater was jammed for a beauty contest featuring thirty-one entrants from the Lower East Side. In February 1911 the Hyperion Theater in Corona presented local Boy Scouts in their own play. The Prospect in Brooklyn gave a special reception for Brooklyn-born Frank Fogarty, whose catch phrase "Am I right, boys?" always sparked the crowd: "From the aspect of the celebrations," *Variety* commented, "one might have concluded that the Brooklyn team had won the National League pennant and that Frank Fogarty was responsible for it."[43]

Small-time theaters were frequently rowdy places, their boisterous humor reminiscent of the earliest variety halls. An act could get big laughs out of flypaper stuck to the seat of a man's pants or an allusion to the wife of the Tsar as the Tsardine.[44] This spirit lived on longest in small-time amateur nights, where aspiring stars competed for prizes in rambunctious events with roaring audiences and sometimes "the hook" to pull off the losers.[45]

When Eddie Cantor appeared at a 1908 Miner's Bowery Theater amateur night, the gallery gods shouted, "Take the muzzler off! . . . Go to work, you bum!" And when he won them over, "there was a rumble of stamping feet, shrill whistling, and a thin shower of coins that pelted the backdrop and rolled toward the gutter of footlights. This was their way of applause, with leather, metal and siren shrieks; they scorned the effeminate clapping of hands." Losers were yanked off with a long hook. At the end of the show the survivors were lined up on stage, and the master of ceremonies walked down the line, holding a five-dollar bill over each performer's head. The one who received the loudest applause won the money.[46]

There was an honesty and egalitarianism about amateur nights, but at their core they were competitions where audiences measured contestants against the standards of big-time vaudeville: they cheered if the act measured up but were merciless if it fell short. One witness recalled occasions when "hopefuls walked the plank for applause and some cash and too often got the hook and perhaps left in tears. But when the patrons liked the talent, they would tear the theater apart and sometimes throw coins. Some thought it funny to heat up the coins with matches."[47] At big-time vaudeville theaters, by contrast, people behaved more as they did at legitimate stage plays. Popular acts were greeted with applause or cheers; unpopular acts received the silent treatment or, if they were particularly bad, a walkout. Booing did occur, but it was rare. Such audience disapproval might be traumatic for the performer, but it was a far cry from the vigorous and vocal assertions common in small-time houses. The Keith-Albee taming of the gallery gods was largely successful.[48]

The theaters farthest from the center of the city were the seaside vaudeville houses of Brighton Beach in Brooklyn, North Beach in Queens, and South Beach in Staten Island. Although open only in the summer months, they were otherwise much like their downtown counterparts: connected to adjacent business districts (in this case the business being amusements) and linked to citywide transit systems. They promised only the best big-time acts, and they appealed to different classes of New Yorkers. They could also be as diverse as their downtown counterparts. South Beach emerged as a resort and entertainment area in 1886, when a new train line opened between urbanized St. George in northern Staten Island and the Arrochar station near South Beach. Working-class pleasure-seekers followed—a "Bowery beer crowd," as one observer put it. Entrepreneurs and builders rushed in, and by 1890, South Beach boasted hotels, boat houses, dance pavilions, shooting galleries, rides, and a carrousel. Ferry service from Manhattan and Brooklyn, plus an 1892 railroad extension, drew crowds that prompted comparisons with Coney Island.[49]

Two vaudeville houses opened in South Beach in the early 1890s: Nunley's Casino at the south end of the boardwalk near the railway terminal, and Hergenhan's Olympia at the north end of the beach. There were others as well, but the contrast between these two is telling. Admission to both houses was free; patrons paid their way by buying beer and soft drinks in thick glasses at double the barroom price of five cents. Both houses featured comics, acrobats, and vocalists left unemployed when other theaters closed for the summer. But the Olympia was apparently something of an island of refinement in rough-edged South Beach—its middle-class patrons seemed to avoid the amusement attractions around it—whereas the Casino attracted more of the "Bowery beer crowd." The visiting habits of soldiers from an artillery regiment stationed nearby followed accordingly. Officers tended to patronize Hergenhan's Olympia; enlisted men frequented Nunley's Casino, where audience behavior was freer.[50]

From Times Square to South Beach, then, vaudeville entrepreneurs recognized that New Yorkers were not one people, easily entertained under one roof. New Yorkers were too divided by class, race, ethnicity, and gender to find satisfaction in one standardized vaudeville theater. In response, owners organized shows with something for everyone and situated their theaters to attract patrons from specific corners of the total vaudeville audience. The showmen who sold vaudeville to the people of New York City had to tailor their appeal to a diverse constituency. No other approach was possible, especially in an industry that grew so symbiotically with the city.

Yet even as the showmen recognized this diversity, they took a giant step toward a mass audience in which many differences would be submerged. Touring acts helped create nationwide standards of performance that were less attentive to individual communities. Indeed, when they took their acts on the road, performers made popular culture less a part of a place and more dependent on the portable offerings of an entertainment industry. In the 1860s, New Yorkers who wanted roughhouse comedy had to go to the Bowery. In the 1920s they could find it at a vaudeville house in almost any neighborhood of the city. The very organization of the industry—with theater circuits radiating out from Times Square booking offices—was a giant step toward a centralized entertainment industry.

Although vaudeville paved the way for forces of centralization and standardization in American culture, it was itself far more attentive to cultural particularities than the electronic forms that followed it. Grounded as it was in live performance, vaudeville could not afford to discard the human, intimate touch that made it a popular form of theater in every sense of the word.

NOTES

1. My thoughts on the configuration of vaudeville have been influenced by Robert E. Park and Ernest W. Burgess, *The City* (1925; rpt. Chicago: University of Chicago Press, 1968), and its introduction by Morris Janowitz, pp. viii–ix; on the fundamental characteristics of popular culture by Lawrence Levine, "William Shakespeare and the American People: A Study in Cultural Transformation," *American Historical Review* 89 (February 1984): 46, and Carlo Ginzburg, *The Cheese and the Worms: The Cosmos of a Sixteenth-Century Miller*, trans. John and Anne Tedeschi (New York: Penguin, 1982), xii, xviii, 130; on the transformation of American popular culture by Susan G. Davis, *Parades and Power: Street Theatre in Nineteenth-Century Philadelphia* (Berkeley: University of California Press, 1988), 181 n. 37, and Daniel J. Czitrom, *Media and the American Mind: From Morse to McLuhan* (Chapel Hill: University of North Carolina Press, 1986), xii, 30–31, 59, 190–92, plus conversations with William R. Taylor of the State University of New York at Stony Brook.

2. See *Vaudeville*, published by the American Vaudeville Circuit (undated), in the Warshaw Collection, National Museum of American History, Smithsonian Institution, Washington, D.C.

3. Discussion of these distinctions may be found in FTC 128 (the records of Federal Trade Commission investigation, docket number 128, which determined that the vaudeville industry had not violated the Sherman Anti-trust Act), housed in the Washington National Records Center, Suitland, Maryland: see John Walsh, box 72, 16 February 1920, p. 3246; Hodgson, box 71, 6 February 1919, pp. 570, 574; box 70, 3 February 1919, pp. 72–74; Goodman, box 72, 17 February 1920, pp. 3380–81. See also statistics in Michael M. Davis, Jr., *The Exploitation of Pleasure: A Study of Commercial Recreation in New York City* (New York: Russell Sage Foundation, 1911), 25, 26, 30.

4. Nellie Revell, "News and Gossip of the Vaudeville World," *Morning Telegraph*, 6 June 1915, p. 2.

5. See Isaac Goldberg, *Tin Pan Alley* (New York: Frederick Ungar, 1961), 108, 111; also Robert Baral, *Turn West on 23rd: A Toast to New York's Old Chelsea* (New York: Fleet, 1965), 38–39.

6. On the vice district's movement, see Lewis Erenberg, *Steppin' Out: New York Nightlife and the Transformation of American Culture, 1890–1930* (Westport, Conn.: Greenwood Press, 1981), 21; on the Tenderloin in the 1890s, see Edward B. Marks (as told to Abbott J. Liebling), *They All Sang: From Tony Pastor to Rudy Vallee* (New York: Viking Press, 1935), 294–311.

7. This description generally corresponds to the trend noted in Mary C. Henderson, *The City and the Theater: New York Playhouses from Bowling Green to Times Square* (Clifton, N.J.: James T. White, 1973), 49. See also William Moulton Marston and John Henry Feller, *F. F. Proctor: Vaudeville Pioneer* (New York: Richard R. Smith, 1943), 50.

8. Edward Renton, *The Vaudeville Theatre: Building, Operation, Management* (New York: Gotham Press, 1918), 12–14. See also "Keith Building Theatres," *Billboard*, 26 June, 1915, p. 6; and a notice on the opening of a Keith theater in a "thickly populated district" at Church and Flatbush avenues, *Billboard*, 8 September 1915, p. 6.

9. Henderson, *The City and the Theatre*, 49.

10. On Hammerstein's role in developing Times Square and the Olympia, see William Morrison, "Oscar Hammerstein I: The Man Who Invented Times Square," *Marquee* 15, no. 1 (1983): 7–9. On the interiors and decor, see William Harvey Birkmire, *The Planning and Construction of American Theatres* (New York: Wiley, 1896), 41–46.

11. See Brian J. Cudahy, *Under the Sidewalks of New York: The Story of the Greatest Subway System in the World* (Brattleboro, Vt: Stephen Greene Press, 1979), 14; and Stephen Jenkins, *The Greatest Street in the World: The Story of Broadway, Old and New, from the Bowling Green to Albany* (New York: G. P. Putnam's Sons, 1911) 256, 270.

12. Jenkins, *Greatest Street*, 256, 262.

13. On marquees, see Renton, *Vaudeville Theatre*, 51.

14. Birkmire, *Planning and Construction*, 16–19, 32–37, 41–46.

15. *Cahn-Leighton Theatrical Guide* (New York: n.p., 1913–14), 433–47; *Theatre and Hotel Directory of the Keith's-Albee Circuit* (Asbury Park, N.J.: R. H. Bowers, 1925), 57; Michael R. Miller, "The Theatres of the Bronx, *Marquee* 4 (Fall 1972): 5; reprinted by Bronx Historical Society.

16. Renton, *Vaudeville Theatre*, 116.

17. See "Palace $2 Vaudeville a Joke; Double-Crossing Boomerang," *Variety*, 28 March 1913, p. 5. On Bernhardt and the early days of the Palace, see Abel Green and Joe Laurie, Jr., *Show Biz From Vaude to Video* (New York: Holt, 1951, 29; also Marian Spitzer, *The Palace* (New York: Atheneum, 1969), 18–19.

18. Norman Hapgood, "The Life of a Vaudeville Artiste," *Cosmopolitan* 30 (1901): 396. For the character of individual theaters' audiences, see the report books of the Keith/Albee Collection, Special Collections Department, University of Iowa Libraries, Iowa City: e.g., Keith's Union Square attracted for its 6 April 1906 show a more aristocratic audience than in many seasons (book 4, p. 25); a holiday audience of confused suburbanites attended Keith's Union Square on 23 February 1903 (undated report book, p. 190).

19. Andre Charlot, "Music Hall Audiences," *Variety*, 25 December 1914, p. 44; Marks, *They All Sang*, 149.

20. Green and Laurie, *Show Biz*, 22–23.

21. Ibid., 18, 20, 22.

22. Ibid., 17–20, 155. Green and Laurie report that eventually the execution acts were canceled because of their lack of "propriety."

23. Spitzer, *The Palace*, 131.

24. My thinking on this point is influenced by Park and Burgess, *The City*, 150–51. On the Riverside audience, see "New Acts 4," *Variety* clipping, c. 1918, Keith/Albee Collection.

25. Birkmire, *Planning and Construction*, 32.

26. "For New Theatre," *Staten Islander*, 7 October 1911, p. 1.

27. See John McNamara, "The Bronx in History," *Bronx Press Review*, 5 April 1962; also Miller, "Theatres of the Bronx," 7.

28. See Ira Rosenwaike, *Population History of New York City* (Syracuse, N.Y.: Syracuse University Press, 1972), 133; Stephen Jenkins, *The Story of the Bronx* (New York: G. P. Putnam's Sons, 1912), 10; Cudahy, *Under the Sidewalks of New York*, 34.

29. See Miller, "Theatres of the Bronx," 7; and the Metropolis report in the Bronx Historical Society theater file, New York.

30. On the Hub, see Harry T. Cook, *The Borough of the Bronx* (New York: Harry T. Cook, 1913), 36; and Lloyd Ultan (with the Bronx County Historical Society), *The Beautiful Bronx* (New Rochelle, N.Y.: Arlington House, 1979), 39. See also "Bronx Adds a House," *Player*, 11 December 1909, p. 1, noting that a vaudeville house, apparently Keith's Bronx, had been opened on Bergen Avenue opposite the Adams-Flanagan department store; also Joseph G. Herzberg, "The Bronx Had Everything, Including Own Shows," *New York Times*, 4 September 1972, p. 17.

31. Miller, "Theatres of the Bronx," 8; information on the National in Bronx Historical Society theater file.

32. *Bronx Theaters*, pamphlet in Bronx Historical Society theater file; and Miller, "Theatres of the Bronx," 8.

33. Joe Williams, "Real Napoleon of the Movies," *Cleveland Leader*, 9 June 1918, in Robinson Locke Collection, ser. 2, pp. 66–67, Lincoln Center Library of the Performing Arts, New York Public Library; and Arthur Prill, "The 'Small-Time' King," *Theatre Magazine* 19 (March 1914), also in Robinson Locke Collection, ser. 2, pp. 63–65; Fred Allen, *Much Ado about Me* (New York: Little Brown and Co., 1956), 216.

34. Alexander Woollcott, "The Life of Marcus Loew," Hearst's *International*, September, October, November 1926, reprinted in *Variety*, 19 October 1927, pp. 5–10; also Donald King, "Marcus Loew, the Henry Ford of Show Business" *Marquee* 17, no. 3 (1985): 3–4.

35. Prill, "The 'Small-Time' King," 63; Williams, "Real Napoleon of the Movies"; *H. B. Marianelli Ltd.* v. *United Booking Offices of America*, C. 12-55, District Court of the United States, Southern District of New York, 15 November 1916.

36. Williams, "Real Napoleon of the Movies"; Woollcott, "Life of Marcus Loew"; and Prill, "The 'Small-Time' King."

37. Prill, "The 'Small-Time' King"; *The Cahn-Leighton Official Theatrical Guide* (New York: 1913–14), p. 421.

38. Prill, "The 'Small-Time' King."

39. Walter Richard Eaton, "The Wizards of Yardville," *McClure's Magazine* 55 (September 1918): 48.

40. "Corona's New Theatre," *Newtown Register*, 5 January 1911, p. 1.

41. "Halsey," *Variety*, 27 December 1912, p. 18.

42. Interview with Harold Applebaum, New York City, 18 January 1984; interview with Terese Klein, New York City, December 1983; Bill Smith, "Vaudeville: Entertainment of the Masses," in Myron Matlaw, ed., *American Popular Entertainment: Papers and Proceedings of the Conference on the History of American Popular Entertainment*, Contributions in Drama and Theatre Studies no. 1 (Westport, Conn.: Greenwood Press, 1979), 110–11; interview with Jack Gross, New York City, December 1983; interview with Norman Steinberg, New York City, 7 December 1983. Unless noted otherwise, all interviews were conducted by the author. When it was impossible to conduct interviews, I sent people questionnaires regarding their vaudeville experiences as performers, audience members, or theater business people. These questionnaires, along with letters I received in response to queries printed in newspapers, were valuable sources of information. See questionnaire from Richard Osk, June 1984; questionnaire from Harold Weintraub, summer 1984; and an anonymous 1984 letter from a Brooklyn man who recalls that when he was a child around 1908, mothers left their children at Keeney's vaudeville house while they went shopping; interview with Norman Steinberg, New York City, 7 December 1983.

43. See "Loew's Beauty Contest," *Variety*, 4 June 1915, p. 5; 5 January 1911, p. 5, and 2 February 1911, p. 5; "Prospect," *Variety* 20 February 1915, p.

19. Keith's Riverside on 96th Street in Manhattan held a toy giveaway at its 13 September 1924 show described in B. F. Keith's Riverside Theatre *News*. On other contests and promotions, see "Bronx Rivalry," *Variety*, 30 July 1915, p. 5.

44. See *So Help Me: The Autobiography of George Jessel* (New York: Random House, 1943), 10; *Some of These Days: The Autobiography of Sophie Tucker*, with Dorothy Giles (Garden City, N.Y.: Doubleday, Doran, 1945), 257; George Jean Nathan, *The Popular Theatre* (New York: Knopf, 1918), 208–9.

45. Interview with Harold W. Engel, New York City, 8 December 1983; Steinberg interview; questionnaire from Joyce W. Zuk, February 1984; Tucker, *Some of These Days*, 33.

46. Eddie Cantor (as told to David Freedman), *My Life Is in Your Hands* (New York: Harper, 1928), 79–80, 82, 85–86.

47. Samuel Komansky, *Daily News*, 5 September 1963, Brooklyn Historical Society clipping files, 145:55.

48. The often restrained conduct in vaudeville theaters is attested in interviews with Gross; Murray Schwartz, New York City, 11 January 1984; Margaret Brown, New York City, December 1983; and Capitola DeWolfe, Queens, N.Y., 23 January 1984; also questionnaires from Weintraub; Osk; Lewis Kornbluth, 1984; and Florence Sinow, 1984. On similar developments in the legitimate theater, see Benjamin McArthur, *Actors and American Culture, 1880–1920* (Philadelphia: Temple University Press, 1984), 91.

49. Henry G. Steinmeyer, "South Beach: The Resort Era," *Staten Island Historian* 9, ser. no. 75 (July–September 1958), 18.

50. Ibid., 19–20.

7

THE MOVIE PALACE COMES TO AMERICA'S CITIES

Douglas Gomery

Important transformations in selling and presentation made movies the most successful commercialized mass entertainment of the first half of the twentieth century. Because of these transformations, the United States moved from a country with a handful of nickelodeons in 1905 to a nation of some 20,000 movie houses during the Golden Age of the 1920s and 1930s. Understanding how theater entrepreneurs shaped movie entertainment goes a long way toward explaining the history of the centralized commercialization of this leisure-time activity and illustrates the changed relationship of audiences to theaters.

One relatively unknown Chicago movie company in particular fashioned a set of strategies that created more profits from movies than anyone had thought possible. We have too long looked to Hollywood to find the locus of fundamental change in the movie business. The transformation from the nickelodeon to the picture palace was fashioned 2,000 miles away, in the neighborhoods of the Windy City.

Movie screenings before the nickelodeon were part of vaudeville shows or entertainment programs in amusement parks and dime museums. But with the coming of the nickelodeon in 1905, a site especially adapted or (later) built to showcase the movies emerged.[1] The nickelodeon was a small, makeshift "theater," usually a converted cigar store, pawnshop, or restaurant fitted out with chairs, a screen, and a projector. Out front, large handpainted posters announced the show of the day. Inside, the entertainment usually began with a sing-along: one member of the owner's family played the piano while another, backed by illustrated, handpainted song slides, led the singing. But the principal attractions were the films, a program of documentary, comedy, fantasy, and dramatic silent shorts that lasted never more than an hour.[2]

In 1905 there were only a few nickelodeons in any one city; by October 1906 the trade press was reporting several dozen in Chicago alone; a year later the grand total in the United States topped 2,000. By 1910 some placed the number over 10,000, and one early expert estimated that some twenty-six million Americans were attending nickelodeons each week—nearly one-fifth of the nation's population at the time.[3] It was not a difficult business to enter. Biography after biography indicates how easily the brothers Warner, Adolph Zukor (later head of Paramount), and Marcus Loew (creator of MGM) got their start in this wide-open market.[4] Only a few thousand dollars in capital was required; no special training or connections were needed. Entrepreneurs in every major American city set up shop in already existing storefronts and watched as millions plunked down millions of nickels and dimes. Only the negative social stigma attached to the "vulgar" movies by the educated classes limited the number of those attending. The nickelodeon had become a national phenomenon—but the era of the small business man and woman offering cheap entertainment to his or her neighbors was about to give way to a twenty-year movement toward the development of a major commercial enterprise.

As early as 1907 reports were filtering back to newly founded trade papers that there were just too many theaters. To retain their business, some nickelodeon owners added vaudeville acts to differentiate their shows from the ones down the street. By moving their nickelodeon operations to premises originally constructed as legitimate theaters or building their own stage facilities, they could offer live entertainment as well as movies. This was the rise of small-time vaudeville.[5] The new wave of combined stage shows and movies brought the era of the nickelodeon to a close.[6]

The transformation to vaudeville and film initiated a change in the audience as well. During the nickelodeon craze, moviegoers tended to be less than affluent. In fact, the movie show was known as the "poor man's theater"; boosters called the nickelodeon "democracy's theater." Entrepreneurs could not afford to turn anyone away, and thus audience behavior resembled the rowdy standards long associated with carnivals, the circus, and the dime museum. Crowds were asked to be quiet but felt no more obligation to do so than they would at the fairgrounds. Educators, disturbed at the amazing popularity of the movies, asserted that these lower-class (in terms of income) audiences often contained rowdy youths who disrupted the shows when they were supposed to be in school.[7] Reformers seized upon this audience behavior to buttress their arguments for the control of the movie show. They wanted films to present refined entertainment modeled on the genteel standards of the legitimate theater and family vaudeville. The audience should spruce up; there would be little talking or shouting; and the atmosphere would be one of respect and refinement.

Theater owners too wanted to attract a higher class (in terms of income) of patrons, urban Americans who had both the time and the money to become regular customers willing to pay higher ticket prices. Hence, by 1910, the owners had taken direct aim at the emerging American urban middle class.

To lure the middle-class trade, the showmen developed strategies to convince mothers that their theaters were proper places for themselves and their children. Half-price afternoon "specials" were designed with the female spectator in mind. A theater that could draw a family audience could make more money and establish a favorable image in the community.[8] Movies were no longer considered some sort of fad that would go the way of bicycle races. In more and more beautiful theaters, in better and better parts of downtown districts, the movie show, especially in the period immediately after World War I, replaced vaudeville as the dominant commercialized form of American mass entertainment. During that time a number of pioneering exhibitors devised ways to cater to the largest possible audiences. Samuel Rothafel in New York and Sid Grauman in Los Angeles symbolized the new breed of movie showman.

In terms of commercial success, however, it was the firm of Balaban & Katz that led the way in developing a package of entertainment that made millions of dollars and put total control into the hands of a few theater owners. All movie exhibitors during the Golden Age of the cinema in the United States took their cues from this Chicago-based corporation; it even inspired the actions of the more flamboyant William Fox and Marcus Loew. To understand the success and innovations of Balaban & Katz is to understand how the movies became a full-fledged big business in America. As late as 1919 the company owned only six theaters; by 1926 it had become the heart of the most powerful chain of movie theaters in the world.

Like hundreds of movie operators in the first decade of the twentieth century, Balaban & Katz started with nickelodeons. Barney and Abraham Joseph Balaban and their parents set up a nickelodeon in Chicago's westside ghetto in 1908, opened their second in 1909, a third in 1914.[9] Samuel Katz acquired his first nickelodeon in 1912; by 1915 he had three theaters and was in the business full time. In 1916 Katz and the Balaban brothers joined to open a theater large enough to take advantage of the growing interest in moviegoing that they had observed firsthand in Chicago.[10] With financing from Julius Rosenwald, president of Sears, Roebuck and the neighborhood's largest employer, the Central Park theater opened in October 1917 and was an immediate success. Katz next put together a syndicate of prosperous Chicago backers—Julius Rosenwald, William Wrigley, Jr., and John Hertz, Chicago's Yellow Cab king—who would soon add to their fortunes as a result.[11]

The firm of Balaban & Katz opened its northside Riviera in October 1918, the southside Tivoli in February 1921, and the Chicago theater downtown in October 1921. All were hugely profitable from the start.[12] At the same time Balaban & Katz was buying up as many smaller theaters as it could in Chicago, and from this base of power began to purchase movie houses in the surroundings states. Remarkably, the company prospered despite having little access to Hollywood's top films in its early years. It did so by not depending on films alone to form the foundation of its theatrical empire. As Barney Balaban and Sam Katz argued:

> We cannot afford to build up a patronage depending entirely upon the drawing power of our feature films as we display them. We must build in the minds of our audience the feeling that we represent an institution taking a vital part in the formation of the character of the community.[13]

Hence, they carefully differentiated their "product" through carefully chosen locations, ornate buildings, splendid service, awe-inspiring stage shows, and the first mechanically air-conditioned movie theaters in the world—a five-factor plan that enabled Balaban & Katz to lead the hawking of movies from a small-time marginal position to center stage in America's Big Business scene.

Balaban & Katz located its theaters close to the audiences it sought in the suburbs of America's biggest cities, with easy access to mass transit. It was not enough to seek the middle class simply by happenstance; one had to take the best of the movie shows to the middle-class neighborhoods. As in other cities, rapid mass transit enabled the middle and upper classes to move to the edge of the urban area (although many of the first suburbs were actually within city boundaries). Thus, as late as 1900 Chicago had been a compact city with most citizens living no more than three miles from the Loop; two decades later that distance had doubled. Balaban & Katz took advantage of this revolution in mass transit by building its first three theaters in the heart of *outlying* business and recreational centers.[14]

The Central Park was in North Lawndale on the far west side, a neighborhood to which friends of the Katzes and Balabans had moved when they "made it." Three-quarters of its population was made up of Russian Jews who had come to the United States in the 1880s and 1890s, settled in the blocks around Hull House, and then resettled in North Lawndale. Louis Wirth documented this residential transformation in his classic sociological study, *The Ghetto*. He found that the children pushed their parents to move to North Lawndale to achieve higher status in life. These children had acquired a strong desire for upward mobility from education in public school, from reformers such as Jane Addams, and from newly acquired Gentile friends and co-workers. The new generation ate nonkosher food, attended synagogue less frequently, shopped outside the neighborhood, and spoke Yiddish only at home. As part of their cultural assimilation, they also embraced the movie show. The Central Park made its fortune catering to the very families Louis Wirth studied.[15]

For its second picture palace Balaban & Katz chose a site in the prosperous northside neighborhood known as Uptown. The thriving bright-lights center of this streetcar transfer point was already filling up with dance halls, cabarets, and arcades. Uptown was the largest outlying center in Chicago in the early 1920s; 100,000 prosperous people lived in apartment building after apartment building within easy walking distance or a short streetcar ride away. Since Balaban & Katz came late to this center, the Riviera was initially several blocks from the elevated train stop. But because the crowds became so big with the opening of the nearby Aragon Ballroom and then another Balaban & Katz theater in 1924 (the Uptown, across the street from the Riviera), the city opened a new station. Uptown became the hottest of Chicago's hot spots in the Roaring Twenties.[16]

The Central Park and the Riviera, because of their proximity to the El lines, were able to draw customers from all parts of the middle-class west and north sides of Chicago. The Tivoli drew from a southside population. It too was convenient to the center of an outlying business and recreational district, and the El was nearby, as were the thousands of potential patrons who worked at or attended the University of Chicago.[17]

The three theaters formed a matrix appealing to all sectors of the city. The Chicago theater in the Loop, built with profits from the suburban theaters, was almost an afterthought but of course gave the company a presence downtown that guaranteed its ability to compete with all rivals. Once these four theaters were in place, Balaban & Katz could advertise that no one need travel more than a half-hour to reach one of its shows. And as the company bought more theaters, the maximum travel time was reduced to fifteen minutes.[18]

Theater owners in every city in the United States copied Balaban & Katz. The Saxe Brothers in Milwaukee, the Skourases in St. Louis, and Loew's Inc. in New York all quickly built theaters in newer sections of the city, choosing sites close to public transportation—subway, elevated line, or trolley—and reaped millions of dollars.[19] During the 1920s, 2,000- to 3,000-seat houses were constructed in the best neighborhoods of all major cities. The only section of Manhattan that saw population growth in the 1920s—the area north of 145th Street, with one-twentieth of the population of the island—had one-fifth of the movie palaces. Because the area offered a high quality of life at affordable prices, the middle class flocked to its newly opened apartment buildings. Second- and third-generation upwardly mobile Americans, educated far in excess of the norm and holding well-paying jobs, had the time and money to spend on the new movie entertainment (even though they did not always find it in their best interest to acknowledge their love for the movie show). Loew's 175th Street theater, now a Hindu-Indochinese temple, still stands as a reminder of this important historical transformation.[20]

But it was not enough simply to locate at the proper crossroads site; a movie theater had to offer a good show, and that show began with the building itself. With the same pride that accompanied the opening of a world's fair or new skyscraper, Chicagoans of the 1920s lauded Balaban & Katz's "wonder theaters." Novelist Meyer Levin, writing in *The Old Bunch*, remembered the impact this way:

> As [they] turned into State Street, the Chicago sign blazed at them. Boy, was that a sign! It made daylight of the whole block. Eight stories high. Three thousand bulbs spelled CHICAGO!
>
> After a wait of forty-five minutes they got inside the lobby. Everything white and gold and mirrored. Up on the promenade was a grand piano, all in white....
>
> And overhead, a magnificent chandelier! The largest in the world! Six tons![21]

Balaban & Katz theater stressed opulence to its patrons. More than simply "going to the movies," it was a treat just to enter these picture palaces.

In order to dazzle the moviegoer, the architects for the Balaban & Katz empire, George and C. W. Rapp, mixed design elements from many periods, including Spanish, Italian, Moorish, and (later) art deco renderings. Their trademarks (influenced by the French) included the triumphal arch, the monumental staircase, and the grand, column-lined lobby.[22]

The architecture of the movie palace was designed to insulate the public from the outside world and create a separate world for the entertainment inside. The theatrical aspect of the entertainment commenced on the street, where the facade of the movie palace with its strong vertical lines lifted high above the shop fronts. Brilliant terra cotta exteriors in purples, golds, azures, and crimsons glowed day and night.

The massive electric marquees could be seen for miles by those riding on trolleys; signs flashing multicolored messages towered several stories in height. The Columbian Exposition had introduced electrical displays to Chicagoans, and lighting displays were still unusual enough to demand public comment; after all, electricity had been accessible in cities for only a few decades and was brand new to many of the citizens of the deep South who had migrated to Chicago after World War I. Balaban & Katz demanded that their theater managers pay special attention to the upkeep of this part of the building's exterior.[23]

Once inside the theater the patrons weaved through a series of vestibules, foyers, lobbies, lounges, upper-level promenades, and waiting rooms designed to impress and excite. The architects insisted that

> the lobby must be a place of real interest, a place where the waiting throng may be transformed.... The walls and surfaces of the lobby should ... [permit] the theatergoers to get one vista after another, which will produce ... a desire to gain admittance to other parts of the house. In other words, the lobby should be so designed and so equipped that the fascination resulting from it will keep the mind of the patron off the fact that he is waiting.[24]

The grand staircase with its massive balustrades, low risers, elliptical treads, and generous width was meant to invite ascent to the balcony seats.[25] Decorations included opulent chandelier lighting, classical drapery, luxurious chairs, fountains, and grand spaces where a piano or organ could entertain the waiting crowds. The rule of thumb was that a lobby should comfortably accommodate ticket holders equal to the number of seats in the auditorium.

The expense of outfitting a theater was considerable, of course. For the 5,000-seat Uptown, opened in 1924, Balaban & Katz spent nearly $25,000 on furniture alone and twice that on drapes and carpets. The restrooms were spacious and clean, decorated with their own drapes, furniture, paintings, and mirrors. In the auditorium itself, all seats offered a clear, unobstructed view of the screen, and acoustical planning ensured that the orchestral accompaniment for silent films could be heard even in the farthest reaches of the balcony. Thousands of bulbs, often in three primary colors, permitted the film and music to be accompanied by changing light motifs—though houselights were generally kept low because too much light would have invited patrons to move about, creating chaos in a full house of 4,000 or more. In any case, since there were no concession stands, one had little reason to leave one's seat. This was a dignified setting; the model for behavior was that of the legitimate theater, catering to the rising aspirations of customers drawn from the better neighborhoods. Patrons responded accordingly.[26]

One reason they did was that Balaban & Katz had a policy of treating movie patrons like royalty. Its services to customers included not only smoking rooms, art galleries in the foyers and lobbies, and organ music for those waiting in line but even widely advertised child care. In the basement of each movie palace was a complete playground with slides, sandboxes, and other toys and equipment; there children could be left in the care of nurses and attendants while parents watched the show upstairs. Special afternoon tea shows attracted women who had been shopping with small children and infants.

Central to the special Balaban & Katz brand of service and its success in shaping a mode of audience behavior to which no one could object was each theater's corps of ushers. Ushers guided moviegoers through the maze of halls and foyers, showed them to their seats, assisted the elderly and small children, asked anyone who misbehaved or disturbed others to leave, and handled any of the emergencies that might well arise in a crowd of 4,000 in the auditorium and another 4,000 waiting for the next show. A picture palace had twenty to forty ushers and doormen in attendance at all shows, with a regular changing of the guard throughout the day. The company recruited its ushers from male college students, dressed them in red uniforms with white gloves and yellow epaulets, and demanded that they be obediently polite even to the rudest of patrons. It was "yes, sir" and "no, ma'am," and all requests had to end with a "thank you." Even the rowdy were led away with propriety and sensitivity to suggest that if they opted to be well behaved, they were welcome to return. Balaban & Katz emphasized that it was an honor to be selected for this job. There was no tipping. The special treatment was "free" to patrons, part of the price of admission.[27]

The company carefully regulated all its employees: cashiers, projectionists, maintenance staff, electricians, stagehands, and musicians. Its goal was to achieve a "high-class" image and yet keep costs to a minimum. For example, having burly white males out front in uniform guaranteed an image that most patrons associated with a fine hotel, country club, or bank. As to labor costs, many people took the minimum wage of the day for the privilege of working in a Balaban & Katz theater. Most employees, from maintenance and cleaning staff to ushers and even managers, were young, female, and/or black. Only musicians, stagehands, and projectionists were union members. All were assigned specific routine tasks so that the management of the chain could regulate their actions like an assembly line, run with a labor efficiency Henry Ford would have surely been proud of.[28]

In the beginning Balaban & Katz could not offer its patrons Hollywood's top films because rival circuits had acquired exclusive booking contracts with the major studios. The company compensated by mounting popular but tasteful stage shows to back up the movies, thus appealing to middle-class audiences that had grown up on vaudeville. The strategy worked so well that in time Balaban & Katz became more famous for its impressive stage attractions, orchestras, and organists than for the films it booked. Putting stage shows and movies together was not a new idea.[29] But Katz and the Balabans made greater use of it, certainly in Chicago, than anyone who had preceded them. The company developed local stars who could then make the circuit in its Chicago theaters. Over time, it signed a stable of talented performers and stage designers, some of whom would go on to international fame. For example, noted Hollywood director Vincente Minnelli, the man behind the camera for many Hollywood musicals of the 1940s and 1950s, began as a set designer in the Balaban & Katz shop.[30]

Balaban & Katz presented a half-film and half-live show to fill a 150-minute program, even shortening a feature film if necessary to fit its allotted time period. The stage performance was an elaborate minimusical with spectacular settings and intricate lighting effects. Much like the more recent stage attractions at Radio City Music Hall, it stood as a separate package of entertainment. Special shows celebrated holidays, fads of the day, and all new forms of popular music. Typical was "Jazz and Opera" week. In an era when jazz was looked down upon by the educational establishment—like rock-and-roll during the 1950s—Balaban & Katz played one form off against the other in a "battle of the sounds." Jazz always won, and by 1925 jazz shows had become regular offerings; classical music was reserved for free Sunday morning concerts in order to appease the reformers and city fathers and mothers. It is hard to overestimate the popularity of Balaban & Katz stage shows. One night when the Chicago's curtain would not rise—and thus, although the movie could still be presented, the stage show could not—more than half of those in the audience walked out and demanded their money back.[31]

Location, architecture, service, and live performances were successful strategies, but they gave Balaban & Katz no specific monopoly advantage. The company did have one unique input throughout most of the 1920s, however. The Central Park, opened in 1917, was the first mechanically air-cooled theater in the world. Others had experimented with blowing air across blocks of ice, but their success was minor. Most movie houses in the Midwest, South, and far West simply closed during the hottest months or played to very small crowds.

Significant progress toward safe mechanical cooling centered in Chicago during the first two decades of the twentieth century because firms in that city slaughtered and processed most of the meat in the United States. The Kroeschell Bros. Ice Machine Company of Chicago developed a carbon dioxide system that efficiently cooled large spaces but required an investment of thousands of dollars for a roomful of apparatus; only the meat packers could afford the necessary investment.[32]

Before entering the movie business, Barney Balaban had worked in the office of the Western Cold Storage Company and thus knew firsthand of the various advances in the art of air cooling. Hence, he contracted with Kroeschell to design a system specifically for movie theaters. The first was installed in the Central Park, another in the Riviera a year later. Both cooled the air and kept it moving by forcing it through vents in the floor and exhausting it through ducts in the ceiling. For the Tivoli and Chicago theaters in 1921, an apparatus was developed to bring in air from the side and to dehumidify it.[33]

These air-cooled fantasy worlds became famous as summertime escapes from brutal Chicago summers. Balaban & Katz publicity constantly reminded Chicagoans of the rare treat awaiting them inside; icicles were depicted in all newspaper advertisements. The city's public health commissioner proclaimed that Balaban & Katz theaters had purer air than Pike's Peak and that anyone with a lung disease or women in the final trimester of pregnancy should regularly spend time "at the movies." The Chicago Chamber of Commerce heralded the city as a wonderland of summer fun, in part because of the cool pleasure to be found inside a Balaban & Katz movie palace.[34]

With the combined strategies of convenient location, opulent architecture, service to patrons, stage entertainment, and air conditioning, then, the Balaban brothers and Samuel Katz fashioned a movie audience of their choice rather than the other way around. Theirs was a carefully crafted package of pleasure designed to maximize profits, a multimedia package calculated to keep audiences enthralled throughout one show and eager to spend money on the next. So clear was their success that by 1925 the major Hollywood movie companies were seeking an alliance. Balaban & Katz chose to affiliate with the largest of all, Famous Players Lasky, soon to become Paramount Pictures Corporation.[35]

This arrangement guaranteed the Chicago company access to Hollywood's top films and secured for the Famous Players management a core of theaters second to none. In October 1925, Sam Katz moved to New York to run what would be known as the Publix theater chain.[36] Under his direction Paramount-Publix set in motion on a national scale the five-point strategy that had worked so well in Chicago, and within five years it had developed the most powerful, most profitable theater circuit in the world, some 1,500 units strong.[37] The Publix chain stretched from North Carolina to Texas, from Michigan to Iowa, and included all of Canada; total daily attendance was estimated at two million. At its peak in the silent film days, Publix employed more musicians than any other organization in the world.[38]

In contrast to the nickelodeon era, when the house manager was also the owner and his or her family helped operate the enterprise, the Balaban & Katz strategy was to maintain control from a central office. Katz and his staff directed every phase of the Publix operation from their headquarters in the Paramount building on Times Square. All decisions were made in New York, based on information passed up the line. The cost of operating each theater fell as the chain expanded—but so did the contact with the public and the feeling that the local theater was part of the community. The movie shows had become another chain store, next to a Woolworth's five and dime, the A&P grocery, and the Sears Roebuck department store, all controlled by faceless business leaders in New York or Chicago.

Publix booked all the films and made deals directly with the major Hollywood studios, obviously giving preference to Paramount productions. Stage shows were staffed, put together, and sent on the road from New York. All major employees were hired by the New York office and even for a time trained in a school run by Katz. The slogan of the company summed it all up: "You don't need to know what's playing at a Publix House. It's bound to be the best show in town." The local manager received instructions about selling the show, prewritten press releases, and a tight budget in which to do everything. Managing a theater had once been a glorious career; now it was a job for a glorified janitor in a tux.[39]

The coming of sound in the late 1920s hardly caused Katz and his staff of experts to miss a step but did bring about changes in format and personnel. Filmed stage shows in the form of shorts of the top vaudeville acts of the day replaced live stage shows in all but the largest theaters. Katz, who had lobbied hard for Paramount to switch to talkies, released hundreds of vaudeville players and musicians and saved thousands of dollars with no drop in demand at the box office. By 1929 all Publix theaters except for a handful in the largest cities offered only films, a more standardized, easily monitored, and profitable product.[40]

The Balaban & Katz formula might have succeeded even longer had it not been for the Great Depression of the 1930s, when too much borrowing and too few customers ended the first great era in the history of American moviegoing. Like the old nickelodeons, theaters again needed to attract all possible ticket buyers, whatever their behavior. To cut expenditures, many ushers were fired and sufficient light left on that patrons could seat themselves. The concession stand became the centerpiece of the lobby, and managers encouraged patrons, whenever the mood struck, to leave their seats for more popcorn, soft drinks, and candy. The prevailing atmosphere changed from an emulation of the legitimate theater to an echo of the nickelodeon era.

Nevertheless, whatever the subsequent changes brought about by depression, war, and (later) television, one Chicago company had defined the Golden Age of the cinema. Balaban & Katz helped to reposition the consumer culture of the United States and to make moviegoing the important historical force that it was for fifty years of this century. The contribution of Balaban & Katz was as important as any film that Hollywood produced or technical change that it instituted.

NOTES

1. For studies of early exhibition, see Robert C. Allen, "The Movies in Vaudeville: Historical Context of the Movies as Popular Entertainment," 57–83; Russell Merritt, "Nickelodeon Theatres, 1905–1914: Building an Audience for Movies," 83–102; and Douglas Gomery, "U.S. Film Exhibition: The Formation of a Big Business," 218–28, all found in Tino Balio, ed., *The American Film Industry*, rev. ed. (Madison: University of Wisconsin Press, 1985).

2. "Moving Pictures and the National Character," *Review of Reviews*, September 1910, pp. 315–20.

3. *Variety*, 6 October 1906, p. 5; 26 January 1907, p. 12; 6 April 1907, p. 18; 27 April 1907, p. 8; also *Moving Picture World*, 4 May 1907, p. 140; *Variety*, 14 December 1907, p. 30; "Moving Pictures and the National Character," 315–20.

4. Adolph Zukor, *The Public Is Never Wrong* (New York: Putnam, 1953), 29–53; Jack Warner, *My First Hundred Years in Hollywood* (New York: Random House, 1964), 32–59.

5. For more on small-time vaudeville see Allen, "Movies in Vaudeville," 80–82, and Robert Snyder, Chapter 6 above.

6. *Variety*, 6 April 1907, p. 18; 11 May 1907, p. 15; *Moving Picture World*, 15 June 1907, p. 231; *Variety*, 5 October 1907, p. 4; *Variety*, 23 November 1907, p. 7.

7. Historians have provided us with interesting case studies. See, e.g., Roy Rosenzweig, *Eight Hours for What We Will: Workers and Leisure in an Industrial City, 1870–1920* (New York: Cambridge University Press, 1983), 190–221; and Kathy Peiss, *Cheap Amusements: Working Class Women and Leisure in Turn-of-the-Century New York* (Philadelphia: Temple University Press, 1986), 139–60.

8. Edward Wagenknecht, *The Movies in the Age of Innocence* (New York: Random House, 1971), 8–24; *Moving Picture World*, 29 August 1908, p. 152.

9. *Motography*, June 1912, p. 247; *Exhibitor's Film Exchange*, 1 July 1915, p. 28; *Exhibitor's Film Exchange*, 21 August 1915, p. 4; *Exhibitor's Film Exchange*, 2 October 1915, p. 5; *Exhibitor's Herald*, 26 February 1916, p. 7; *Motion Picture News*, 15 July 1916, p. 315; *Motography*, 7 April 1917, p. 704.

10. *Motography*, March 1912, p. 105; *Motography*, 17 April 1915, p. 620; *Exhibitor's Film Exchange*, 9 October 1915, p. 23; *Motography*, 2 December 1916, p. 1220; Joseph P. Kennedy, ed., *The Story of Films* (Chicago: A. W. Shaw, 1927), 349–50; *United States of America* v. *Motion Picture Patents Co. et al.*, 225 F. 800 (1915), 5:2737.

11. *Who's Who in Chicago and Illinois* (Chicago: A. N. Marquis, 1917), 75, 584; *Who's Who in Chicago and Illinois* (Chicago: A. N. Marquis, 1926), 107, 625; Paul M. Angle, *Philip K. Wrigley* (Chicago: Rand McNally, 1975), 11–41; M. R. Werner, *Julius Rosenwald* (New York: Harper, 1938), 20–22; "Paramount Pictures," *Fortune* 15 (March 1937): 87–96; *Exhibitor's Herald*, 24 November 1917, p. 23; and 15 December 1917, p. 217; *Motion Picture News*, 1 June 1918, pp. 3327–28.

12. *Moving Picture World*, 19 October 1918, p. 366; *Exhibitor's Herald*,

7 June 1919, p. 35; *Motion Picture News*, 5 April 1919, p. 4; *Exhibitor's Herald and Motography*, 31 April 1919, p. 37; *Motion Picture News*, 31 May 1919, p. 3574; *Exhibitor's Herald and Motography*, 6 September 1919, p. 46; *Motion Picture News*, 6 December 1919, p. 4065; *Exhibitor's Herald and Motography*, 4 October 1919, p. 47; *Motion Picture News*, 24 January 1920, p. 1038; *Motion Picture News*, 265 February 1912, p. 1615; *Motion Picture News*, 6 August 1921, p. 759.

13. Barney Balaban and Sam Katz, *The Fundamental Principles of Balaban and Katz Theater Management* (Chicago: Balaban & Katz, 1926), 54.

14. James L. Davis, *The Elevated System and the Growth of Chicago* (Evanston, Ill.: Northwestern University, Department of Geography, 1965), 11–49; Homer Hoyt, *One Hundred Years of Land Values in Chicago* (Chicago: University of Chicago Press, 1933).

15. Chicago Plan Commission, *Forty-Four Cities in the City of Chicago* (Chicago: Chicago Plan Commission, 1942), 27–28; Louis Wirth, *The Ghetto* (Chicago: University of Chicago Press, 1928), 241–52; Meyer Levin, *The Old Bunch* (New York: Citadel Press, 1937).

16. T. V. Smith and Leonard D. White, eds., *Chicago: An Experiment in Social Science Research* (Chicago: University of Chicago Press, 1929), 113–18; M. J. Proudfoot, "The Major Outlying Business Centers of Chicago" (Ph.D. diss., University of Chicago, 1936), 16–50, 100–224; Hoyt, *One Hundred Years*, 227–31; Balaban and Katz, *Fundamental Principles*, 87.

17. Chicago Plan Commission, *Forty-Four Cities*, 118–19.

18. Michael Conant, *Antitrust in the Motion Picture Industry* (Berkeley: University of California Press, 1960), 154–55; Chicago Recreation Commission, *The Chicago Recreation Survey*, 1937, vol. 2, *Commercial Recreation* (Chicago: Chicago Recreation Commission, 1938), 36–37; Hoyt, *One Hundred Years*, 262.

19. For detailed studies of how others aped Balaban & Katz, see Douglas Gomery, "The Skouras Brothers: Bringing Movies to St. Louis and Beyond," *Marquee* 16, no. 1 (1984): 18–21; and Gomery, "Saxe Amusement Enterprises: The Movies Come to Milwaukee," *Milwaukee History* 2, no. 1 (1979): 18–28.

20. Federal Writers Project, *New York City Guide* (New York: Random House, 1939), 226–52; *The New York Market* (New York: New York Herald, 1922), 60–63; Allan Nevins and John A. Krout, eds., *The Greater City* (New York: Columbia University Press, 1948), 148–72; Walter Laidlow, *Population of the City of New York, 1890–1932* (New York: Cities Census Committee, 1932), 51–58; Harold T. Lewis, *Transit and Transportation*, Regional Survey (New York: Regional Plan of New York, 1928), 4:19–69.

21. Levin, *The Old Bunch*, 58.

22. Ben M. Hall, *The Best Remaining Seats* (New York: Bramhall House, 1961), 136–42.

23. "Uptown Theatre," *Marquee* 9, no. 2 (1977): 1–27; Balaban and Katz, *Fundamental Principles*, 99–100.

24. Quoted in E. C. A. Bullock, "Theater Entrances and Lobbies," *Architectural Forum* 42, no. 6 (1925): 372.

25. Joseph M. Valerio and Daniel Friedman, *Movie Palaces: Renais-*

sance and Reuse (New York: Educational Facilities Laboratories Division, 1982), 21–29.

26. "Uptown Theater," 1–27; Theatre Historical Society, *Chicago Theater* (Notre Dame, Ind.: THS, 1975), 1–20; "Special Issue on the Balaban & Katz Tivoli Theater," *Marquee* 17, no. 4 (1985): 1–36; John W. Landon, *Jesse Crawford* (Vestal, N.Y.: Vestal Press, 1974), 19–44.

27. Arthur Mayer, *Merely Colossal* (New York: Simon & Schuster, 1953), 71; Ira Berkow, *Maxwell Street* (Garden City, N.Y.: Doubleday, 1977), 201.

28. Kennedy, *The Story of Film*, 269–73; *Exhibitor's Herald and Motography*, 21 December 1918, p. 25.

29. Robert C. Allen points out in "Vaudeville and Film 1895–1915: A Study in Media Interaction" (Ph.D. diss., University of Iowa, 1977) that live performance and movies had worked together from the beginning of the introduction of cinema before the turn of the century.

30. Vincente Minnelli, *I Remember It Well* (New York: Doubleday, 1974), 52–56; *Variety*, 12 April 1923, p. 30; *Variety*, 12 July 1923, p. 27; *Variety*, 1 November 1923, p. 26; *Variety*, 8 November 1923, p. 21.

31. *Variety*, 22 September 1922, p. 1; Hall, *Best Remaining Seats*, 208; *Variety*, 25 October 1923, p. 18; *Variety*, 14 June 1923, p. 21; *Variety*, 11 March 1925, pp. 39–40; Carrie Balaban, *Continuous Performance* (New York: A. J. Balaban Foundation, 1942), 46–60.

32. Fred Wittenmeyer, "Cooling of Theatres and Public Buildings," *Ice and Refrigeration*, July 1922, pp. 13–14; Fred Wittenmeyer, "Development of Carbon Dioxide Refrigerating Machines," *Ice and Refrigeration*, November 1916, p. 165; R. E. Cherne, "Developments in Refrigeration as Applied to Air Conditioning," *Ice and Refrigeration*, January 1941, pp. 29–30; Walter L. Feisher, "How Air Conditioning Has Developed in Fifty Years," *Heating, Piping, and Air Conditioning*, January 1950, pp. 120–22.

33. Barney Balaban, "My Biggest Mistake," *Forbes* 50 (1 February 1946): 16.

34. "Air Conditioning," *Ice and Refrigeration*, November 1925, p. 251.

35. *Motion Picture News*, 10 May 1924, p. 2085; *Variety*, 14 January 1925, p. 21; *Motion Picture News*, 14 February 1925, p. 708; *Motion Picture News*, 14 March 1925, p. 1150; *Variety*, 2 September 1925, p. 33.

36. *Variety*, 15 July 1925, p. 23; *Variety*, 4 November 1925, p. 29; *Variety*, 16 December 1925, p. 29; *Variety*, 7 April 1926, pp. 24, 28; Kennedy, *The Story of Films*, 75.

37. *Variety*, 28 October 1925, p. 27; Mason Miller, "Famous Players in Transition Period," *Magazine of Wall Street*, 23 April 1927, p. 1178; *Variety*, 26 June 1929, p. 5; "Review of Operations—Paramount Famous Lasky," *Commercial and Financial Chronicle*, 21 April 1928, p. 2490.

38. Maurice D. Kann, ed., *The Film Daily Yearbook, 1931* (New York: Film Daily, 1931), 823–44; *Variety*, 7 August 1929, pp. 3–10, 50; *Wall Street Journal*, 11 June 1927, pp. 1, 4; *Film Daily*, 26 August 1927, pp. 1, 4.

39. Kennedy, *The Story of Films*, 275; Mayer, *Merely Colossal*, 106–11; Howard T. Lewis, *Cases on the Motion Picture Industry*, Harvard Business

Reports, vol. 8 (New York: McGraw-Hill, 1930), 516–21; *Variety*, 7 August 1929, pp. 2–10, 189.

40. *Film Daily*, 8 April 1929, p. 1; *Film Daily*, 16 April 1929, pp. 1, 4; *Variety*, 29 May 1929, p. 30; *Variety*, 14 May 1930, p. 4; Hall, *Best Remaining Seats*, 251–53.

THE UNITED STATES FOREST SERVICE AND THE POSTWAR COMMODIFICATION OF OUTDOOR RECREATION

L. Sue Greer

An advertisement in the May 1988 issue of *Travel and Leisure* magazine shows a sunset-tinged panorama of verdant springtime in the Arizona desert. The copy reads, "The setting, by nature. The resort, by us. Rockresorts, the natural."

Outdoor recreation provides a market for a variety of products, such as camping paraphernalia, outdoor sports equipment, and clothing, as well as a bewildering array of trail bikes, four-wheel-drive vehicles, and snowmobiles. There are also transportation, tours, lodging, and dining intended for outdoor recreationists. The profitable production and sale of these recreational goods and services requires the existence of certain kinds of physical settings and an elaborate infrastructure of roads, trails, ski runs, and campsites. Even the physical setting becomes a commodity to be consumed in all its beauty, grandeur, or peace via the purchase of a particular recreational good or service.

Private commercialization is inhibited by the costs of acquiring, developing, and maintaining the physical setting, but government spending on parks and recreation areas—for campgrounds, trails, roads, lakes—creates the conditions required for the private accumulation of capital in recreation-related industries. This is part of the *accumulation* function of the capitalist state.[1] State spending on outdoor recreation also contributes indirectly to capital accumulation in the economy as a whole. Moreover, outdoor recreation provides leisure opportunities that are believed to refresh and revitalize workers, thus increasing the productivity of labor.

Accumulation is not the only function of the capitalist state, however. The state must also maintain or establish the *legitimacy* of the distribution of resources and power resulting from private accumulation. The state is not structured solely by the accumulation needs of the capitalist class. Workers are not merely the passive recipients of recreational commodities. Government planners must take into consideration the recreational preferences of potential users and purchasers in order to satisfy accumulation functions. The state may undergo reforms or develop programs responsive to democratic pressures and extend benefits to the working class or middle class at the expense of the capitalist class as the price of legitimacy.[2] To the extent that urban workers want increased opportunities for outdoor recreation, the provision of greater facilities and opportunities meets legitimation as well as accumulation functions. On the other hand, government recreation planners may find it necessary for the sake of legitimacy to respond to the environmental concerns of citizens, even when those concerns undercut capital accumulation considerations in the short term.

Still, the state cannot mirror the class struggle entirely. A capitalist society must of necessity be dominated by capital. Failure to reproduce the social relations whereby one group expropriates the surplus created by another group would mean the demise of capitalism. The decision-making process has been structured to limit the issues and concerns that can be raised, presented, and considered. A variety of barriers to public input and participation operate to shape and contain potential conflicts within relatively well-defined limits. Thus, the involvement of the United States federal government in the development and provision of outdoor recreation, bringing together the functions of accumulation and legitimization, also illuminates their potential contradictions.

The contribution of the Forest Service to the commercialization of outdoor recreation has taken three primary forms. First, Forest Service *expenditures* on roads, trails, campsites, lakes, ski slopes, and other major infrastructures have been an important condition for the growth of such recreation-related industries as hotels, restaurants, equipment outfitters, ski operators, recreational vehicles (RVs), and even automobiles as instruments of leisure. Second, the centralization of recreation planning in a bureaucratic organization under the control of "experts" has tended to *objectify* the physical environment and recreation activities into discrete "packages" or "events" that are amenable to measurement and control. This process of objectification is an important step in commodification, because before a "product" can be sold, it must first be differentiated as an object. Before there is any opportunity to commercialize sightseeing, the activity must be carved into packages or commodities, through the construction of "scenic overlooks," for example, or by the presentation of specific events such as "fall foliage tours." Third, the *rationalization* of public input into government decision-making through the National Environmental Policy Act of 1969 has given precedence in the planning process to the recreation interests of organized recreation user groups, especially those that can marshal the backing of an industry or of other national organizations.[3]

The Forest Service interest in the promotion of capital accumulation through recreation has not been limited to recreation or leisure industries. Clearly implied in government recreation planning was the intention to promote general capital accumulation through increasing the productivity of the workforce. The Forest Service would provide, on a national scale, healthy outdoor leisure opportunities for urban white- and blue-collar workers, much as turn-of-the-century urban reformers had tried to do on a local level.[4]

This chapter examines Forest Service activities since the 1960s, focusing particularly on the development of the Mount Rogers National Recreation Area in the Jefferson National Forest in Virginia. The Mount Rogers case demonstrates that the same centralization and rationalization of planning that facilitate commodification also determine what issues can be raised and limit whatever conflict may occur.

THE FOREST SERVICE AND THE NATIONAL RECREATION AGENDA

The first true federal involvement with outdoor recreation was the creation of Yellowstone National Park in 1872. Spurred by the shrinking availability of urban park land, individuals in the municipal park movement came together with early conservationists to urge the preservation of non-urban areas as national parks.[5] For several decades the administration of each park was an individual and often haphazard matter. Some parks came under the control of the army; others were overseen by the supervisors of adjacent national forests—a sore point to many supporters of national parks, because the Forest Service was perceived as anti-park.

It is true that the reservation of national forest land and the parallel reservation of parks were motivated by different factors. The national forests were designed and administered as reserves for economic resources: timber, minerals, and grazing. Hence, the national park idea was anathema to most Forest Service officials, not because they opposed recreation per se but because the parks were viewed as "locking up" crucial resources. Forest Service policymakers, says historian Harold Steen, were "commodity oriented and reluctant to make irreversible decisions that would prevent future generations from drawing upon needed resources."[6] Consequently, national park supporters inside and outside government continued to lobby for the creation of a separate, independent bureau to administer the parks and promote outdoor recreation.

The formal organization of the Park Service in 1913 caused Forest Service officials to reconsider their stance on recreation in national forests. Competition with the Park Service for funding and the threat of losing more productive national forest land to new national parks gave support to recreation advocates within the Forest Service ranks and prompted the hiring of new experts whose interests coincided with the advancement of recreation. The conception of recreation developed by the Forest Service, however, was different from that promoted by the Park Service; it was both more active and more open to commercial recreation development.

The first major link between Forest Service recreation development and commercial interests involved the promotion of automobile access to national forests for recreational purposes. When the Forest Supervisors' conference in 1917 considered the "popularization of the national forests," two of the steps proposed were road building to increase auto accessibility, and an advertising campaign to "sell" recreational use of the forests to the public.[7] To emphasize the connection between the two, the supervisors were taken to the Ford Motor Company plant in Denver to see the new mass production process. In line with the goals outlined at this conference, a total of $33 million was designated for road building in the national forests over the next four years.

At the same time, the Forest Service took a new approach to recreation development and planning that would contribute to the process of objectifying recreation activities and transforming the physical recreation environment into a commodity. The new position of "recreation engineer" was created in 1919 and filled by an enterprising young landscape architect named Arthur Carhart, who laid the groundwork for much of the agency's future recreation activity.

Carhart, a social reformer, stressed the importance of outdoor recreation for maintaining the industrial workforce. Outdoor recreation would provide the proper moral benefits for the working man, benefits not found in urban dissipations. More important, Carhart strongly advocated a rationalized approach to the development of recreation resources, a task requiring specialists and experts to develop, in his words, "systematic plans for the *manufacture of recreation as a commodity*."[8] Carhart's philosophy and the specific projects he developed became the basis for a structure of decision-making that, over the years, would promote "packaging" of recreational activities for convenient consumption, measurement, and control.

It was not until the post–World War II period, however, that economic and social changes pushed the federal government into extensive recreation development. Among the social changes that stimulated a national recreation program were (1) the rapid concentration of population in metropolitan areas brought about by the massive growth of suburban communities between 1946 and 1970; (2) the reduction of the work week and increased leisure time for many workers; (3) the beginning of the shift from a manufacturing to a service sector economy. These changing conditions of work and community prompted an intensified concern with recreation planning at the national level.

Federal attention was stimulated in part from below, by public demand for outdoor recreation. The rapidly expanding use of existing resources resulted in the overcrowding of existing facilities. Between 1950 and 1960, visits to state parks more than doubled (from 114,291 per year to 254,772), as did visits to national parks (from 33,253 per year to 79,229). But the greatest rate of increase was in the recreational use of the national forests, where visits trebled from 26,368 to 95,592 per year.[9] To accommodate the increasing demand, the Park Service began a program in 1956 to update the national parks. Not to be outdone, in 1957 the Forest Service launched its own program, called "Operation Outdoors," to accommodate and encourage more visits to the national forests.[10] Thus, on one important level, expansion of federal involvement in outdoor recreation was a response to public pressure. But other concerns also shaped federal recreation planning and development, among them the uses of recreation for social control of the workforce, and of federal expenditures for the stimulation of private investment in recreation-related industries.

Federal leadership both inside and outside the agencies directly involved with recreation agreed that a comprehensive national recreation policy was needed. This view was promoted by corporate leadership and influential members of the upper class, as demonstrated by their leadership and financial support of the planning movement in the 1950s and 1960s. Laurance Rockefeller, chair of the Rockefeller Brothers Fund, urged Congress to create the Outdoor Recreation Resources Review Commission (ORRRC) in June 1958 and was appointed to chair the commission.[11] The report of the ORRRC begins with social control concerns:

> Outdoor activity . . . is essentially a renewing experience—a refreshing change from the workaday world. This is true *no matter what an individual actually chooses to do in the outdoors. . . .* Latent energy is tapped, unused powers of the body, mind, and spirit are employed, the imagination works on fresh material, and when all these things occur, the individual *returns to his work with a sense of renewal.*[12]

The emphasis on setting rather than activity opened the door for the commercialization of outdoor recreation.

The same report stressed that federal recreation development would—indeed, should—lead directly to a greater demand for goods and services from private industry. Such development, in the commission's words,

> enhances community values by creating a better place to live and increasing land values. In some underdeveloped areas it can be the mainstay of local economy. And it is a basis of big business as millions and millions of people seeking the outdoors generate an estimated $20 billion a year market for goods and services.[13]

The ORRRC reports make clear that through the funding of recreation developments, in particular the infrastructure of roads, campgrounds, ski runs, and so on, the federal government would underwrite a whole new area of investment for private enterprise.

The ORRRC recommendations, all of which were eventually adopted, included coordinated national outdoor recreation development; standardized guidelines for management; creation of the Bureau of Outdoor Recreation to coordinate development; and a federal grants-in-aid program to stimulate state-level development. Key concepts underlying these proposals were long-range planning, centralized decision-making, and coordination. Given the emphasis on standardization and measurement, this rationalization of recreation planning has been a major contributor to the commodification of leisure activities.

Upper-class and corporate support for recreation development was demonstrated by the formation of the Citizens' Committee for the Outdoor Recreation Resources Review Commission Report, which received substantial industry and private foundation funding.[14] ORRRC chairman Laurance Rockefeller also used private funds to promote the adoption of the commission's recommendations.[15] Congress responded quickly to these lobbying efforts by creating in 1962 both the Bureau of Outdoor Recreation and the Recreation Advisory Council (consisting of cabinet officers and federal bureau heads). Congress also established in 1965 the Land and Water Conservation Fund (LWCF) to assist states, local governments, and federal agencies to acquire land for recreation.

The Recreation Advisory Council mandated a whole new concept in federal recreation development: the national recreation area or NRA, which would bypass the barriers to commercial recreation development inherent in both the national parks and the national forests. The criteria for the new NRAs were spaciousness (more than 20,000 acres); high recreation carrying capacity; broad service area; large scale; accessibility to urban areas; and the dominance of recreation over all other uses. The advisory council specified that the size and carrying capacity of the NRAs was to be such that federal investment would be a major stimulus to private recreation investments: hotels, restaurants, ski resorts, and other services and activities for vacationers. The council also issued a major position paper urging a program of road building to encourage increased recreational use of automobiles.[16] The ORRRC predicted that the tourism and sightseeing promoted by scenic drives would result in substantial local economic benefits.

It was these two policy statements—on the criteria for national recreation areas and the importance of scenic roadways—that set the conditions for the specific development of the Mount Rogers National Recreation Area by the Forest Service.

THE MOUNT ROGERS NATIONAL RECREATION AREA

The Forest Service development of the Mount Rogers National Recreation Area highlights the themes outlined above.[17] The project illustrates the accumulation function of the state in several ways. First, Forest Service plans for the Mount Rogers NRA placed an emphasis on the stimulation of private investment through federal expenditure on infrastructure. Second, the rationalization of Forest Service administration and planning contributed to packaging the outdoor recreation experience into discrete, measurable units. Third, the procedures for public input that resulted from the National Environmental Policy Act of 1969 (NEPA) gave precedence to organized user groups that had industry and national organization backing. Finally, the NRA was specifically designed to attract urban white- and blue-collar workers and to provide them with a revitalizing respite from modern industrial life in "Rural Americana."

The Mount Rogers NRA case also shows that the Forest Service must address questions of legitimacy and may be forced to modify recreation development plans. At the same time, it demonstrates that not all citizen concerns have access to the public decision-making arena. The structure of centralized, bureaucratic planning severely limits the amount and nature of public participation in decision-making. Even when such specific legislation as the NEPA does increase public access to decision-making, it contains biases that control conflict and shape the permissible issues to be addressed. This case history provides evidence that federal involvement in recreation development can change the relationship of people to leisure activities. The change can occur even when the commodification of the physical setting and of the attendant activities does not lead directly to a major increase of commercial recreation investment in the local area.

The Mount Rogers NRA is located in the Jefferson National Forest in the southwestern tip of Virginia. The boundaries of the NRA stretch across five Virginia counties—Carroll, Grayson, Smyth, Washington, and Wythe—in an area of high mountains and fertile valleys. Between 1890 and 1925 logging was the region's major industry, and vast acreage was owned by a few large companies such as U.S. Spruce Company, Hassinger Lumber Company, and the largest landowner, the Douglas Robinson Land Company. The logging methods used during that time left largely denuded mountainsides, and during the 1920s and 1930s much of this barren, cutover land was sold. Some went to local private owners for farming, residences, *and recreation*—although the recreational activities of hunting, fishing, and berrypicking also performed important economic functions for local residents, especially during the Great Depression. The integration of leisure and economic necessity was an important characteristic of community life.

Far more of the former timberland was sold in enormous tracts to the U.S. Forest Service, and by 1940 thousands of acres in the five-county area had become part of the Jefferson National Forest. During the early decades the Forest Service task was primarily custodial. Not until the 1950s were there any developed recreation sites.

Through the early 1960s these national forest lands were used informally for family and community picnicking, hunting, and rough camping (much as the surrounding private lands were, although less frequently), chiefly by local residents. The few outside users were primarily hikers following the Appalachian Trail and others interested in primitive camping experiences. This situation changed considerably in the later 1960s.

The Mount Rogers National Recreation Area, authorized by Congress in May 1966, was proposed as a means of stimulating the flagging economy of the region by utilizing the NRA legislation and the funding available for land acquisition and recreation development. The boundaries of the new NRA encompassed 154,000 acres of land in the five counties, though only about half of this acreage was actually owned by the federal government. The enabling legislation included condemnation authority to acquire additional private land.

The recreational planning of the 1960s focused on national policy more than on local needs and conditions. This emphasis contributed directly to the rationalization of planning through more centralized decision-making and the reliance on specialists and experts. The plans drafted by the Forest Service were based on the research and policy recommendations of the ORRRC and the Recreation Advisory Council. When Forest Service officials met with residents of the region, questions and concerns about the specific nature or impact of the proposed developments were deflected by references to the highly "technical" nature of the planning process. A local booster organization, the Mount Rogers Citizens Development Corporation, took the position that its members should not criticize or question the Forest Service, because Forest Service officials, *as experts,* were better able to make decisions.

The first, very ambitious master plan for the area, completed in 1968, clearly reflected capital accumulation concerns. The plan called for a major ski slope on White Top Mountain developed and maintained by the Forest Service, while private capital built the lodging, restaurants, shops, and other facilities. Additional high-cost, low-return recreation development envisioned in the plan included large campgrounds, man-made lakes for swimming and fishing, and a sixty-eight-mile scenic highway; the Forest Service expected these projects to stimulate hotel, restaurant, and service development in communities bordering the NRA.

The early plans also showed the desire to objectify or package the outdoor recreation experience. The theme chosen to tie the NRA together was "Rural Americana," and there was a clear preoccupation with creating discrete scenic "views," like picture postcards, each framed by rustic split-rail fences. To this end the Forest Service used the right of eminent domain to condemn farms whose homes and trailers cluttered the countryside. Dozens of families and individuals in several small communities were moved out, and at least two tiny hamlets disappeared entirely.

Thus, even before any actual recreation development began, the Forest Service conception of a "Rural Americana" scenic theme had had a significant negative impact on a number of rural American residents and small communities. This came about because the Forest Service wished to exchange the untidy, dynamic reality of farm life for a neatly packaged but static bucolic image served up as a recreational commodity. The effort to do so affected not only the living and working space but also the recreational and leisure space of the people removed from the land and their relatives, friends, and neighbors. The transfer of land from private to public ownership contributed to the divorce between leisure and other activities by erecting boundaries between "recreation" lands and private homes.

Ironically, the attempt to "freeze" these rural views by removing the occupants has done just the opposite. By the 1980s even the Forest Service officials admitted that without the former inhabitants there to maintain the fields, gardens, and orchards, what had been picturesque was quickly becoming choked with weeds and brush. The Forest Service could not care for the land as its former residents had done, and it was already being reclaimed by scrub forest.

Scarce funding during the late 1960s and early 1970s did not alter the plans for Mount Rogers NRA development. These remained constant, waiting for federal pursestrings to loosen. Not until the legitimacy of the plans was challenged directly by local and national groups in the late 1970s and 1980s did the Forest Service consider altering its proposals. Interestingly, this occurred at a time when more money, rather than less, was actually available for recreation development.

Whatever funds it could obtain for Mount Rogers between 1968 and 1978 were used by the Forest Service to enhance existing facilities and create a few new areas for camping and picnicking. One larger campground, Grindstone Branch in the Fairwood Valley, was completed in 1970, with paved parking spaces at each campsite, hot showers in the restrooms, a central septic dumping facility for RVs, and a large amphitheater for nature presentations and religious services. A few years later a stone-banked wading pool and sandy "beach" area were added. Grindstone Branch was considered a model for even larger future campgrounds.

No movement was made toward the development of the ski area, with the important exception of land acquisition; the available money was not sufficient to demolish the structures on the site or provide for upkeep. Road building also fell far short of the original plans. No funds had been voted to begin the scenic highway, and only a few small roads were improved during the first fifteen years. The only fully realized parts of the original plan were the hiking and horse trails.

Forest Service statistics showed an increase in visitor days at the Mount Rogers NRA from 290,700 in 1975 to 429,700 in 1978, lower than the Forest Service had projected in 1968. Still, it had an impact on the region and on the recreational activities of local residents, largely from the concentration of visitors in the small number of developed areas, (three of which were close together) and the concentration of most visits on midsummer weekends and holidays. Local people found themselves avoiding outdoor recreation in areas that had once been very popular and during those times when their outdoor recreation had been greatest. Residents in the eastern end of the Mount Rogers NRA, in Wythe and Carroll Counties, reported that roads and trails that had been used by hunters for decades, while the land was under private ownership, had been closed. Forest Service officials claimed that the closings were necessary to stop the erosion and environmental damage that increased use of those areas had caused. The creation by the Forest Service of stream impoundments to provide "lake" fishing had a negative impact on fishing above and below the impoundments, even in stocked streams. Thus the attempt to produce a recreational commodity—lake fishing—in some places damaged the accessibility to stream fishing and fishing in general.

The overall activities of the Forest Service support the private accumulation of capital in many industries such as timber, oil, natural gas, and mining. Consequently, the Forest Service has managed the Mount Rogers NRA so that recreation is simply one of a number of competing commodities. In some cases, the incorporation of private lands into the NRA has resulted in the compromise of their recreation potential by competing uses. A primary example has been the extensive destruction of hardwood tree stands to make way for white pine, which is more valuable to the timber industry because it matures more quickly and provides a more uniform lumber. But hardwood forests provide a better environment for such popular game species as deer, turkey, and squirrel—and as a representative of the local Big Walker Game and Fish Club pointed out, hunting is more than a sport for many local residents; it can also be an important supplement to the food budget for many low-income families. A more isolated example occurred, as a native of the area explained, when "the Forest Service gave a contract to a local timber operator... [who] killed all the blueberry bushes... great huge blueberry bushes.... That's one of the main things that local people have always done on the mountain—pick blueberries."

In many different ways, then, the commodity orientation of the Forest Service, for both recreation and other industries, has resulted in limited and altered access for local residents. Moreover, surveys and anecdotal evidence from Mount Rogers officials and residents suggest that outside recreational users are more likely than local people to have a college education and to be middle-class professionals. The bulk of the local population is composed of working-class or blue-collar workers, clerical workers, and farmers. Thus the shift in recreational use tends to be along class lines.[18]

The changes in local recreation and leisure patterns that resulted from land acquisition, development, and private investment raised questions in the minds of many residents about the desirability of further change. Ultimately, the decision of the Forest Service to eliminate extensive infrastructure developments from the NRA plan was due to its concern to maintain legitimacy in the face of changing local and *national* views on recreation and the environment. The population is not simply a passive mass upon which leisure activities and recreation development can be imposed in any manner desired by government planners. Forest Service intentions of underwriting capital accumulation had to be balanced against questions of legitimation.

CONFLICT OVER RECREATIONAL DEVELOPMENT

The 1968 master plan for the development of the Mount Rogers NRA was prepared by experts and bureaucrats with no input from local residents or potential user groups. Even after the master plan was completed, it was not widely disseminated to the public. A single-page popularized version, published in local newspapers, attempted to distill the highlights of the two-volume document, describing each project in the most general terms and presenting glowing estimates of the positive impact on the local economy. There was no indication how much acreage was involved or any hint of potential negative environmental or social effects.

However, the passage of the National Environmental Policy Act of 1969 made it necessary for the Forest Service to rewrite its 1968 plan in order to include an environmental impact statement (EIS). NEPA regulations required that a draft EIS be released to the public and public input be sought before a final EIS and management plan could be written.

The Forest Service began the required review of the Mount Rogers plan in 1972, accompanied by two "public listening sessions" in May. But because so little information on the nature and scope of the NRA development had been made available to the public in the first place, very few people of the region had sufficient knowledge to make the "constructive criticism" sought by the Forest Service. As a result, attendance was very low at the listening sessions; fewer than a dozen individuals were present, and most of those were representatives of such organizations as the University of Virginia, the Holston Valley Conservation Congress, Mead Corporation (a timber products company), and the Mount Rogers Appalachian Trail Club. Each of these groups had limited and concrete concerns, and the expertise available to represent its interests. Only one man spoke to the more general public concerns about land acquisition.[19]

The Forest Service also received letters from residents that represented a wide range of serious concerns: objections to the ski area and scenic highway developments, and anxiety about increased traffic, overcommercialization, the endangerment of wildlife species, and the extent of land acquisition. But because there were only a few such letters, Forest Service officials discounted them as isolated complaints and concluded that the public was solidly behind the recreation proposals.

There followed a six-year lag before the draft EIS was completed and released, during which the planners had little or no contact with the local population.[20] Consequently, the 1978 draft EIS presented development proposals nearly identical to those in the 1968 master plan. This time, however, the Forest Service did distribute copies of the full two-volume report to local elected officials, prominent citizens, and the owners of stores and other locations where area residents congregated. These people quickly passed on the information to their friends and neighbors. Moreover, since by law the document had to detail the potential negative as well as positive effects of the proposals, the draft EIS gave substance to the vague concerns and questions that had existed privately for some time.

Hence, public response was vociferous in opposing the scenic highway, the ski complex, the overall size of the proposed campsite development, the number of stream impoundments, and *most of all* the continued acquisition of private land by the Forest Service—concerns that the rationalized planning process had previously prevented from being publicly articulated. The NEPA had changed the process so that more people had access to more information on which to base criticism and specific forums through which to voice complaints. The new public listening sessions held by the Forest Service in February and March 1978 immediately following the release of the draft EIS attracted large, often angry crowds.

There were roughly two major categories of those in opposition, with different interests and different motivations.[21] The division fell roughly (and only roughly) along class lines. The first group consisted of small landholders, mostly natives of the area, whose income derived from low-wage blue-collar and clerical jobs supplemented by part-time farming. Their objections to the scenic highway, ski area, and scale of development focused primarily on the loss of "their" land. It is important to note that though some of this opposition was the result of self-interest, much of it had to do with concern for family, friends, neighbors, and the fate of the community as a whole. The second category comprised primarily college-educated white-collar and professional workers, fairly evenly divided between area natives and recent (within fifteen years) immigrants. This group's objections focused on environmental damage and the potential for overcommercialization of the area.

As the roll call of existing local organizations and governments opposing the Forest Service plans for the Mount Rogers NRA grew, an ad hoc group formed to coordinate protests and opposition. This disparate collection of people called itself Citizens for Southwest Virginia (CSV), with a majority of active members from the second opposition category. Composed equally of natives and more recent arrivals, most of them educated and middle class, the core group that planned strategy and organized and carried out activities focused primarily on environmental concerns. However, the CSV also tapped into the broad reservoir of local opposition and, initially, made Forest Service land acquisition an important issue on its agenda.

The NEPA provides a basis for public opposition based on the failure of government agencies to assess adequately all the environmental impact of a proposed development; therefore, the CSV marshaled the services of experts—biologists, geologists, economists, regional planners, and transportation specialists familiar with the region—for a critical review of the draft EIS. Perhaps of greatest significance was the CSV's successful enlistment of technical, legal, and moral support from national groups: the Environmental Defense Fund, the National Wildlife Federation, the Sierra Club, Trout Unlimited, the National Parks and Conservation Association, the National Rifle Association, the Defenders of Wildlife and Rural

America, the Appalachian Trail Club. The citizens' group even turned to other government agencies, such as the U.S. Department of Commerce, for expert technical assistance.

As the CSV became more involved in meeting the technical requirements of the NEPA, it gradually shifted its emphasis away from land acquisitions. The transfer of land per se from private to public ownership, for whatever purpose, is not viewed legally as "development" or an environmental change that falls within the jurisdiction of the NEPA. No environmental impact assessment is required, even when land is acquired by condemnation. Once outdoor recreation has been established as being in the "public interest" and within the jurisdiction of the federal government, there is little or no legal way to prevent eminent domain from being used. Thus, the issue most frequently mentioned by the public slowly disappeared from the active agenda of the CSV.

For the first few months of the controversy, Forest Service officials adamantly held their ground, insisting that the plan in its entirety was not only good but necessary to national recreation policy. Officials on the scene also maintained that the opposition was ephemeral and instigated largely by "outsiders" who had only recently moved to the area. But as opposition mounted, and especially as the voices of local organizations and government bodies were supplemented by those of national organizations and agencies, the Forest Service began to talk of reevaluation. The opposition of nationally based organizations suggested that national recreation policy itself needed updating, that the expansive proposals of the early 1960s no longer served a legitimizing function.

The process of overhauling the plans was considerably different from that of previous planning. When the official public response period closed in August 1978, the Forest Service established interdisciplinary teams to consider changes and modifications for the final unit plan and environmental impact statement. The teams dealing with trails had formal and informal input from outside interests such as hiking clubs, equestrian and horse breeder groups, and off-road vehicle users. The CSV had no official representation on these Forest Service teams but achieved significant input in other ways. In September 1978, CSV representatives and their legal counsel met in Washington with Robert Cutler, assistant secretary of agriculture. Also present were representatives of the National Wildlife Federation, the National Parks and Conservation Association, the Conservation Council of Virginia, the Environmental Defense Fund, the Defenders of Wildlife and Rural America, and the Appalachian Trail Club.

Signs of success for the CSV and other organizations came in June 1979, when the Forest Service announced that it had decided to reduce the scope of the project. The final plan for the Mount Rogers NRA, released in March 1980, eliminated the scenic highway and the ski area. All the campgrounds were to be smaller and the proportion of Level 4 (the most highly developed) sites lower. The number of roads to be built on the NRA was reduced, limiting the number of acres to be disturbed. The specific interests of the organized user groups that had had input to the revision process were also apparent. There was an extensive plan for the maintenance of game species such as deer, grouse, turkey, and native trout—a major concern of local as well as national groups—and a projected expansion of riding trails, trail heads, and primitive trail camping with horse facilities, plus attention to the interests of off-road-vehicle users.

Plans for land acquisition, on the other hand, remained unchanged. The Forest Service insisted that the new proposals for dispersed recreation made additional land all the more necessary. In short, what was perhaps the most deeply felt concern of local residents was entirely ignored in the final plan for the Mount Rogers NRA, since the NEPA process itself, which rationalized public input, did not permit all the issues and concerns of the public to be addressed in the public decision-making arena.

DISCUSSION AND CONCLUSIONS

The final plan for the Mount Rogers NRA reflects a complex interplay of the accumulation and legitimation functions of the state. Middle-class groups such as the CSV and the Sierra Club were largely successful in achieving their goals, primarily because of the National Environmental Policy Act. Representatives of off-road-vehicle (ORV) organizations also used the legal structures set up by NEPA to gain more ORV trails and facilities, despite the strong opposition of the same citizens and environmental groups that successfully challenged the scenic highway and ski resort. The Mount Rogers NRA thus provides a physical recreation setting conducive to the consumption of such commercial recreational commodities as four-wheel-drive vehicles, trail bikes, and snowmobiles, even with the changes in development plans.

The simple transfer of private land to public ownership contributes enormously to turning the physical setting into a commodity that can be consumed via the purchase of a particular recreational good or service. The transfer of land takes acreage open to many possibilities and makes it into a formally designated "scenic vista," "hunting area," or "picnic site," carefully monitored and preserved. The transfer of land creates a greater separation between everyday family and community activities and "recreation."

This is most clear in the cases of those families that lost land. For them, hunting, berrypicking, walking (rather than "hiking"), and picnicking were an extension of daily household life, activities that spilled out in available moments into the woods "back of the house" or by the stream "down the hill." Other residents have experienced the same effect. In the smaller communities, private land boundaries had been fairly permeable: children especially, but adults as well, paid little mind to whose property the swimming hole was on, or the blueberry bushes and blackberry brambles. But as more of the land became specifically designated recreational sites, or areas in which certain kinds of activities were restricted, the lines between daily living and recreation or leisure became more clearly drawn. Previously casual and spontaneous activities are now likely to be turned into planned events and saved for specific occasions.

The ultimate example of how the Mount Rogers NRA contributed to the commodification of leisure comes from an elderly woman, a native of the area. Her kitchen window looks out over the spectacular vista of the mountain region—yet she provided an enthusiastic description of how her local ladies' group had paid to go on a chartered "fall foliage" tour around the Mount Rogers region. The process of paying and joining a guided tour made a specific recreational "event" out of the commonplace enjoyment of the region's changing seasons.

NOTES

1. James O'Connor, *The Fiscal Crisis of the State* (New York: St. Martin's Press, 1973).

2. Manuel Castells, *The Economic Crisis and American Society* (Princeton, N.J.: Princeton University Press, 1980); Alan Wolfe, *The Limits of Legitimacy: Political Contradictions of Contemporary Capitalism* (New York: Free Press, 1977).

3. Robert Goldman and John Wilson, "The Rationalization of Leisure," *Politics and Society* 7, no. 2 (1977): 159.

4. Paul Boyer, *Urban Masses and Moral Order in America, 1820–1920* (Cambridge, Mass.: Harvard University Press, 1978); Francis Couvares, *The Remaking of Pittsburgh: Class and Culture in an Industrializing City, 1877–1919* (Albany, N.Y.: SUNY Press, 1982); Roy Rosenzweig, *Eight Hours for What We Will: Workers and Leisure in an Industrial City, 1870–1920* (New York: Cambridge University Press, 1983).

5. Carlton S. Van Doren, *America's Park and Recreation Heritage*, for U.S. Department of Interior, Bureau of Outdoor Recreation (Washington, D.C.: Government Printing Office, 1975), 15.

6. Harold K. Steen, *The U.S. Forest Service: A History* (Seattle: University of Washington Press, 1976).

7. Donald N. Baldwin, *The Quiet Revolution: Grass Roots of Today's Wilderness Preservation Movement* (Boulder, Colo.: Pruett, 1972), 14.

8. Ibid., 77 (emphasis added).

9. Outdoor Recreation Resources Review Commission, *Outdoor Recreation for America: A Report to the President and to the Congress by the ORRRC* (Washington, D.C.: Government Printing Office, 1962), 50.

10. Van Doren, *America's Park and Recreation Heritage*.

11. Gerald O. Barney ed., *The Global 2000 Report to the President*, vol. 2, prepared by Council on Environmental Quality and U.S. State Department (Washington, D.C.: Government Printing Office, 1981). Ten private citizens appointed to an advisory council by the ORRRC itself represented major businesses or industries, including Standard Oil of New Jersey, International Paper, and New England Power.

12. ORRRC, *Outdoor Recreation for America* (emphasis added), 23.

13. Ibid., 4.

14. Citizens' Committee for the Outdoor Recreation Resources Review Commission Report, *Action for Outdoor Recreation for America* (Washington, D.C.: CORC, 1963).

15. Barney, *Global 2000 Report*.

16. Recreation Advisory Council, *Federal Executive Branch Policy Governing Selection, Establishment, and Administration of N.R.A.'s*, Circular no. 1 (Washington, D.C.: Government Printing Office, 1963); Recreation Advisory Council, *A National Program of Scenic Roads and Parkways*, Circular no. 4 (Washington, D.C.: Government Printing Office, 1964).

17. I gathered the material for this paper during two different field studies: a community study of Troutdale, Virginia, (near the center of the Mount Rogers NRA), carried out between 1976 and 1978, including a total of six months in residence there; and a study of the Mount Rogers NRA development as a whole between 1978 and 1982, with a total of eight months in residence in the region. I visited the site again in 1984 and continue to correspond with Forest Service officials and area residents about further developments. My data sources include interviews with residents, activists, and Forest Service officials; newspaper accounts, Forest Service documents, and documents of opposition organizations; participant observation and the responses to survey questionnaires mailed to a random sample of residents from the five-county region.

18. Eugenie C. Scott and Billie R. DeWalt, *Landowners, Recreationists, and Government: Cooperation and Conflict in Red River Gorge*, Research Report no. 134 (Lexington: University of Kentucky Water Resources Research Institute, 1982).

19. *Bristol Herald-Courier* (Bristol, Virginia-Tennessee), 30 April 1972; *Smyth County News* (Marion, Va.), 30 May 1972.

20. Even the Mount Rogers NRA administrator eventually admitted that both the planners and the local Forest Service officials had been out of touch with local sentiment. There had been a formal liaison between the Forest Service and the Mount Rogers Planning District Commission during those six years, but even that contact had been mostly with the commission's professional planning staff, not the locally elected or appointed commissioners. Only twice in the six years did Forest Service officials meet with county supervisors, and reports from participants suggest that communication in these meetings was largely one way: from the Forest Service officials to the local officials.

21. The plan did have some proponents. The greatest support came from small businessmen and public officials in communities that stood to gain the most economically and were likely to feel the least direct effect of land acquisition. On the other hand, some individuals who themselves had nothing to gain thought the recreation construction promised economic growth for the region as a whole; and some businessmen (like one sporting goods retailer) who would profit from the development nevertheless opposed it on principle.

PART IV
COMMERCIALIZATION AND MASS MEDIA

A HISTORICAL COMPARISON OF CHILDREN'S USE OF LEISURE TIME

Ellen Wartella and Sharon Mazzarella

The notion that our ideas of childhood are constructed socially and change through history is the hallmark of recent studies of the history of childhood.[1] Philippe Aries's *Centuries of Childhood* (although criticized for his particular reading of the construction of childhood in the late Middle Ages) sparked interest in examining the changing nature of childhood experience.[2]

What influence might the enormous social and technological innovations of the twentieth century have had on the social construction of childhood? Several recent books—Neil Postman's *The Disappearance of Childhood* and Joshua Meyerowitz's *No Sense of Place*, as well as more general treatises on child care such as David Elkind's *The Hurried Child*[3]—argue that, among other influences, television in late twentieth-century America has thrust children into the adult world at an earlier and earlier age. These books hint at our thesis here: that during the twentieth century independent, autonomous youth cultures developed around leisure activities, and that the mass media became the social catalysts promoting, sustaining, and commercializing the leisure of each succeeding youth culture. We believe that such youth cultures, complete with their own distinct leisure-time activities, are part of the social construction of childhood.

This chapter addresses two questions: generally, how children's leisure-time activities have changed over the decades of the twentieth century; more specifically, what influence the introduction of media technologies has had on how children spend their time.

1900–1930

The social constructions of our notion of childhood have undergone certain shifts during the twentieth century as a result of two profound innovations that marked the Progressive era. The first was the sense of the public meaning of childhood and children that began in this century. Reformers and civic leaders between 1880 and 1920 came to view children (as distinct from families) as the future of American culture and argued that children's needs and interests needed to be met by the society, if not the government. As one historian observes: "By the 1890's a new perception of children and of the national population had emerged as the basis for public policy action and intervention. Children constituted a distinct group within the national population."[4]

The second innovation was the social definition of adolescence as a distinct period of the life cycle. Although during the nineteenth-century social commentators made reference to the biological changes of puberty, it was not until the turn of the twentieth century, and most notably the period between 1900 and 1930, that adolescence as a stage in the life cycle became institutionalized.[5]

These two social facts—the identification of children as a group that was of concern to reformers, and the definition of adolescence as a distinct period of human development, brought attention to how children spent their time. It is important to note that the concept of leisure, too, had only recently developed and during this period was becoming institutionalized.[6] Consequently, concern with children's leisure was part of a list of child-related interests among Progressive reformers: public education was institutionalized (between 1900 and 1930 high school attendance increased from 11 to 51 percent of the high school–age population); children became the focus of scientific studies apart from parents and families with the growth of child psychology and the establishment of Child Welfare Stations for ongoing research on children and childhood; federal social legislation was in place to monitor the health and welfare of children and families with White House Conferences on children held in 1909,

1919, and 1913 and the establishment of the federal Children's Bureau in 1912; and our society's interest in "youth" as a distinct category took on visible social meanings.[7] As Paula Fass has pointed out, the 1920s marked the beginning of the socially articulated "youth culture," a culture of older adolescents (then college students) who organized their social life separately from the family and as a distinct social category in the society.[8] The youth culture broke from the parents' generation by how its members set fashions, oriented themselves toward their peers, and innovated social practices in dance, hair, language, and social mores.

This was also a period of sweeping technological and social changes. The first three decades of the century saw the widespread introduction of the automobile, the growth and development of the movies, and the invention and establishment of radio. As Robert and Helen Lynd discovered in their study of *Middletown* in 1923, "the major invention reinventing leisure is the automobile... it has revolutionized leisure; more, perhaps, than the movies or any other intrusion new to Middletown since the nineties, it is making leisure time enjoyment a regularly expected part of every day and week rather than an occasional event."[9] The automobile allowed families, even poor families, to take vacations, something unthinkable in the previous generation; it took people out of town and away from community-sponsored parades and socials associated with holidays; it also represented a way of passing time, going for rides with the family or with peers.

Again, according to the Lynds, "like the automobile, the motion picture is more to Middletown than simply a new way of doing an old thing; it has added new dimensions to the city's leisure." For instance, in January 1890, the Middletown Opera House opened for four performances; by contrast, during 1923 while the Lynds were conducting their study, nine motion picture theaters in Middletown were offering more than 300 performances every week of the year.[10]

How did children spend their time during this period? Although it is always difficult to reconstruct the nature of children's (or, for that matter, anyone else's) lived experience from the past, the nature of the child study movement during the Progressive era made more documentary evidence available on children's lives in the twentieth century then we have for previous centuries. Moreover, concern about how youths did spend their time was a central part of the debates about children and media that began with debate about the movies in the mid-1910s.[11] The earliest critics of movies focused on the fact that children were early and heavy users of this new mass medium. For instance, when M. M. Davis surveyed 1,140 children between the ages of eleven and fourteen about their moviegoing behavior, 713 (62 percent) reported attending movies once a week or more.[12] Other studies conducted in the 1910s and 1920s further documented the popularity of movies among young people.[13]

In addition, societal interest prompted more general research into how children were spending their leisure time. At least two major studies are available from the 1920s. First, in 1924, the Boy Scouts of America published *Boy Facts: A Study from Existing Sources* by H. W. Hurt, very much in the "child-saving" spirit of the late Progressive era. As the foreword noted, the motivation for the study was the effort to understand the nature of "boy culture": "Childhood is the key to the future of civilization—yet civilization as a whole is illiterate, unlearned in child culutre. The culture of childhood is our most basic human task—yet most of us know little about it."[14] Then, in 1927, the National Committee for the Study of Juvenile Reading (supported primarily by the Payne Fund, a private foundation that also funded a multifaceted investigation of the effects of movies on children and youth between 1929 and 1934) sponsored a study of juvenile girls to serve as a companion report to that of the Boy Scouts. Published as *Girl Life in America*, by Henriette R. Walter, it reviewed the findings of various other social scientific studies and reported on three surveys of girls age five through twenty, compiled from questionnaires sent to public school principals, the leaders of Girl Scout and other youth groups, and librarians at public and school libraries.[15]

Both reports give the impression that youth in the 1920s had a lot of leisure time but did not use it constructively; both urged action to channel youth's leisure into organized activities: clubs, neighborhood playground associations, scouting. Hurt reported that the schoolboy had twice as much leisure as school time, and the employed youth 41 percent more leisure than job time. But according to a study by the Playground Association in nineteen cities, most of boys' leisure time was spent away from the home—68 percent in streets and alleys, 6 percent in parks, schoolyards, and playgrounds, 7 percent in vacant lots, and 22 percent in private yards—and when these boys were observed on the streets, half of them were found "doing nothing or hanging around." Other away-from-home activities included such commercialized recreation as frequenting movies, public dances, poolrooms, and theaters for vaudeville and burlesque. According to Hurt, little time was spent in sports, reading, churchgoing, or other "morally uplifting" pursuits. The picture he painted of "boys' culture" was bleak: "This great hazard of leisure... greater because of weakness of home, withdrawal from school, desertion from church and misfit in job, must be met. It cannot be met unless fathers and others with real manhood step into the gaps left by our social order." He saw scouting as the answer.[16]

The proselytizing tone is more subdued in the study of girls, but a similar picture emerges in at least one respect: "Through the growth of commercialized recreation, the use of the automobile and the congestion of city life, the home is ceasing to be the center of the recreational life of girls."[17] The automobile was drawing youth out of the home to movies and public dances. Still, though this study found that six to nine hours per weekday of the adolescent girl's time (whether she was in school or working) was spare time, home duties were the most frequently mentioned spare-time activity—and helping with child care, housework, and meal preparation was seen as teaching girls to become wives and mothers. Sports and outdoor exercise took second place after household chores; social events (parties, dances, motoring) tied for third with reading books; moviegoing and magazine reading ranked fourth and fifth.

These two books articulate the Progressive era's concern about adolescent youth's leisure time. In general, young people of fourteen to eighteen were seen as having too much time simply to hang around with their peers, unsupervised, or to spend in commercial activities, like the movies, that were thought to have questionable moral standards. Child savers were concerned that such ill-spent leisure would lead to moral degeneration, particularly in the absence of control by family, church, and school. The reformers argued that unless young people occupied their leisure more constructively, leisure could become a hazard, breeding delinquency and crime outside the home.

Neither of these studies, however, refer to adolescents of high school age as constituting a "youth culture," a designation reserved in the 1920s for an older group. Fass asserts that the first identifiable youth culture of the twentieth century developed among 1920s college students whose life style represented a distinct break with the values and behaviors of their parents' generation, prompting newspaper and magazine articles to decry the moral degeneration of the youth of the day. Fass argues that one factor leading to societal concerns about wayward youth was the changing nature of the urban middle-class family of the 1920s:

> A very specific kind of family style had developed among the native urban middle class. Families were small, planned, and actively concerned with the welfare of children. The relations between husband and wife and parents and children were increasingly democratic

> and emotionally responsive. Fathers had become more involved with their children and more affectionate toward them. Women expected that marriage and family would provide them with a variety of personal satisfactions and scope for personal expression. There was at once an increase in the emotional bond and a decrease in the amount of physical interdependence. Children were less tied into a household routine of work and place and permitted to partake freely in peer centered activities. The very nature of dependence had been changed as parents permitted their children personal freedoms and assumed financial burdens associated with extended education. There is moreover every indication that these patterns were becoming more and more common.[18]

The youth culture of college students of the twenties involved, as Fass notes, a change in the norms of behavior: women bobbed their hair, wore short skirts, dated, and became independent-minded and sexual beings. Premarital sex characterized the independence of the youth culture, at least for a large minority: Fass reports that one-half of college men and one-fourth of college women experienced premarital intercourse. More generally, college students showed a reorientation toward new institutions and groups: the movies, the peer group, and youth clubs. In addition, college students devalued academic work in favor of such extracurricular activities as campus clubs, fraternities and sororities, and what Fass calls a third tier of campus functions: dances, bonfires, bull sessions, proms, house parties—the social life of the campus. The image of the short-skirted, bobbed-haired flapper smoking a cigarette and wildly dancing to jazz at the all-night fraternity party has become synonymous with youth of the 1920s. This sort of social life, moreover, was portrayed in and encouraged by movies, music, radio, magazines, and popular fiction. These media both reflected and promoted the 1920s college students' mores; indeed, turning the youth culture into a leisure consumer culture was central to the media's attention to youth, according to Fass.[19] Most clearly for college students, leisure time was synonymous with peer-oriented social activities, many of which incorporated the mass media.

By the end of the 1920s the American public was clearly concerned about how youth spent its leisure time. The college "youth culture" was the target of public outrage and media publicity, but even younger children's leisure-time pursuits were under scrutiny, as the Hurt and Walter books make clear. The moral panic arose out of the fact that adolescents were developing an autonomous peer-oriented leisure-time culture, a culture independent of adults, outside the home, unsupervised, and increasingly commercialized.

Indeed, the late 1920s established a pattern of public concern about all children's use of media for leisure time that would continue in succeeding decades.

1930–1950

The Great Depression of the 1930s and World War II in the 1940s changed children's and adolescents' lives. Although the outside influences of the automobile, films, and radio were still present, these leisure-time pursuits were eclipsed first by the exigencies of hard economic times and later by war. Public concern about the impact of the movies on children's morals had by the mid-1930s been somewhat assuaged by the industry's introduction of self-regulatory codes.[20] The Lynds' *Middletown in Transition,* their ten-year follow-up to their 1923 analysis of an American small town, found that just as in the mid-1920s, leisure time was becoming increasingly passive, more formal, more organized, more mechanized, and more commercialized. By the mid-1930s, however, radio had eclipsed movies and automobiles: "If a comparative time count were available, it would probably be found that the area of leisure where change in time spent has been greatest since 1925 is listening to the radio."[21]

To what extent did children's leisure activities shift during the Depression? First, high school attendance increased: by the early 1930s, 60 percent of high school–aged students were in school and tended to stay in school.[22] Thus, the high school, like the college of the earlier decade, was increasingly able to provide a place for an age group to spend time together in activities to establish their own culture. There is also evidence that many adolescents attending school were also working during the Depression. According to G. H. Elder's analysis of interviews conducted with families during the mid-1930s as part of the Oakland Growth Study at the University of California, two-fifths of the children of the more than 200 families surveyed were working in part-time jobs. Boys were twice as likely as girls to hold paying jobs outside the home. Further, Elder found that both after-school employment and performance of domestic tasks were related to economic deprivation. Boys from deprived homes were more likely to work outside the home (72 percent of boys with nonworking fathers) than were boys from nondeprived homes (42 percent). For girls, the economic situation of the family made a sharp difference in work-related activities: over 90 percent of the girls from deprived families contributed to the family economy either through work in the household, thus freeing the mother to work outside the home, or by working at a paid job. In contrast, only 58 percent of the girls from nondeprived homes had household or paid job obligations.[23]

Elder found that the economic hardship of the Depression increased youth's involvement in the affairs of the family: boys were more likely to take full-time or part-time jobs, and girls became much more involved in domestic duties. Class background made a difference, however, in that middle-class youth tended to respond to hardships with greater effort and higher ego strength and problem-solving techniques, lower-class youth with a greater sense of fatalism. Elder reports that the Depression did have one major effect on both classes: it tended to restore conservative, traditional family values. Young people of the Depression, unlike the flappers of the 1920s, were not rejecting their parents' traditional values. Indeed, the Depression may have staved off the pressure for high school students to become the new flapper generation, the new youth culture.[24]

Elder notes that even with school and work activities, youth of the 1930s still had time to socialize with friends. For time use data, we look at one of the earliest investigations of American leisure time, *Leisure: A Suburban Study*, by sociologists George Lundberg, Mirra Komarovsky, and Mary Alice McInerny. During 1932 and early 1933, Lundberg and his colleagues conducted extensive field research in affluent suburban Westchester County, New York. They asked 2,460 individuals to keep diaries of how they spent their time for several days; included in this sample were 795 high school students. They found that suburban adolescents averaged seven hours and twenty-five minutes of leisure time per weekday; on Sundays, the boys averaged eleven hours and fifteen minutes; the girls, eleven hours (comparable to Walter's 1927 estimate of six to nine hours per day for juvenile girls in the 1920s).[25]

Much of this spare time was spent away from home: 58 percent for boys; 47 percent for girls in the laboring classes; and 52 percent for girls from professional homes. As Elder noted, girls from the more economically deprived families were more likely to be engaged in domestic work at home. But even during the Depression, the trend toward a peer-oriented youth culture was clear: when these high school students were asked to describe a recent "good time," the vast majority recounted an occasion away from home and with a small group of three to ten friends.

There were strong gender differences in leisure activities. Girls reported that 26 percent to 41 percent of their leisure time was spent at the movies, typically with peers. The major activities for adolescent boys involved sports, which accounted for 34 to 41 percent of their weekday leisure time. Other outside activities for both included visiting and talking with friends, attending club meetings, going to dances, motoring, and, for girls, church-related activities.[26]

At home, the number one pastime was listening to the radio:

> So general is the practice... that two-thirds of a sample group of children spent at least one half hour listening in on everything from detective stories to the Lucky Strike Orchestra. This pursuit occupies more of the boys' time than of the girls', and takes up from 17 to 30 percent of all the leisure which the children spend at home. As the income of the family increases, the girls spend less time listening to the radio, but not the boys. On Sunday, the radio gives way to reading on the part of the boys and visiting on the part of the girls.[27]

When the Lundberg and Elder studies are considered together, it appears that the Depression tended to increase the time adolescents spent working but did not much affect their tendency to spend lesiure time with their friends away from home. Their quantity of leisure time may have decreased somewhat, but the range of leisure pursuits seems similar to that reported in the 1920s: sports, social activities, mass media. Moreover, adolescents of the 1930s were using media—movies, radio, magazines, and books—much as did their cohorts of the earlier decade, though it is unclear whether that use was greater in the 1930s than in the 1920s. If anything changed, it appears that youth spent less time just hanging around; perhaps the late Progressive era's attempts to get youth off the streets and involved in organized activities were successful. Adolescents in the 1930s did report engaging in organized clubs, youth groups, and sporting teams. Indeed, in 1939 an associate of the Child Study Association of America decried the "extinction" of children's free time by the increase in scheduled, organized activities.[28]

By the 1940s, high school students as a group were labeled, identified, and the subject of popular attention and concern. The creation of *Seventeen* magazine in 1944 highlighted the fact that "teenagers" had developed an identifiable culture with attendant dress, morals, and behaviors. Much as in the 1920s, concern about youth in the 1940s turned to the morals of adolescents. Public displeasure was voiced over juvenile delinquency, wild swing music, sexual activity, and the development of a culture among teenagers that diverged from that of their parents. As Leroy Ashby notes: "Throughout the depression and especially the war, adults anxiously fretted over the increase in juvenile crime and socially unacceptable conduct. In a 1946 poll, 42 percent of the adult respondents were convinced that teenagers behaved worse than their parents' generation; only 9 percent thought that youthful behavior had improved."[29]

And how did these teenagers spend their time? According to data collected in 1947 and reported in 1949 by E. B. Olds, high school students from an affluent suburb of St. Louis spent their time much as had their 1930s cohorts in Westchester County. For boys, loafing around (both with peers and alone), working part time, and playing sports were the top three activities, followed closely by listening to the radio. For girls, loafing around and listening to the radio outranked housework. School activities took up a fairly large share of time as well: studying, club activities, and various out-of-school classes filled some fifteen hours a week for both boys and girls, adding to the time spent with peers. Likewise, radio listening, reading for fun, and moviegoing averaged about fifteen hours per week for boys and girls.[30]

During the 1930s and 1940s, then, high school students increased the time spent outside the home, in peer-oriented pursuits, and with mass media that were coming to be specifically marketed to them. The fact that during this period adolescents were increasingly likely to attend and stay in high school helped bring peers together to coalesce into a youth culture. The anxiety about the bobby soxer of the 1940s who swooned to Frank Sinatra and watched her own teen movies and read her own teen magazines was somewhat eclipsed by depression and wartime concerns. After the war, however, the tendency of high school students to take on after-school and weekend jobs increased their economic independence and solidified the peer network, since many of these jobs involved working with other teenagers in the burgeoning drive-ins and record shops and movie houses. The youth culture that developed around high schools in the 1930s and 1940s would be the focus of the next round of what J. B. Gilbert calls a "moral panic" about how youth spent their leisure time in the 1950s and subsequent decades.[31]

1950 TO THE PRESENT

The outcry about the morals of American youth in the postwar era was similar to the lament about the wayward youth of the 1920s. But there was a major difference: although movies got part of the blame in the 1920s, they were not the only focus of concern. Beginning in the 1950s, however, the public responded to increases in juvenile delinquency and the teenage youth culture by implicating the influence of the mass media: television, comic books, movies, rock-and-roll.[32] Indeed, since the 1950s, concern about how children spend their time has been nearly synonymous with concern about the effects of the mass media, and television in particular.

What generated this new round of moral panic? First, the rise of rock-and-roll, the growth of television, and the popularity of comic books in the 1950s brought public attention to the multiple media outlets for popular culture. Second, as Gilbert argues, the postwar years brought increased economic prosperity to the country as a whole and to adolescents in particular as they acquired economic power independent of their parents. Through part-time jobs and the general affluence of postwar society, teenagers in the 1950s "often tied themselves into a separate network that undercut links to family and community. Already set apart in high schools, they constructed a subculture that drew energy from the group culture of schools, retail stores, drive-in theaters, and early versions of fast food restaurants where many of them worked."[33] Third, as school and work physically segregated the generations so that the young spent the greater portion of their day in a world dominated by peers, so the mass media ideologically segregated them; youthful language, style of dress, values, goals, and behavior became more and more foreign to adults—as well as more and more commercialized. The mass media, by targeting the teenage market for cultural products, helped to create a separate teen culture. In his analysis of the public panic about juvenile delinquency in the 1950s, Gilbert contends that "teenagers, by erecting barriers of fashion and custom around adolescence, had walled off a secret and potentially antagonistic area of American culture."[34]

In response, the 1950s spawned the still-prevalent trend in studies of how young people use the media, with most giving special attention to the use of television. In fact, a number of studies documented that American youth—both adolescents and younger children—were spending a great deal of time with the new medium, at the expense of more creative or active pursuits such as participating in sports or playing musical instruments. Perhaps more important, the time spent watching television accompanied an increase in time spent with mass media overall.[35]

One debate that has raged among academics since the earliest days of the medium is whether television served to "displace" other media as a leisure-time pursuit or whether it brought about a total reorganization of children's leisure-time activities. A number of studies of children's use of the mass media, going back to the classic Schramm, Lyle, and Parker study, have examined the "displacement" versus the "reorganization" hypothesis by attempting to analyze the impact of television when it is first introduced into a community. Such studies have been conducted over the years in England,[36] in Scotland,[37] in Australia,[38] and most recently in northern Canada,[39] affording comparison across the decades through the late 1970s. They tend to find a consistent pattern that when television is introduced into a community, it tends to displace some kinds of leisure activities and not others; however, there is disagreement about the nature of what is displaced and how. Moreover, there is some suggestion that television radically changes the structure of children's free time.

J. W. Riley, F. V. Cantwell, and K. F. Ruttiger, for instance, surveyed 278 television families and 278 matched nontelevision families in an eastern industrial city in the late 1940s and found that television's most immediate effect on families was to "reduce the number of hours devoted to other leisure time activities." Children age six to twelve with access to television spent more than two hours viewing in the evenings but averaged only two minutes listening to the radio in the evenings. Their non-TV counterparts spent half an hour listening to the radio in the evenings. Thus, there was an increase of one and a half hours in television over radio use. From this the authors concluded:

> It cannot be said that television in this situation is displacing radio, as is so often the case with adults; on the contrary, there is good reason for believing that the children who now devote more than two hours to television probably spent not much above one-half hour listening to radio prior to family purchase of television. In short, television is adding a completely new dimension to the experience of these children.[40]

Similarly, in an early survey in Cambridge, Massachusetts, conducted during the winter of 1950–51, E. E. Maccoby found that children of four to seventeen in homes with television viewed two and a half hours on a given weekday and lost interest somewhat in other mass media. Again, "the amount of time spent looking at TV is so much greater than the amount of radio-listening, etc., which is given up, that there is a very substantial net gain in the total amount of time spent in externally controlled fantasy activity (i.e., the mass media)." Specifically, children with television spent a total of 2.6 hours per weekday and 4.0 hours on Sunday with the various mass media, while children without television spent only 1.2 hours per weekday and 2.9 hours on Sunday with mass media. Maccoby's findings support those of Riley et al. that television was displacing more than other media; that in fact it was leading to an increase in children's use of media overall. According to Maccoby, this increase came at the expense of both indoor and outdoor play as well as household chores. Thus, television was not simply a functionally similar alternative but was chosen over "active and perhaps more 'creative' play."[41]

More recently, investigators of television's introduction into communities in Scotland and Canada have argued that television reorganizes all of children's leisure-time use.[42] The strongest evidence comes from T. M. Williams and A. G. Handford:

> Television's role in facilitating or hindering participation in leisure activities is complex. Some, such as active participation in sports, apparently are displaced more or less directly, but others, especially those which can be time-shared with television, are not. To what extent, how and for whom does television displace other activities simply because it is so readily available? What are the processes involved in choosing to watch television versus playing sport, reading or attending a club meeting? We suspect that most people do not typically consider 5 to 10 activities and choose television as the preferred option, rather they think immediately of television and the other possibilities never surface.

Williams and Handford go on to cite Aimee Dorr's report of the response of a second-grader who was asked why television programs are available: "To entertain. And to help me think. If they don't have TV, when you come in and you sit down and you just want to do something, you don't have anything to do."[43]

Further evidence for the reorganization hypothesis comes from a direct comparison of time-budget studies across the decades. In particular, one can compare 1930s data from Lundberg et al. with those from a 1985 survey by Susan Timmer, Jaqueline Eccles, and Keith O'Brien, another diary study of time use among adults and youth, though the latter used a national sample.[44] Table 9-1 presents a direct comparison of fourteen to eighteen year olds' reported use of leisure time in these two studies. All data are given in a common metric of hours and minutes per activity per week. Two findings are noteworthy: first, there has been a slight decrease in the amount of leisure time among this age group from the 1930s to 1980s, from nearly forty hours to nearly thirty-one hours per week; second, media use takes up a larger proportion of the teenagers' leisure time, rising from 38 percent to 51 percent. In support of the reorganization hypothesis, these data suggest that the increase in media use is primarily time spent with television. The table indicates a decrease in all other leisure-time activities, with the exception of "free play," or time doing nothing in particular. Further support for the reorganization hypothesis is the observation that the pattern of the adolescents' nonleisure activities remained reasonably similar across the fifty-year span.

Television's dominance in the leisure time of youth, then, would appear to be occurring at the expense not only of other media but of other leisure-time activities as well. As Haluk Sahin and John Robinson have argued with respect to a study of adults, television is "colonizing" American's leisure activities, encroaching on more and more leisure time.[45]

Another question raised about television's impact on the leisure activities of children and youth has been the degree to which television has served since the 1950s to bring young people back into the home with their families and to reverse the trend toward age segregation in leisure-time pursuits. Early studies found evidence that the new medium actually increased time spent with family.[46] Though on the surface this finding seems to conflict with Gilbert's youth segregation hypothesis, the two are not so contradictory as they first appear. In his review of the 1950s research, T. E. Coffin explained the double-edged nature of television and family life: while the medium brought family members back into the home, their interaction became more passive. He concluded that television was "both credited with increasing the family's fund of common experience and shared interests, and blamed for decreasing its conversation and face-to-face interaction."[47] H. T. Himmelweit's and Maccoby's research too provided evidence that the interaction of families with television tended to be more passive than active. Maccoby concluded that instead of fostering family interaction, "the increased family contact brought about by television is not social except in the most limited sense: that of being in the same room with other people," and Himmelweit et al. observed that the older children get, the more likely they are to view silently.[48] The change with age has been corroborated in later studies. Jack Lyle and Heidi Hoffman found that although watching television was frequently a family social event, "solitary viewing did appear to be considerably higher among sixth graders than first graders and a further increase was shown among tenth graders."[49] According to G. B. Blain, "Television not only inhibits family communication, but it can also physically separate the adolescent from his parents, especially if he has his own television set."[50] And indeed, since the 1950s there has been spectacular growth in the percentage of households with two or more television sets. According to C. R. Sterling and T. R. Haight, 1 percent of households had multiple sets in 1948, 8 percent in 1958, 29 percent in 1968, and 47 percent in 1977.[51] Data from the *Broadcasting Yearbook* indicate that by 1988, 57 percent of American households had two or more television sets.[52] Typically, parents and children have their own sets and consequently separate viewing patterns. Thus, there is some evidence that television, instead of promoting family unity, may actually over time have contributed to the age segregation of American youth, especially adolescents, from adults.

This age segregation, it has been suggested, goes well beyond parents and children to extend into the relationship between youth and adults across society. In their study of the introduction of television into a Canadian town in the mid-1970s, Tannís Williams and A. Gordon Handford found that residents of Notel, a town still without television, participated in more community activities than did the residents of two similar towns that had television. More important, the authors found that such effects were mediated by age: the contribution of television to decreases in attendance at community dances, suppers, and parties was greater for youth than for adults—although television also seemed to decrease adult attendance at clubs and meetings. These "age-related findings," the authors conclude, "suggest that television may affect the degree of age segregation characteristic of a community."[53]

Age segregation also emerged as a major finding of Mihalyi Csikszentmihalyi and Reed Larson's experience sampling (beeper) method study as reported in *Being Adolescent* (1984). With this method, people's activities are sampled randomly across the day with the aid of a beeper programmed to go off at unexpected moments. When subjects are "beeped," they record their activities in a diary. The authors found that the largest single activity engaged in by adolescents was socializing (three times as much with friends as with adults). In addition, 52 percent of adolescents' time was spent with peers (friends and/or classmates), and of the 21 percent of time spent with adults, only 2 percent was with nonfamily members. The authors conclude that "in terms of sheer amount of time, peers are by far the greatest presence in adolescents' life."[54] The importance of peers in the lives of American adolescents is clearly seen in adolescent preferences for such peer-oriented media as rock music and motion pictures, which frequently accompany socializing with peers.[55]

A third major impact of television on children's leisure is the manner in which it has commercialized their leisure-time activities. Although marketing to youth is an enduring trend that began with the role of media in the development of the 1920s college youth culture, television has brought commercialization into the lives of ever younger children. With the onset of "kidvid"—Saturday morning limited-animation cartoon shows interspersed with many ads for child-oriented food and toy products[56]—in the early 1960s, television began marketing to grade school and even preschool children. Moreover, during the 1980s, as Thomas Engelhardt has shown, marketing to children took on even greater emphasis with the development of toy-related programming: *HeMan, Masters of the Universe, Strawberry Shortcake, Gobots, Jem, Ghostbusters,* and other "program-length commercials."[57] These shows, available both through syndication on local stations during weekday hours (typically late afternoon) and on Saturday morning network television, signal a new strategy for marketing to children because they typically are funded by the toy companies themselves, and their introduction to television is timed to coincide with the introduction of the toy lines into the marketplace. Substantial public outcry by consumer groups, Action for Children's Television and others, led to government inquiries into, but no regulation of, children's television by the Federal Communications Commission in 1987 and the House of Representatives Subcommittee on Telecommunications, Consumer Protection, and Finance in 1987 and 1988. Critics of such programming/marketing strategies decry the commercialization of young children's entertainment and the tendency of toy-related programming to monopolize television for children.

Just as college students and then teenagers acquired a youth culture characterized by autonomous dress, mores, and leisure-time pursuits, such critics as Postman, Meyerowitz, and Elkind fear that television has now reached down to grade school children and promoted a similar commercialized youth culture for this age group.[58] Television not only provides shows for young children to watch but intrudes into other parts of their leisure time by providing the source and objects of their play (Ghostbusters, HeMan, and other action figures). Like earlier and older generations of youth before them, grade schoolers constitute a major national market for commercial products, sold through today's major mass medium, television. Moreover, at present there appears to be little evidence that the mushrooming of videocassette use as a new leisure-time pursuit will stop this trend. A recent examination of all the available videotape rental offerings in one upscale midwestern community found that whereas videos for adults tend to be based on Hollywood films, the vast majority for children are based on television programming—most often, the animated, toy-related product that critics of television lament.[59]

We draw two conclusions from this survey of children's use of leisure time during the twentieth century. First, as we have tried to demonstrate, since the 1920s young people have developed increasingly autonomous, peer-oriented, and commercialized leisure-time pursuits that have recurringly been criticized by their parents. Moreover, the mass media have served to promote, identify, and help create these national youth cultures over the various decades. Further, it is significant that the public anxiety or moral panic about youth cultures has with each successive generation since the 1920s concerned younger and younger groups, from the college students of the 1920s to the teenagers of the 1940s and 1950s to the grade school children of the 1980s.

Second, although each new mass medium of the twentieth century has been ushered in with public debate about its negative influence on children and adolescents and with suggestions that it has "added a new dimension" to the user's leisure-time pursuits, there is some evidence that in forty years of television, this medium has had a more profound effect on children's leisure time than earlier mass media had. In particular, evidence that television has brought about a reorganization of children's and adolescents' leisure-time practices, reducing the amount of time devoted to non–mass media activites, is important here. As Bruce Watkins has argued, television appears to have become a "dominant activity" of American childhood, a behavior engaged in by virtually all American children and a central agent of socialization to American culture—one that requries skills in decoding and is associated with certain cognitive and behavioral outcomes. Watkins thus considers television comparable in the Vygotskian sense to a dominant activity provided by the society to "define important issues, events and values and insure practice in developing socially valued behaviors and thoughts."[60] Thus, the nature of television's influence on children's knowledge about the world as well as its influence on their leisure-time activities is of paramount importance.

As this chapter has argued, our notions of children and youth during the twentieth century have been shaped and influenced by the activities in which children participate. Among these, the mass media have been central in shaping successive generations of youth cultures.

TABLE 9-1. *Activity Comparisons for Youths Age 14–18 in Average Hours:Minutes/Week (and Percent of Leisure Time)*

	Lundberg et al., 1930s (suburban sample)	Timmer et al., 1980s (national sample)
Leisure Activity		
Medium		
Television		14:14 (46%)
Radio	4:40 (11.7%)	
Movies		
Reading	4:54 (12.2%)	1:36 (5.0%)
All media entertainment (including movies, concerts, records)	5:39 (14.2%)	
Total media	15:13 (38.1%)	15:50 (51%)
Free play		1:52 (6.0%)
Organized Activity		
Lessons/practice		
Clubs	1:03 (2.6%)	
Team sports	7:14 (18.2%)	5:04 (16.4%)
Motoring	1:24 (3.5%)	
Shopping		
Visiting/talking with friends	8:20 (20.9%)	3:32 (11.4%)
Other	6:35 (16.5%)	4:39 (15.0%)
Nonleisure Activity		
Church/religious observance		1:11
Household chores	4:33	4:50
Paid work		3:56
Sleeping	60:54	60:19
Eating	11:57	7:45
Homework		5:15
Personal care	5:36	6:42
Transportation	4:33	

Sources: George A. Lundberg, Mirra Komarovsky, and Mary Alice McInerny, *Leisure: A Suburban Study* (New York: Columbia University Press, 1934); Susan G. Timmer, Jaqueline Eccles, and Keith O'Brien, "How Children Use Time," in F. T. Juster and F. P. Stafford, eds., *Time, Goods, and Well-Being* (Ann Arbor: University of Michigan Survey Research Center, 1985).

NOTES

1. For a bibliographic review, see the introduction to J. M. Hawes and N. R. Hiner, eds., *American Childhood: A Research Guide and Historical Handbook* (Westport, Conn.: Greenwood Press, 1985), 3–13.

2. Philippe Aries, *Centuries of Childhood: A Social History of Family Life,* trans. Robert Baldick (New York: Vintage Books, 1962).

3. Neil Postman, *The Disappearance of Childhood* (New York: Delacorte Press, 1982); Joshua Meyerowitz, *No Sense of Place* (New York: Oxford University Press, 1985); David Elkind, *The Hurried Child: Growing Up Too Fast Too Soon* (Reading, Mass.: Addison-Wesley, 1981).

4. Hamilton Cravens, "Child-Saving in the Age of Professionalism, 1915–1930," in Hawes and Hiner, *American Childhood,* 415.

5. Hawes and Hiner, *American Childhood,* introduction.

6. D. A. Somers, "The Leisure Revolution: Recreation in the American City, 1820–1920," *Journal of Popular Culture* 5, no. 1 (1971): 125–47.

7. See Cravens, "Child-Saving."

8. Paula Fass, *The Damned and the Beautiful: American Youth in the 1920s* (New York: Oxford University Press, 1977).

9. Robert and Helen Lynd, *Middletown: A Study in Modern American Culture* (New York: Harcourt, Brace & World, 1929), 260.

10. Ibid., 263.

11. Ellen Wartella and Byron Reeves, "Historical Trends in Research on Children and the Media, 1900–1960," *Journal of Communication* 35, no. 2 (1985): 118–33.

12. M. M. Davis, Jr., *The Exploitation of Pleasure: A Study of Commercial Recreation in New York City* (New York: Department of Child Hygiene of the Russell Sage Foundation, 1911).

13. J. S. Johnson, "Children and Their Movies," *Social Service Review* 6 (1917): 11–12; D. B. Nutting, "Motion Pictures for Children," *Woman Citizen* 5 (1920): 659–60; H. E. Jones, "Attendance at Movie Pictures as Related to Intelligence and Scholarship," *Parent-Teacher* (1928): 75–80; A. M. Mitchell, *Children and Movies* (Chicago: University of Chicago Press, 1929); R. F. Woodbury, "Children and Movies," *Survey* 62 (1929): 253–54.

14. H. W. Hurt, *Boy Facts: A Study from Existing Sources* (New York: Boy Scouts of America, 1924), 5.

15. Henriette R. Walter, *Girl Life in America* (New York: National Committee for the Study of Juvenile Reading, 1927).

16. Hurt, *Boy Facts,* 44, 45, 65. Hurt's own figures, cited here, add up to 103 percent.

17. Walter, *Girl Life,* 8.

18. Fass, *The Damned and the Beautiful,* 89–90.

19. Ibid.

20. Garth Jowett, *Film: The Democratic Art* (Boston: Little, Brown, 1976).

21. Robert Lynd and Helen Lynd, *Middletown in Transition: A Study in Cultural Conflicts* (New York: Harcourt, Brace & World, 1937), 31, 263.

22. Fass, *The Damned and the Beautiful,* 211.

23. G. H. Elder, *Children of the Great Depression: Social Change in Life Experience* (Chicago: University of Chicago Press, 1974).

24. Ibid.

25. George A. Lundberg, Mirra Komarovsky, and Mary Alice McInerny, *Leisure: A Suburban Study* (New York: Columbia University Press, 1934).

26. Ibid., 181.

27. Ibid.

28. J. Frank, "Children and Their Leisure Time," *Childhood Education* 15 (1939): 389–92.

29. L. Ashby, "Partial Promises and Semi-Visible Youths: The Depression and World War II," in Hawes and Hiner, *American Childhood,* 508.

30. E. B. Olds, "How Do Young People Use Their Leisure Time?" *Recreation* 42, no. 10 (1949): 458–63.

31. J. B. Gilbert, *A Cycle of Outrage: America's Reaction to the Juvenile Delinquent in the 1950s* (New York: Oxford University Press, 1986).

32. Fass, *The Damned and the Beautiful;* Gilbert, *Cycle of Outrage.*

33. Gilbert, *Cycle of Outrage,* 216.

34. Ibid., 15.

35. See G. S. Besco, "Television and Its Effects on Related Interests of High School Pupils," *English Journal* 41 (1952): 151–52; A. L. Lazarus, "Pupils' TV Habits," *Educational Leadership* 13 (1956): 242–52; E. E. Maccoby, "Television: Its Impact on School Children," *Public Opinion Quarterly* 15 (1951): 421–44; J. W. Riley, F. V. Cantwell, and K. F. Ruttiger, "Some Observations on the Social Effects of Television," *Public Opinion Quarterly* 13 (1949): 223–34; W. Schramm, J. Lyle, and E. Parker, *Television in the Lives of Our Children* (Stanford, Calif.: Stanford University Press, 1961).

36. H. T. Himmelweit, A. N. Oppenheim, and P. Vince, *Television and the Child* (London: Oxford University Press, 1961).

37. William Belson, *The Impact of Television* (London: Cheshire, 1967).

38. John P. Murray and Susan Kippax, "Children's Social Behavior in Three Towns with Differing Television Experience," *Journal of Communication* 28, no. 1 (1978): 19–29.

39. Tannís M. Williams and A. Gordon Handford, "Television and Other Leisure Activities," in T. M. Williams, ed., *The Impact of Television: A National Comparison in Three Communities* (New York: Academic Press, 1986), 143–213.

40. Riley, Cantwell and Ruttiger, "Social Effects of Television," 227–28, 239.

41. Maccoby, "Television," 436.

42. J. R. Brown, J. K. Crammond and R. J. Wilde, "Displacement Effects of Television and the Child's Functional Orientation to Media," in Jay Blumler and Elihu Katz, eds., *The Uses of Mass Communication* (Beverly Hills, Calif.: Sage, 1974), 93–113; Williams and Handford, "Television."

43. Williams and Handford, "Television," 186–87.

44. Susan G. Timmer, Jaqueline Eccles, and Keith O'Brien, "How Children Use Time," in F. T. Juster and F. P. Stafford, eds., *Time, Goods, and Well-Being* (Ann Arbor: University of Michigan Survey Research Center, 1985).

45. Haluk Sahin and John P. Robinson, "Beyond the Realm of Necessity: Television and the Colonization of Leisure," *Media, Culture, and Society* 3, no. 1 (1981): 85–95.

46. T. E. Coffin, "Television's Impact on Society," *American Psychologist* 10 (1955): 630–41; Maccoby, "Television"; Riley, Cantwell, and Ruttiger, "Social Effects of Television," among others.

47. Coffin, "Television's Impact," 634.

48. Maccoby, "Television," 427; Himmelweit, Oppenheim, and Vince, *Television.*

49. Jack Lyle and Heidi R. Hoffman, "Children's Use of Television and Other Media," in E. Rubenstein, G. Comstock, and J. Murray, eds., *Television and Social Behavior,* vol. 4, *Television in Day-to-Day Life: Patterns of Use* (Washington, D.C.: Government Printing Office, 1972), 163.

50. G. B. Blain, cited in M. D. Baranowski, "Television and the Adolescent," *Adolescence* 6 (1971): 379.

51. C. R. Sterling and T. R. Haight, *The Mass Media: Aspen Institute Guide to Communications Industry Trends* (New York: Praeger, 1978).

52. *Broadcasting Yearbook* (New York: Broadcasting Publications, 1988).

53. Williams and Handford, "Television."

54. Mihalyi Csikszentmihalyi and Reed Larson, *Being Adolescent: Conflict and Growth in the Teenage Years* (New York: Basic Books, 1984), 71.

55. See, among others, R. Avery, "Adolescents' Use of the Mass Media," *American Behavioral Scientist* 23 (1979): 53–70; George Comstock, Steven H. Chaffee, Natan Katzman, Maxwell E. McCombs, and Donald R. Roberts, *Television and Human Behavior* (New York: Columbia University Press, 1978); U. Johnsson-Smaragdi, *Television Use and Social Interaction in Adolescence* (Stockholm: Almquist & Wiksell International, 1983); J. W. C. Johnstone, "Social Integration and Mass Media Use among Adolescents: A Case Study," in Blumler and Katz, *Uses of Mass Communication,* 35–47; Reed Larson and Robert Kubey, "Television and Music: Contrasting Media in Adolescent Life," *Youth and Society* 15, no. 1 (1983): 13–31; James Lull, "The Naturalistic Study of Media Use and Youth Culture," in K. E. Rosengren, Lawrence A. Wenner, and Philip Palmgreen, eds., *Media Gratifications Research: Current Perspectives* (Beverly Hills, Calif.: Sage, 1985); Lyle and Hoffman, "Children's Use of Television"; J. M. McLeod and J. D. Brown, "The Family Environment and Adolescent Television Use," in Roger Brown, ed., *Children and Television* (Beverly Hills, Calif.: Sage, 1976), 199–233.

56. William Melody, *Children's Television: The Economics of Exploitation* (New Haven, Conn.: Yale University Press, 1972).

57. Thomas Englehardt, "The Shortcake Strategy," in Todd Gitlin, ed., *Watching Television* (New York: Pantheon, 1986), 68–110.

58. Postman, *Disappearance of Childhood;* Meyerowitz, *No Sense of Place;* Elkind, *The Hurried Child.*

59. Ellen Wartella, Katherine Heintz, and Amy Aidman, "Beyond TV: Children's Use of Cable and VCRs, a Case Study of One Community," paper presented to the International Communications Association, May 1988.

60. Bruce Watkins, "Television Viewing as a Dominant Activity of Childhood: A Developmental Theory of Television Effects," *Critical Studies in Mass Communication* 2 (1985): 326; see also L. S. Vygotsky, *Thought and Language* (Cambridge, Mass.: MIT Press, 1962).

10

"HOW DOES IT FEEL WHEN YOU'VE GOT NO FOOD?" THE PAST AS PRESENT IN POPULAR MUSIC

George Lipsitz

During the winter months of 1982–83, eleven-year-old Kelvin Grant attracted international attention among television viewers. Staring directly into the camera, the black Jamaican youth raised in England announced that "this generation rules the nation" to begin his reggae band's energetic music video version of the song "Pass the Dutchie." The engaging singing and dancing by Grant and the other four teenagers in the group called Musical Youth helped "Pass the Dutchie" sell more than two million units (records and tapes) worldwide within two weeks of its release, and their video brought reggae music to new audiences. Industry insiders credited the "freshness of the video" for the song's surprising commercial success, noting that it became one of the rare videos by black musicians to secure regular rotation on U.S. cable television's MTV network. The president of MCA Records International Division told a trade journal that his company's marketing strategy for "Pass the Dutchie" focused on aggressive promotion of the video on local and national television in the United States, and most reviews of Musical Youth's recorded and live performances made reference to the popularity of the memorable video.[1]

As one of the first hit songs whose popularity in the U.S. market rested on the appeal of its music video, "Pass the Dutchie" called attention to the strengths and weaknesses of the emergent video medium. On the one hand, the video enabled Musical Youth to achieve a degree of commercial success in North America that had eluded previous reggae musicians. In this respect, music video enabled a historically grounded oppositional subculture to reach a mass audience in new and effective ways. On the other hand, the content of the video seemed to direct attention away from the historical and social traditions of reggae, substituting instead a narrative story line shaped to the contours of conventional mass media messages. In that respect, music video smoothed off the rough edges of an oppositional subculture, delivering it to a mass audience only by bending its discourse toward the preexisting expectations of viewers and listeners. Thus the music video of "Pass the Dutchie" illumines both positive and negative characteristics of the video medium, and it provides an appropriate focus for an examination of the generation and circulation of cultural messages through the machinery of today's electronic commercial mass media.

COMMERCIAL SUCCESS AND CULTURAL QUESTIONS

Despite the genre's commercial viability in the Caribbean, Europe, and Africa, relatively few reggae songs have reached the U.S. top forty best-selling singles charts.[2] Yet if "Pass the Dutchie" was one of the most successful reggae songs of all time in the U.S. market, it was also one of the tamest—a quality that disturbed many American critics. A *Los Angeles Times* reviewer categorized it as "prepubescent pop," suggesting that "reggae purists might be pulling out their dreadlocks over the fact that these kids—ages 11 to 16—are now taking the Jamaican pop sound into areas of the U.S. charts that major figures like Bob Marley and Toots and the Maytals have yet to enter."[3] A *Rolling Stone* commentator wondered if "Pass the Dutchie" represented a new genre, "reggae bubblegum," and claimed that "the five Musical Youth have reduced reggae's musical vocabulary to a dependable bag of licks removing many of the stylisms that prevent the music from being accessible to a mass audience."[4] In a similar vein, the popular music critic for *High Fidelity* contended that Musical Youth had succeeded only by purging "whatever people find threatening about reggae—the dreadlocks, the simmering radical anger and religious imagery, the reference to ganja ... the dub techniques that stretch songs out hypnotically."[5] The most serious critical complaints arose from the ways that Musical Youth changed lyrics to make the record acceptable to a mass (and presumably white) audience, and from the way that the music video superimposed a new visual narrative on the song, altering its original message and meaning.

Musical Youth took "Pass the Dutchie" from the reggae group the Mighty Diamonds, who had used the melody of an older song, "Full Up," as the basis for a hit record titled "Pass the Kouchie." In their version, the Mighty Diamonds celebrate the ritual passing of a *kouchie*, a pipe used for smoking marijuana by the Rastafarian cult in Jamaica. Smoking *ganja* (marijuana) has religious significance for the Rastafarians because the ritual employs the natural herbs made by *Jah* (God) to help blot out the oppressions of colonialism and poverty. "Pass the Kouchie" lyrics ask, "How does it feel when you've got no food?" and the answer comes in the sound of a smoker inhaling on a *kouchie* to the rhythms and chord progressions of the song.[6] Connected to an illegal act (drug use) by an oppositional subculture (Rastafarianism) and rooted in a rejection of colonialism and racism, "Pass the Kouchie" remains embedded in "the fabric of tradition" and tied to "the location of its original use value" as an icon of resistance for Jamaican black nationalists.[7] Musical Youth's song substitutes a "dutchie" (a pot used for cooking) for the Mighty Diamonds' *kouchie*. With this change, the refrain's question "How does it feel when you've got no food?" becomes one-dimensional and literal, while the answer now presents eating rather than rebellion as the proper response to deprivation.

In Musical Youth's video, Rastafarian themes fade far into the background, and a seemingly contextless universal playfulness takes its place. We see Musical Youth setting up guitars and drums in a park, but then the boys are confronted by a truant officer determined to send them back to school. While trying to apprehend them, the officer trips over their amplifiers and guitar cords. Consequently, he takes them to court on charges of assaulting him. Led by Kelvin Grant, the five "defend" themselves by singing and dancing in the courtroom. A delighted judge and jury feel the spirit of their music and set them free—to the consternation of the defeated truant officer.

On the surface the compromises incorporated into "Pass the Dutchie" seem to reveal the corruption of organic folk music by the apparatus of commercial popular culture. A song with origins in a historically specific subculture becomes "mainstreamed" by muting the oppositional character of its lyrics and by adding a visual narrative that converts profound social alienation into slapstick comedy.[8] By wrenching reggae music out of its anticolonial and antiracist contexts, "Pass the Dutchie" appears to trivialize the rich textures of Jamaican resistance into little more than eccentric local color, into a novelty that offers only diversion and escape for an uncomprehending mass audience. By substituting innocent youthful rebellion for Rastafarianism, by making the "enemy" an individual state functionary rather than systemic oppression, and by seeking ideological and narrative closure through the approval of the judge and jury, the video transposes divisive issues of class and race into a universally accessible scenario about a harmless form of rebellion. It forges a false unity between the reggae subculture that spawned it and the mass audience receiving it, masking the real exercises of power and authority against aggrieved populations.

Yet underneath the very real co-optation and misappropriation basic to "Pass the Dutchie" lies a sedimented consistency. Even mainstreamed for commercial success, the content of Musical Youth's song retains overt and covert references to Rastafarianism, disseminating them to a wider audience than ever before. Both the revised lyrics and the video contain Rastafarian imagery as well as signs and symbols from other oppositional cultures. The anti-authoritarian sentiments and class resentments may lie beneath the surface, but they nonetheless spoke directly to the circumstances of audiences facing the severe economic crisis that coincided with the song's popularity. Far from representing the elimination of oppositional content from popular culture, the success of "Pass the Dutchie" displayed the creative plurality, plasticity, and persistence of oppositional traditions and symbols. Commercial pressures and political self-censorship altered the content, but the ingenuity of Musical Youth and the resilience of the culture they drew upon combined to leave significant historical, semiotic, and social oppositional content within their hit song. Specifically, it retains elements of the collective history of the Rastafarian movement, icons and images encoding oppositional meanings, and a message of immediate relevance to its American audience.

RASTAFARIAN HISTORY AND "PASS THE DUTCHIE"

In fairness, Musical Youth cannot be accused of diluting the organic purity of a folk music and a folk religion, because no such purity ever existed. The imperatives of capital that transform religious and cultural traditions into commodities like phonograph records created the very fissures and dislocations that brought Rastafarianism into existence in the first place. Musical Youth stands on traditional ground in adapting an old song to new realities. Indeed, the camouflaging of subversive messages within appealing and seemingly harmless images constitutes an essential part of the Rastafarian heritage. Born of the dislocations of international capitalism and nurtured in nations around the globe, Rastafarianism has always involved complicated negotiations among diverse cultural symbols. Thus, the adaptation to commercial pressures fashioned by the members of Musical Youth in England in 1982 marks them as legitimate heirs to the reggae/Rastafarian tradition more than as apostates from it.

Although a long tradition of "Ethiopianism" influenced Jamaican religion and black nationalism, the core doctrines of Rastafarianism emerged from the cultural creations of Jamaicans dispersed around the globe. Work in the mines of South Africa, on the construction and maintenance of the Panama Canal, and in the factories of the United States drew Jamaican laborers overseas in the first part of the twentieth century. Under these circumstances, the oppressions of race and nation took on new meaning, while biblical accounts of exile and return provided powerful metaphors for current conditions. The precursors of Rastafarianism emerged among these exiled Jamaicans in dialogue with the politics and cultures of other countries. David Athlyi Rogers enunciated the core doctrines in *The Holy Piby,* sometimes referred to as "the Black Man's Bible," which he wrote and published in Newark, New Jersey, in 1924. Rogers's followers included Jamaicans working in the factories of northern New Jersey, but his "Afro-Athlican Constructive Gaathly" church had its headquarters in Kimberly, South Africa. Grace Jenkins Garrison and the Rev. Charles F. Goodbridge discovered *The Holy Piby* among Jamaican workers in Colon, Panama, and upon their return to Jamaica founded the "Hamatic Church," the Jamaican branch of Rogers's Afro-Athlican Constructive Gaathly. *The Holy Piby* declared Marcus Garvey an apostle of a new religion that looked to the crowning of a black king in Africa and an eventual return home to that continent for oppressed Jamaicans.[9]

In the 1930s, Jamaican Ethiopianist sects began to stress claims of divinity for Emperor Haile Selassie, whom they called by his given name, Ras Tafari. Leonard Percival Howell played an important role in popularizing the idea of Selassie's divinity and Garvey's status as his prophet. In the years immediately after World War I, Howell had been a porter and a construction worker in New York, where he dabbled in radical politics and mystical faith healing. He corresponded with the West Indian George Padmore, at one time a leading intellectual in the Communist Party, U.S.A., and sought (without success) Marcus Garvey's approval for his black nationalist activities. Other Jamaicans with histories of religious and political activism overseas also spread the word about Ras Tafari, including David and Annie Harvey, who had lived in Costa Rica, Panama, the United States, and Ethiopia before establishing a sect they called "the Israelites" in Jamaica in 1930. These activists drew upon biblical psalms as justification for prophecies of a divine punishment of evil that they envisioned as coming in the form of Ras Tafari's reign, which would "scorn" the nation. Coupled with indigenous folk traditions and elements of Hindu and East Indian mysticism, the Rastafarian cults provided important ideological legitimation for the 1938 labor uprisings in Jamaica as well as for rural millennial movements.[10]

Initially, the Rastafarians had no distinctive music of their own, but they gradually absorbed a variety of folk music styles from other cults. In the slums of Jamaican cities they encountered members of the Burru cult, who celebrated the return to their community of discharged prisoners with a ceremonial dance accompanied by three drums. The bass, *funde,* and repeater drums of Burru music became the basis for subsequent Rastafarian musics, including reggae. Important Rasta musicians such as Count Ossie of St. Thomas Parish also drew upon the drumming styles of the Kumina cult. But all available kinds of music, both religious and popular, found their way into Rastafarian celebrations. Instruments ranged from native thumb pianos to imported trumpets and saxophones played by jazz musicians; popular melodies and revival-meeting-style handclapping provided determinate features. Just as their religion blended African and Christian images and beliefs, just as their politics blended class, racial, and national themes, Rastafarians' music drew upon an eclectic mixture of styles and forms.[11]

Jamaican popular music borrowed freely from the diverse repertoires of Rastafarian musicians, who provided the basic components for "ska," "rock steady," and reggae music. Reggae guitar patterns evolved out of Burru *funde* styles, and the reggae bass line emanated from the Burru bass and repeater drums.[12] But reggae artists also borrowed from Anglo-American popular music, especially from the instrumentation and arrangements popularized by Detroit's Motown artists in the 1960s. Fusing the folk musics of Jamaica with the international commercial musics they heard on the radio (and encountered on their travels to England and the United States as workers and musicians), reggae artists created in the field of music the same kind of international/national fusion that Rastafarians forged in the realms of religion and politics. Although not all reggae artists considered themselves Rastafarians, nearly all employed some Rasta forms and ideas in their multicultural fusions. Born in Jamaica, attuned to the popular cultures of England and North America, and ideologically focused on Africa for inspiration and identity, reggae musicians quickly grasped the possibilities for cultural mixing latent in all commercial popular culture. At the same time, their fusions remained rooted in specific historical and social concerns. They wished to participate in the making of a global popular culture by bringing the particular traits and tendencies of their own culture into dialogue with those from other nations. Economic and cultural imperialism extended the reach of global media monopolies into Jamaican folk culture, but the same conduit that brought North American and British popular styles into Jamaican music also carried the moral concerns, self-respect, and revolutionary nationalism of Rastafarians in Jamaica out to the rest of the world.

In both form and content, Musical Youth carried on the eclectic traditions of the reggae past in their approach to "Pass the Dutchie." Their group's adaptation of a previous hit record reflects a folk consciousness that privileges clever modification of collective forms over the invention of "new" and "original" ones. In the reggae tradition, "toasters" prove their mettle by creating "version" or "dub" renditions of existing songs. On the streets, this process can be done by turntable and sound system operators who distort or combine existing music recorded by others. In the recording studios, it takes the form of "version" adaptations of already familiar songs. Musical Youth's reformulation of "Pass the Kouchie" by the Mighty Diamonds, then, was less a watering-down of a traditional song than an improvisation on it—an ingenious application of a work written under one set of circumstances to a similar but not identical set of circumstances. The lyrical changes made by Musical Youth in actuality *extended* rather than limited the radical social content of the Mighty Diamonds' record by encoding multiple meanings in the new version.

Though critics derided the group for changing "Pass the Kouchie" to "Pass the Dutchie," Musical Youth's true relationship to the song is quite complicated. "Pass the Kouchie" originated not with the Mighty Diamonds but rather with a 1968 instrumental by Sound Dimension titled "Full Up," written by Jamaican musician Leroy Sibbles (later with the Heptones). As was their custom, Fitzroy Simpson and L. Ferguson of the Mighty Diamonds used "Full Up" as a basic "riddim" or instrumental track for the lyrics that became "Pass the Kouchie." Musical Youth learned the song from reggae artist Jackie Mittoo, the keyboardist for Sound Dimension, whom they incorrectly credited with authorship of the original tune when they changed the lyrics. Musical Youth's Michael Grant told *Billboard* that "Jackie Mittoo did the original version, so the song has been passed around a bit, you see."[13] Although misidentifying the song's exact lineage, Grant's comment shows that Musical Youth recognized the song as part of a collective tradition. The band did not break with that tradition in supplying an old song with new effects or lyrics; Mittoo, Ferguson, and Simpson had already borrowed Sibbles's melody for their own purposes.

Nevertheless, the nature of Musical Youth's changes, especially the apparent sanitizing of the lyrics, did seem to some critics like a break with the past, a difference not just in degree but in kind. By substituting "dutchie" for *kouchie*, Musical Youth's lyrics talk about eating rather than marijuana smoking. In fact, censorship influenced this change: producer Peter Collins demanded new lyrics in order to make the adolescent group's record more marketable. By excising explicit references to Rastafarianism and by stressing youthful innocence in the video, the record company encouraged the youths to hide their true identity and seek a more neutral public image in order to avoid offending potential customers. Such pressures are routine in commercialized mass media, and aggrieved populations often find their artists forced to disguise their identity in order to please those in charge of marketing mass culture. But Musical Youth drew upon sedimented currents of opposition within the reggae past to devise a form of camouflage that would satisfy those in power even as it subtly conveyed oppositional messages. The new lyrics and video extended some of the original messages of "Pass the Kouchie" even while tampering with its content.

By declaring that "this generation rules the nation—with version" at the beginning, Kelvin Grant announces that "Pass the Dutchie" is a rendition of an existing song rather than a new composition. But this "version" involves a transformation of social consciousness more than an obliteration of it. "We write songs about what's happening," boasted fourteen-year-old bass player Patrick Waite in explaining the song to a reporter. Conceding that the group enjoyed the song's rhythm and "happy" sound, Waite nonetheless insisted that "it's also about things today—the words are true."[14] Those words include a "toast" in which Kelvin Grant claims that "music happen to be the food of love" as he promises listeners some "sounds to really make you rub and scrub." Music, food, and love become interchangeable; passing the dutchie involves related acts of pleasure and passion. For audiences familiar with Rastafarian language, this connection contains logical and political significance as well. In the Rasta lexicon, "dub" not only means "to mix," in the sense of putting together different sounds and musics into "version," but also refers to cooking. "Sip" can mean "to eat or drink" but also connotes drawing on a pipe. Thus the substitutions that appear in standard usage to reflect a capitulation to censorship actually undermine censorship by using the Rasta vernacular to encode multiple meanings.[15]

Throughout the song the lyrics resonate with ambiguous meanings. Passing the dutchie results in music that "make me jump and prance," blending the "dub" practices of cooking with those of musicmaking. Background voices caution "it a gonna burn," not making clear whether they mean the music or the food or both. As in "Pass the Kouchie," the narrator encounters a "ring of dreads" (a circle of Rastafarians with their hair matted into dreadlocks) who provide the answer to the question "How does it feel when you've got no food?" The dreads answer, "Pass the dutchie,"—sharing their food and their love, their music and their spirituality. To complete the message, the lyrics celebrate the pervasive presence of this music—"the food of love"—on the radio, on the stereo, and at the disco.

Although listeners equipped with special competence in Rastafarian terminology can easily decode "Pass the Dutchie," the song's complicated subversions of language offer a challenge to others. The Rasta argot relies upon a radical undermining of univocal narratives and linear descriptions, replacing them with ambiguous and layered multivocal meanings. As Dick Hebdige notes, Rasta speech succeeds by threatening "to undermine language itself with syncopated creole scansion and an eye for the inexpressible." In his view, this comes from the origins of reggae music in a "culture which had been forced, in its very inception, to cultivate secrecy and to elaborate defenses against the intrusions of the master class."[16] Consequently, part of the meaning of any reggae song lies in creative wordplay designed both to disguise and gradually to disclose that meaning, to nurture an oppositional vocabulary incapable of control by outside authorities.

It is not unusual for oppositional subcultures to cultivate artistic ambiguity as a means of resisting unambiguously undesirable power relations. The Armenian painter Arshile Gorky counseled other artists that "what the enemy would destroy, he must first see," adding that "to confuse and paralyze his vision is the role of camouflage."[17] Subsurface Rastafarian elements in "Pass the Dutchie" retain their own kind of camouflage in order to enter mainstream discourse without fully internalizing mainstream values. Whether by replicating in speech the musical practices of "dub" and "version" with their creative adaptations and seemingly inappropriate juxtapositions, or by direct references to "dreadlocks" and "the spirit of Jah," the lyrics set limits on outside appropriation. This is not to assert that every listener receives the intended message of the song, but the tropological subversions and layers of ambiguity reveal a link to historical traditions and a capacity for employing multiple meanings as a form of protective coloration.

Just as Rastafarianism itself represents a religious form of "version," taking the Judeo-Christian bible and "flinging it back rude,"[18] reggae musicians play upon commonly accepted pop music forms and idioms in order to subvert them. Musical Youth accepted one form of censorship by allowing direct references to marijuana to be excised and adapting to standardized pop music conventions. Yet these changes disguise rather than compromise the ethical core of reggae's culture; traditional meanings remain encoded in the song, waiting to be discovered by listeners. In the same fashion, the video reached a mass audience by adding another story line and by transposing Rastafarian resistance into schoolboy slapstick. At the same time, however, subordinated oppositional elements permeate the video as well, providing a visual subtext appropriate to the complexity of the already multilayered musical messages encoded in the song.

SEMIOTICS AND "PASS THE DUTCHIE": THE SPECULAR TEXT

The successful MCA Records strategy of using the video to "break" "Pass the Dutchie" in the U.S. market raised questions among critics about whether audiences responded to the music itself or to the video. Some reviewers saw the group as a television novelty act rather than a rock-and-roll band, dismissing them as "Reggae Chipmunks" and "Rasta Smurfs."[19] A record store clerk in Chicago complained that "people don't buy that record because they like the music; they buy it because they saw those kids on TV."[20] A preteen in Houston disclosed that he bought the record "because I like the way that kid [Kelvin Grant] jumps around."[21] These reactions seem to confirm critical fears that the video decontextualized the song, severing its links to reggae and Rastafarian traditions and foregrounding it as an atomized media artifact. Yet the video emerged from the same forms of negotiation between commercial pressures and cultural traditions that gave determinate shape to the lyrics, and a careful examination of the video reveals an abundance of sedimented historical and cultural referents.

Initially, Musical Youth and video director Don Letts collaborated on a video of the song "Youth of Today," which showed the boys being chased by a policeman. But their record company ordered them to come up with a different video, one with a less insurrectionary theme. In response, they did "Pass the Dutchie," substituting a truant officer for the policeman. Yet both Letts and the band refused suggestions that they totally drain their work of oppositional content. As one of the few commercially successful black video directors, Letts felt an obligation to inject social commentary into his work, and he proudly wore his hair in Rastafarian dreadlocks to proclaim his antiestablishment views. Letts had been an important figure in the development of punk rock music in England when he worked as a disc jockey in London night clubs in the 1970s, and his skillful work directing a motion picture documentary on punk bands had led him to assignments making videos for rock groups, including the Clash and the Pretenders. "I'll only work with a band or a song that I like," Letts vowed, "and that means they or the song have to be saying something, doing something honest and with quality,"[22] In "Pass the Dutchie" he found a means of fulfilling those commitments.

The video opens with a full-frame shot of Kelvin Grant's face as he announces "This generation rules the nation—with version." The camera pans back as he "toasts" music as the food of love, revealing him to be standing on the bank of the Thames in front of the Parliament buildings in London. Along with the other members of Musical Youth, Grant starts setting up equipment, evidently to play their music for tourists. The opening connection between "this generation" ruling "the nation" and images of the Parliament immediately introduces a provocative tone. It connects music and politics, and it underscores the incongruity of five black teenagers from Birmingham claiming to rule. The claim raises the issue of what it means to be black in Britain and how that identity relates to concepts of the nation at large. Reggae musician and poet Linton Kwesi Johnson has eloquently discussed the core tensions involved in those questions:

> What does it mean to be black in Britain? It means that you have to wage a tremendous amount of struggle over things that other sections of society take for granted, like housing, education, trade union rights and so on. It means that even though you were born in England, you're

> forever being referred to as an immigrant. It means that you are at the very bottom of this society, forever trying to break out of the colonial mode.[23]

The oppositions endemic to being black in the U.K. form the opening visual contrast in the "Pass the Dutchie" video, juxtaposing five black teenagers with the majestic government buildings. In conjunction with the song's lyrics, the video draws a clear distinction between the state as embodied in Parliament and the nation as represented by a young generation practicing "version" in the streets.[24] It constitutes the streets as a site of cultural contestation and challenges national iconography with an oppositional prestige from below. The next scene underscores that contrast by cutting to a judge's gavel striking a desk, then panning back to reveal a courtroom in which the youths appear as defendants before a jury—on trial by the state. The first three shots are not really a narrative; rather, they introduce questions to be answered by the narrative to follow. What is the connection between Kelvin Grant's claim, a band setting up, and a courtroom scene?

As he does throughout the video, Kelvin Grant provides the dramatic action that pushes the story to its next stage. He jumps up in court, singing the first verse—and his action magically transports the camera back to the park, where we see closeups of the band members playing their instruments. Grant is "testifying" in this scene, both in the literal sense of giving testimony in court and also in the way black religion and music define the term: speaking from the heart about true feelings. A crowd of appreciative white adults gather around the band, delighted by the singing and dancing of sixteen-year-old lead singer Dennis Seaton and the others. At this point, a quick cut shows the truant officer arriving on the scene, followed by a cut back to courtroom, judge, and jury.

On the witness stand, Kelvin resumes his testimony. Springing out of his chair and singing with enthusiasm, his words seem to push the prosecuting attorney right off the screen. The jury watches sympathetically as the youths "testify," the camera panning each of them individually as they sing at the defense table. Then quick cuts show us the five defendants and their adversaries: the prosecutor, the judge, and the truant officer.

The next scene unravels the narrative. In the park we see the truant officer running toward the band, intent on ending their fun. He trips over their guitar cords and amplifiers, giving himself a black eye. Immediately we see a black man with dreadlocks on the jury, nodding and smiling knowingly. The earlier reference in the song to "the ring of dreads" takes on new meaning with this shot; in retrospect it reveals a subordinated Rastafarian current in the entire video.

As narrator, guide, and mischievous trickster, Kelvin Grant takes on the role of Anansi the Spider, a stock character in West Indian folklore. Like other tricksters in the Afro-Caribbean tradition, Anansi uses guile and pluck to conquer more powerful opponents.[25] Grant's boast about ruling the nation seemed incongruous in the first scene with his tiny frame dwarfed by the government buildings behind him, but his simple and direct affirmations about love and music incite the truant officer to rage, and that rage provides the force that defeats the officer in the end. His zeal to capture the youths propels him into their equipment, leaving him with injuries. The musicians direct no violence at the officer; it is his own anger that trips him up. That scenario plays out a basic theme of Rastafarianism as moral jujitsu—as a withdrawal that lets the system destroy itself by its own force. The role played by the musical instruments in the "Pass the Dutchie" video bears special relevance to this theme. Bob Marley once explained that "destruction come outta material things," illustrating his point by saying that an electric guitar can make joyful music, but it can also kill if there is a short circuit. But Marley's point resonates with broader Rastafarian themes, identified by Hebdige as an ideology whereby "technology capitulates to belief; belief succumbs to knowledge, and thought is really felt."[26]

As the video concludes, the camera takes us back inside the courtroom, where Kelvin demonstrates the power of "material objects correctly used." He joyfully describes the ubiquitous presence of music, introducing as "evidence" an assortment of "boom box" radios and personal cassette players. Another leap by Kelvin launches the band into performing its song in court, followed by a quick cut showing the truant officer telling his story to the jury—which laughs at his account and declares the defendants not guilty. The five members of Musical Youth jump up and dance in the courtroom, and despite the judge's call for order their enthusiasm provokes pandemonium. The dancing in this segment displays the high kicks and leaps off the ground that Marjorie Whylie, head of the division of folk music research at the Jamaica School of Music, has identified as characteristic of traditional Rastafarian dance.[27]

What is important here is not Rastafarianism as doctrine but Rastafarianism as a symbol of resistance. As Linton Kwesi Johnson explains:

> I'm not a religious person myself, but Rastafarianism is the most important positive cultural movement that we have experienced in Jamaica and whose impact has been much wider than Jamaica in fact.

> What the Rasta have succeeded in doing is to correct the imbalance of colonial brain-whitening—as some people would call it—brainwashing. Rasta made Jamaicans proud of their history, their culture, their African heritage and their roots. As a spiritual force, it has brought a tremendous amount of creativity into reggae music. And it has contributed to the popular language of the people. A lot of people who are not even Rastas use Rasta words.[28]

The claims that Johnson makes for the influence of Rastafarianism on black Jamaicans can be extended to a mass audience as well. Even when the particular vocabulary does not resonate with immediate experience, the resistance to authority and the affirmation of moral force central to Rastafarianism offer an appealing voice to audiences with similar if not identical grievances.

"PASS THE DUTCHIE" AND AUDIENCE RESPONSE

The existence of sedimented Rastafarian signs and symbols in "Pass the Dutchie" hardly guarantees their comprehension by the audience. People watched and listened to the song in a variety of contexts, and they brought diverse frames of interpretation to it. As a second-order sign system, mass communication represents ideas and experiences imperfectly—through allusion rather than exact representation. Mass-mediated myths take on some of their powerful influence precisely because they are open to interpretation, capable of being related to varying personal values and experiences. The very openness that allows artists like Don Letts and Musical Youth to inject a sedimented layer of politics into mass-marketed cultural commodities also allows audiences to interpret those artifacts in the contexts of their own experiences and aspirations.

For more than a decade, Dick Hebdige's *Subculture: The Meaning of Style* has served as the definitive scholarly work on the meaning of reggae and Rastafarianism as cultural practice. Hebdige demonstrates that in the context of the disappearance of familiar symbols of British working-class culture, some segments of white working-class youth turned to reggae music and Rastafarian imagery as a means of restoring a lost sense of community. Quoting John Clarke, Hebdige sees the white youth as attracted by the "defensively organised collective" in West Indian communities, which no longer existed in their own neighborhoods. Yet for Hebdige one of the most important aspects of white working-class interest in reggae was the subculture's ultimate failure to arbitrate enduring tensions of class identity. In his view, reggae music's association with black nationalism posed insurmountable barriers to lasting acceptance among white youths, who, logically enough, saw themselves excluded from a collective past that involved the experiences of slavery and anticolonial rebellion. As allegiance to race superseded points of class unity, Rasta imagery failed to serve as the basis for a classwide counterhegemony. Reggae continued to influence the subsequent punk subculture, but even in that context, according to Hebdige, the centrality of commodity form to subcultural revolt reduced its potential for rebellion into trivial questions of fashion and style.[29]

As a model for social analysis, Hebdige's work opened up new possibilities for cultural criticism, yet some of the contradictions in his argument now disguise more than they disclose. Hebdige's grasp of semiotics enables him to see the ways in which dominant ideology can be encoded within ordinary objects of everyday life, as well as the ways in which dress, grooming, and music can serve as signs of latent opposition. Yet his overview of social relations, his insistence on regarding subcultural practices largely as blocked class politics, compels him to see cultural discourse as less dialogic than it actually is. Why should the encoding of dominant ideology be treated as more powerful than the encoding of oppositional messages? If dominant powers require cultural legitimation as a precondition of continued rule, why wouldn't challenges to that legitimacy be of great significance, even if they disguise themselves in the form of commodities? Hebdige's grounding in a class analysis enables him to see the white working-class youth appropriation of reggae as a manifestation of "blocked" class politics, but he sees no autonomous identity for that appropriation other than a substitution of race for class. Why should the "defensively organised collective" aspect of Rastafarian culture necessarily form the sole basis of its appeal to white working-class youths?

As Stuart Hall explains, the loss of Empire, deindustrialization, and the growing Asian and Afro-Caribbean populations in England have all combined to create a crisis of legitimation for traditional symbols of British cultural identity.[30] In an age of decolonization worldwide, the white youth's appropriation of reggae can be an identification with the culture of the colonized rather than with the culture of the colonizers. In the face of late capitalism's legitimation crisis, it calls attention to the original plunder endemic to the capitalist system. For a population bombarded with messages explaining how to fit into society and conform with its imperatives, Rastafarian imagery offers an experience of detachment through drugs, avoidance of authority, and celebrations of sensuality and collectivity. In a society whose univocal cultural narratives are being undermined by profound social change, the multivocality and multiculturalism of "Pass the Dutchie" offer a significant alternative, a competing set of signs and symbols proclaiming prestige from below. Most important, in an age of unparalleled emphasis on commercial mass media, the internal ideological tensions of any one center of cultural production become available to alienated groups in other societies; real and invented memories of colonial societies help shape the contours of popular culture in contemporary England; the unresolved racial and cultural conflicts of Great Britain play a role in racial and class consciousness in the United States.

Hebdige is so concerned with the white "appropriation" of reggae that he underplays the creativity within the reggae community that successfully fashions signs and symbols capable of appealing to members of the dominant community. Entrepreneurs and "skinheads" may both "appropriate" Rastafarian symbols, but their appropriation is limited and constrained by the internal authority of the signs themselves. Of course, all icons and images can be misappropriated and ripped out of context, but all have an internal logic providing guidelines for preferred readings that can be defended as "correct." Rastafarian imagery is not just some bizarre "otherness" to be appropriated by white youth and capitalist record companies. It is a historically sanctioned language that skillfully unmasks the internal contradictions and historical sins of Western colonialism and racism. As a heavily coded subculture it is not easily translated into direct political action, but for precisely that reason it retains a freedom of action that enables it to insinuate its message into the discourse of its enemies.

Don Letts felt that the pressure from the record company to make Musical Youth more acceptable to a mass audience displayed the racism of the recording industry. "That's the kind of politics you have to deal with," he complained in reference to their request to drop "The Youth of Today."[31] It angered Letts that his track record of success as a filmmaker meant little to white businessmen who assumed that black artists had to look and sound more like white artists in order to be commercially successful. As he saw it, record company executives tried to eliminate all content that might offend the imagined consciousness that they attached to the mainstream, white record-buying audience. But Letts felt obligated to fight that kind of censorship and get as much oppositional content into his videos as possible. He described his battles with record company executives as essentially racial:

> First of all, me being black and over six feet and wearing dreadlocks like a Rastafarian, and usually wearing shades and combat fatigues—when I walk into a record company, they just bug out, man. I'm there

trying to explain a concept to them and they can't believe I can speak English. In a way, that sort of attitude carries over to the way they do black artists' videos, even to the way they do all videos.[32]

In order to make "Pass the Dutchie," Letts and Musical Youth did compromise—no doubt one reason their record penetrated markets that had resisted Bob Marley and Peter Tosh. But they did not compromise completely. The youths presented the song in the context of a battle with authority (the truant officer and the courts); they presented their own faces and performed their own songs with a dignity and legitimacy that undermined any expectations of deference; and they showed themselves as beating the system by drawing upon their internal resources. In the final analysis, the amount of black nationalism, class consciousness, and self-affirmation that remains in the video is far more significant than what has been purged from it. The young musicians dealt with their blackness by acting as if it didn't need to be explained and by building upon it to fashion universal values open to all regardless of race. But they also spoke to frames of reception other than race—especially youth.

Nearly every account of Musical Youth's concerts in the United States in April 1983 mentioned the youthfulness of the audiences. The crowds might have a preponderance of white faces or black faces, but they always had a majority of young faces. A writer for the *Village Voice* described an audience composed of preteens, teens, and their parents; the reviewer for *Billboard* spoke of "a biracial crowd largely of youngsters under 16."[33] Yet the reviewers also stressed that the band's appeal made it more than a youth phenomenon. *Variety*'s "New Acts" column noted that "there is nothing cloying or precocious about Musical Youth's presentation," adding that the performers displayed "an engaging sense of understatement that's diametrically opposite to the show-offishness indulged in by other kid groups." In a similar vein, the *Village Voice* reviewer argued that "Musical Youth is less a novelty or child labor routine than a good working reggae band that happens to be a bunch of kids."[34] Still, that bunch of kids obviously served as role models for other kids: a friend of the *Village Voice* reviewer working in a Harlem day care center related that many of the four-year-olds in her play group knew each member of the band by name.

In sum, the published reviews of "Pass the Dutchie" indicate that the members of Musical Youth came across both as legitimate reggae musicians and as social critics. Even the *Rolling Stone* reviewer who worried that the group might be the harbinger of a new "reggae bubblegum" genre conceded that their reggae retained "much of the form's original feeling."[35] Michael Shore described

Musical Youth in his *Rolling Stone Book of Rock Video* as "both adorable and potentially unlawful," with a group persona in keeping with "Pass the Dutchie," which "itself disguises hard-bitten social protest ('How does it feel when you got no food?') with lilting pop-reggae."[36]

Within the U.S. market, the popularity of "Pass the Dutchie" came from a serendipitous confluence of circumstances: the emergence of music video as a new vehicle for reaching audiences; the economic crisis of deindustrialization; the ascendancy of black artists who were mastering the forms and styles of pop music, as exemplified by Michael Jackson and Prince; the popularity of British groups with traces of reggae in their music, like the Clash and the Police; and the desire of young audiences to escape the demographic tyranny of the 1960s and have pop heroes of their own. "Pass the Dutchie" arbitrated tensions of class, youth, race, and culture in the short run, and its success helped create space for the subsequent successes of Eddy Grant and UB40 on the U.S. pop charts with politically trenchant reggae songs of their own.[37] Musical Youth's historical codes enabled them to speak powerfully to crucial issues in the lives of their listeners and viewers, to insert the experiences of young Jamaicans living in England into the consciousness of rock music fans in the United States. The vocabulary and imagery of reggae enabled them to "trip up" a system that threatened to deny them a future as legitimate citizens and artists, and it provided the vehicle for liberation by transmitting their message to sympathetic audiences around the globe. U.S. audiences may have known little about the inverted symbols of British democracy or the tropes of Rastafarian language in the video, but when Kelvin Grant looked them in the eye and proclaimed that his generation ruled the nation, they did not blink. Instead, they accepted a performance that encouraged them to sympathize with Grant and to see the world through his eyes. In the process, they acknowledged the shifting sands of authoritative discourse in the modern world and joined in the creation of families of resemblance and prestige from below that has characterized the Rastafarian project from the start.

NOTES

1. Richard Gold, "Juvenile Music Acts Blossom Worldwide: U.K., Latin Groups Head Invasion of U.S. Market," *Variety*, 12 January 1983, p. 199.

2. Joel Whitburn, *The Billboard Book of Top 40 Hits* (New York: Billboard, 1985); Joel Whitburn, *Top Pop Albums, 1955–1985* (Menomonee Falls, Wis.: Record Research, 1985); Gold, "Juvenile Music Acts."

3. Richard Cromelin, "Reggae by the Younger Generation," *Los Angeles Times*, 22 January 1983, calendar sect., p. 1.

4. J. D. Considine, "Youth of Today," *Rolling Stone*, 3 March 1983, p. 51.

5. Mitchell Cohen, "Youth of Today," *High Fidelity*, April 1983, pp. 182–83.

6. Stephen Davis, *Reggae Bloodlines* (New York: Anchor Books, 1977), 10, 131; *Variety*, 26 January 1983, p. 67; Dick Hebdige, "Reggae, Rastas, and Rudies," in Stuart Hall and Tony Jefferson, eds., *Resistance through Ritual: Youth Subcultures in Post War Britain* (London: Hutchinson, 1976), 138–39.

7. See Walter Benjamin's essay "The Work of Art in the Age of Mechanical Reproduction," in *Illuminations* (New York: Harcourt, Brace & World, 1968), pp. 225–26.

8. This is not to assert that slapstick humor lacks political content; it adheres to the notions of humor as "uncrowning power," advanced by Mikhail Bakhtin, among others.

9. Robert A. Hill, "Dead History: Leonard P. Howell and Millenarian Visions in Early Rastafari Religions in Jamaica," *Epoche: Journal of the History of Religions at UCLA* (1981): 32–34.

10. Ibid., 37, 41–45, 51.

11. Wendell Logan, "Conversation with Marjorie Whylie," *Black Perspective in Music* 10, no. 1 (n.d.): 86, 89, 92; Hebdige, "Reggae, Rastas, and Rudies," 142–43.

12. Logan, "Conversation with Marjorie Whylie," 86, 88.

13. Davis, *Reggae Bloodlines*, 131; *Billboard*, 18 December 1982; *Variety*, 26 January 1983, p. 67. According to the liner notes for Heartbeat Records' *Best of Studio 1* (HB–14), however, producer Clement Dodd remembers Robert Lyn as the keyboardist for Sound Dimension the day they recorded "Full Up."

14. *Musician*, no. 52 (February 1983): 44–45.

15. Davis, *Reggae Bloodlines*.

16. Hebdige, "Reggae, Rastas, and Rudies," 147.

17. Quoted in Michael M. J. Fischer, "Ethnicity and the Postmodern Arts of Memory," in George Marcus and James Clifford, eds., *Writing Culture* (Berkeley: University of California Press, 1986), 207.

18. Hebdige, "Reggae, Rastas, and Rudies," 138.

19. See *Trouser Press*, no. 10 (June 1983): 12–14; *Musician*, no. 52 (February 1983): 44–45.

20. Personal conversation with the author, 8 January 1983, Chicago.

21. Personal conversation with the author, 15 January 1983, Houston, Tex.

22. Michael Shore, *The Rolling Stone Book of Rock Videos* (New York: Quill, 1984), 125.

23. "Interview: Linton Kwesi Johnson," *Los Angeles Weekly*, 13–19 July 1984.

24. I am grateful to Ronnie Serr of the Theater Arts Department of the University of California, Los Angeles, for pointing out this connection.

25. Davis, *Reggae Bloodlines,* 10; George P. Rawick, *From Sundown to Sunup* (Westport, Conn.: Greenwood Press, 1972), 98–100.

26. Hebdige, "Reggae, Rastas, and Rudies," 140.

27. Logan, "Conversation with Marjorie Whylie," 90–91.

28. "Interview: Linton Kwesi Johnson."

29. Dick Hebdige, *Subculture: The Meaning of Style* (London: Methuen, 1985), esp. 92–94.

30. Stuart Hall, "Culture, The Media, and the Ideological Effect," in James Curran, Michael Gurevitch, and Janet Woollacott, eds., *Mass Communication in Society* (Beverly Hills, Calif.: Sage, 1979).

31. Shore, *Rolling Stone Book of Rock Videos,* 125.

32. Ibid., 45.

33. John Piccariella, "Little Big Youths," *Village Voice,* 26 April 1983, p. 66; Leo Sacks, "Talent in Action," *Billboard,* 23 April 1983, p. 38.

34. "New Acts," *Variety,* 20 April 1983, p. 184; Piccariella, "Little Big Youths."

35. Considine, "Youth of Today."

36. Shore, *Rolling Stone Book of Rock Videos,* 296.

37. Whitburn, *Billboard Book.*

11

HOME VIDEO AND CORPORATE PLANS: CAPITAL'S LIMITED POWER TO MANIPULATE LEISURE

Richard Butsch

The 1980s witnessed the dismantling and reshaping of an American ritual of three decades, the nightly ritual of tens of millions of Americans watching the same programs at the same time on network television. During the 1980s the U.S. television set, no longer simply a receiver of broadcast signals, became a screen for cable and satellite television, videocassette and videodisc playback, video games, and home computers. More than half of American households acquired cable and/or a videocassette recorder (VCR). The videodisc player came–and went. Cable television became an industry with its own networks, paralleling and competing with broadcast television. VCRs surpassed theaters as the primary exhibition medium for movies, linking the movie industry more closely to television. Music video added both a new dimension to the music industry and a new link to video industries. Broadcast television itself underwent changes. The FCC deregulated; the number of independent stations not affiliated with a network increased dramatically; and the networks' share of the audience plummeted.

Such dramatic changes in the pre-eminent mass medium are in themselves important to an appreciation of the commercialization of leisure. Beyond that, examination of the effectiveness of the industries involved in reshaping this most time-consuming of American leisure activities is of direct interest to the question of hegemony. These developments reveal a multiplicity of interests of various corporations and industries and consumers—interests sometimes compatible, sometimes conflicting even within the same corporation. What was the relative impact of consumers and corporations in shaping the leisure practices associated with television viewing and in reshaping television industries?

A variety of critics and scholars have considered capital or the capitalist classes or the mass media so powerful, or the working classes or audiences so passive, that only the one side need be understood. Others, though tending to exaggerate the extent of the power of people to resist corporate and media manipulation, have celebrated consumer resistance, reminding us that people do not simply swallow whole what is presented to them.[1]

To assess leisure accurately as a medium of hegemony, we must move beyond claims and counterclaims that people are or are not manipulated and see that the answer lies not just in one force or even in a struggle between two forces but in a complex interplay of forces that vary in their influence. Capital is not a monolith; it consists of many actors whose momentary interests may differ even while they have common class interests, and the variety of capitalist actors and structures affects the ability of any of them to control people's leisure. Similarly, people's control can take different forms, from organized boycotts to style movements to the simple result of many persons individually making the same consumer decision at the same time. It is meaningless to cite any of these variations alone as resistance or power without elaborating on what kind or extent of power, and how it differs from other kinds.

What better way to begin to understand the complexities of hegemony as a process, rather than simply ascertaining its presence or absence, than by studying that pre-eminent mass medium, television, with its huge audiences and centralized programming? Here capital would appear to have the advantage, yet in the dramatic changes of the 1980s, corporations did not always get their way. Some were in fact soundly defeated by consumer preferences or forced to move in a different direction. Central to these events was the development of home video, where these multiple interests intersected and collided.

Let us begin by identifying the many actors in this drama. First the multiple uses of television mean that it involves not one but several industries. The three major ones I am concerned with are broadcast, cable, and home video. Each of these utilizes electronics hardware and thus involves the consumer electronics industry. Each uses programs or, in today's parlance, software; thus the movie and the music industries are involved. Then there are the channels of distribution—movie distributors, networks, cable program suppliers, syndicators, videotape and disc distributors, wholesalers, and retailers—and the exhibitors: broadcast stations, cable systems. Finally there are the audiences: those with television sets, those with cable subscriptions, those with VCRs.

VIDEOTAPE COMES OF AGE

The story begins with the spread of videocassette recorders. VCR sales developed slowly through the 1970s but grew rapidly in the 1980s (see Table 11-1). In 1980, five years after their introduction, only 2.4 percent of U.S. television homes had a VCR. By the end of 1987 more than half had a VCR. Americans adopted the VCR as a common household product almost as quickly as they did television itself in the 1950s.[2]

TABLE 11-1. Changes in Television Use, 1976–1987

Year	TV Households with VCR (%)	TV Households with Cable (%)	Network TV Share (%)	Average TV Use (hr/day)	Theater Admissions (millions)
1976		15.1		6.18	
1977		16.6		6.10	
1978		17.9		6.17	
1979		19.4	92	6.28	
1980	2.4	22.6	90	6.36	1,022
1981	3.1	28.3	85	6.45	1,060
1982	5.7	35.0	83	6.48	1,175
1983	9.9	40.5	81	7.02	1,197
1984	17.6	43.7	78	7.08	1,199
1985	27.3	46.2	77	7.10	1,056
1986	40.0		76		1,020
1987	52.0	49.3	75		1,083

Sources: VCR households from *1985 U.S. Economic Review* (New York: Motion Picture Association of America, 1986), 8; "Electronics Group Paints a Rosy Picture," *Variety*, 14 January 1987, p. 1; "VCR Sales Down," *Variety*, 2 March 1988, p. 54. Cable households and television use from Neilsen Inc., personal communication. Network prime-time share for September–April season from "Network Scorecard, 1952–87," *Variety*, 30 September 1987, p. 36. Theater admissions from *1985 U.S. Economic Review*, 2; "Total '86 Box Office at $3.83 Bil," *Variety*, 14 January 1987, p. 9; "Box Office Yr for the Record Books," *Variety*, 13 January 1988, p. 3.

In the 1970s the introduction of cable programming as a competing new use for television kept VCR sales slow, as did the limited choices of prerecorded cassettes (predominantly X-rated), competing recording formats, and high cost. As VCR prices dropped from an average of about $1,200 in 1978 to under $300 in 1985, blank tapes from $18 in 1980 to $10 by 1984, and rental from $8 in 1980 to $3 in 1984, the new technology came within the reach of more people.[3] (Owners did remain slightly upscale through 1985: households with incomes above $35,000, professionals and managers, people with college degrees, and those between twenty-five and forty-four years of age were overrepresented.)[4]

The establishment of a dominant format may also have helped. Several incompatible recording technologies (formats) were developed by different manufacturers. Sony introduced the modern VCR in 1975 with its Betamax, priced at $1,300. Matsushita had introduced two formats in 1977, one by Quasar (which was not long lived) and JVC's VHS. Matsushita, by licensing to many manufacturers, rapidly gained dominance for its VHS format, which was outselling Beta two to one by 1978 and four to one by 1985. Only two Beta manufacturers remained in 1985; by the end of the year some prerecorded cassettes (PRCs) were not even produced in Beta format, and many stores ceased to carry Beta at all.[5]

Sales increased still further with the availability of more material to play on VCRs. Although recording television programs in order to play them back at a time more convenient to the viewer was their primary use initially, this ability alone did not make VCRs an instant market success. Rather, the introduction of hit movies on prerecorded cassettes and, in particular, their availability for a two- or three-dollar rental fee was an important programming factor in boosting sales.[6]

The capabilities of VCRs, combined with more available programming and lowered prices, explain the explosive increase in sales by 1985. Their capabilities created new relationships between people and their television sets and had considerable impact on the involved industries.

TIME-SHIFTING: CONSUMER PROGRAMMING

VCRs made it possible for the first time for television users to watch programming at times of their own choosing, instead of at the will of the broadcaster or cable system. Three-fourths of purchasers in 1978 and again in 1984 gave this time-shifting capability as their primary reason for buying a VCR. Even after rental PRCs became widely available, time-shifting remained an important use: in 1985 Nielsen found that almost three hours per week were spent watching taped programs and less than one hour watching prerecorded cassettes. Nielsen also found that viewing PRCs dropped by half after two to three years of VCR ownership, while playback of taped programs remained stable.[7]

About 70 percent of the taping is done when the owners are not watching TV or are watching another program.[8] Thus, it allows people to see shows they would otherwise miss, expanding the audience for that program—but not the audience for commercials, which viewers often skip, thanks to the VCR's fast-forwarding capability. About three-fourths of taping has been of network programs, with the heaviest emphasis on the fall and winter prime-time season. Television series, particularly daytime serials, are the programs most frequently time-shifted, followed by movies. Owners who are also cable subscribers tend to use the VCRs even more for time-shifting.[9]

Because time-shifting has added flexibility to people's leisure, giving them independence from broadcasters' and cablecasters' control of their time, the viewing audience has begun to create some difficulties for advertising-based television. Time-shifting contributes to audience fragmentation, making it more difficult to measure, predict, and deliver an audience of specific demographics to advertisers. Previously, audience demographics could be predicted by what groups were at home during certain hours and advertising matched to these groups. Time-shifting eliminates the connection between scheduled air time and the demographics of the audience. The effect on advertisers, broadcasters, and cablecasters is an unintentional byproduct of VCR use; it does not arise from any consumer move to resist or affect those parties. On the other hand, it does reflect the cross-cutting interests of the consumer electronics industry, which markets time-shifting VCRs for profit, and the broadcast and cable television industries, whose control over their audiences is lessened.

Even more threatening to television advertising is the VCR user's ability to skip commercials, a process known as "zapping." Audiences have traditionally switched stations or left the room during commercial breaks, but the VCR allows viewers to separate commercials from the entertainment entirely. Surprisingly, Nielsen's first study of VCR use in 1980 found that only about a third of users zapped any commercials. But in 1984 Neilsen found that half skipped commercials "regularly," a third skipped three-fourths of all commercials and 5 percent of the total audience of any given commercial was lost through zapping. At least some in the industry considered this loss significant. One advertising agency claimed in 1984 that General Foods lost $1 million in paid advertising time as a result of zapping, yet only 17.6 percent of television homes had VCRs at that time. In 1985, with VCRs in 28 percent of homes, 44 percent of users always fast-forwarded past commercials. This could mean that 12 percent of the audience of any given commercial was lost to zapping in 1985.[10]

Whatever the actual figures, the spread of VCRs makes zapping a very real danger to broadcast—and increasingly cable—television based on advertising. An obvious solution for advertisers is to embed commercial material into the entertainment itself so that it is not separable. This is already done in children's programming, with shows built around a toy, and in movies, with products prominently displayed for a fee.

THE RETAILERS' RENTAL REBELLION

VCR use changed with the appearance of hit movies on prerecorded cassettes. In 1979, 83 percent of VCR use was taping television programming and only 9 percent playing prerecorded cassettes; by 1982, 41 percent was taping and 52 percent playing PRCs.[11] Twentieth Century–Fox had released movies on cassette as early as 1977, and Paramount in late 1979, but most of the major studios—Warner, Universal, MGM, Columbia, and Disney—made their first releases in 1980. Hundreds of titles were licensed for release in 1980 as distribution arms for the major studios' film libraries were formed.[12] By early 1981, two-thirds of PRC dealers' inventory consisted of movies.[13] But what the studios had not anticipated was the dramatic clash with retailers occasioned by the new possibility of going to the movies at home.

In its early days, the prerecorded cassette retail business was composed primarily of small stores. Surveys in 1982 indicated that 62 percent of retailers owned only one store; an additional 18 percent owned only two.[14] Two factors chiefly accounted for the ability of small business people to enter the market with little capital and little competition from larger dealers. One was the early predominance of X-rated films in PRC retail. During the late 1970s, X-rated tapes began to move from adult theaters and bookstores to become an important part of the video stores' business. In 1979, before the release of major movies, 71 percent of PRCs purchased were X-rated material.[15] Bigger retailers showed little interest in what was not only a relatively small market but one that might stain their image. With the appearance of first-run movies on cassette, however, the X-rated share of the market dropped rapidly; moreover, suppliers who held the distribution rights for movie cassettes constituted an oligopoly, dominated by the major film studios. Several joint ventures were involved: CBS/Fox, RCA/Columbia, Thorn/HBO. Karl Video, owner of the Jane Fonda workout cassettes, was acquired by the Lorimar Studio in October 1984. The four largest suppliers in 1982 accounted for 64 percent of retail sales. The top four in 1983, 1984, and 1985 accounted for half of wholesale PRC sales.[16]

Second, and more important to small stores, was the rapid popularity among VCR owners of renting rather than buying movie tapes. Rental is a labor-intensive mode of retailing that requires considerable paperwork and involves the difficulties associated with overdue and damaged cassettes. Nevertheless, rental requires a smaller inventory than sales and thus less initial capital. In 1982, 79 percent of video stores had fewer than 800 tapes in stock.[17]

It is difficult to ascertain precisely when and how small retailers began renting cassettes.[18] It may simply have been that they were unable to sell enough PRCs, which were priced at $50 or more, to stay in business. In any case, despite no-rental clauses in their contracts with cassette suppliers, 80 percent of retailers were renting by late 1980, and retailers who abided by earlier agreements not to rent were suffering. In early 1981, 52 percent of retailers' income was coming from PRC sales, 48 percent from rental; by 1982, 75 to 95 percent of transactions were rentals. Three-fourths of VCR owners rented an average of three cassettes a month in 1983, compared with 20 percent in 1980. Retail rental revenues in 1983 were $800 million; in 1984, $1.74 billion; in 1985, $3.6 billion. Rentals rose from 30 million in 1983 to 262 million in 1985.[19] *Rental was a fait accompli.*

The rental runaway proved to be legally possible as a result of the "first sale" doctrine of copyright law. Since the studios were selling the prerecorded cassettes to wholesalers and retailers—instead of leasing them, as they leased film to theaters—they found that they could not prohibit the buyers from renting the cassettes, nor could they demand a share of rental revenue. The major film studios attempted numerous schemes to regain control of their product. First, some simply raised the price of their cassettes to as much as $100. But this fueled rental trade even more and caused large retail chains to halt their entry into videocassette retail. Then, during late 1981 and early 1982, Warner, Disney, MGM/CBS, and Twentieth Century–Fox's Magnetic Video introduced various rental-only plans in which they leased cassettes to retailers, for rental only.[20] According to *Variety*, these plans were "thoroughly defeated." Retailers wanted to own the cassettes they rented; apparently they objected to the costs and paperwork involved in leasing from a studio. Retailers boycotted Warner's rental-only plan, for example, forcing Warner to replace it with a policy allowing retailers a choice of purchase or lease.[21]

In 1984 Paramount Pictures initiated an alternative strategy of lowering hit movie cassette prices to $25, hoping to encourage customers to buy rather than rent. The plan resulted in good sales for Paramount but did not deter the rental trend. Also in 1984 a major distributor, Media Home Entertainment, introduced a line of feature films (not hits) at $19.95, well below the previous lowest price of $39.95 for features. The expressed goal was to "open up new markets" such as major chain stores and thus combat rental. RCA/Columbia Home Video reduced prices on six of its best-selling movies, from $79–$89 to $29.95; Walt Disney marked down twenty-one of its old hits to $29.95 at the end of 1985; Vestron tagged twenty-seven of its best sellers at $24.95 or less. Thus, the trend by 1985 was not to try to capture a share of rental but to increase retail sales, or "sell-through."[22]

None of these strategies enabled the studios to regain control of their product. For one thing, retailers organized and took concerted action to protect their interests, forming retailers' associations, boycotting Warner's rental plan, opposing repeal of the first-sale doctrine.[23] For another, the video retailers' interests coincided with those of consumer electronic companies. As long as rental boosted VCR sales, small retailers had powerful allies in the VCR manufacturers; the Electronic Industry Association too opposed the Motion Picture Association of America's efforts to get Congress to repeal the first-sale doctrine.[24] Most effective of all was the day-to-day business of thousands of mom-and-pop stores—most of which did not participate in or even belong to the dealers' associations.

But the sweet victory of small over large was short-lived. As the number of outlets rapidly increased—from about 14,000 in mid-1984 to 25,000 or 30,000 in 1985—large retailers began to enter the market, and some smaller ones grew into regional chains. Before long, small retailers were being squeezed out as prices and profits dropped and inventory of a wider variety of tapes began to be necessary. Rental prices were driven down as low as $0.99 by the fierce competition, and retail associations even began pushing sales, for fear of the price competition in rental.[25] By late 1985 the average retailer owned five stores; National Video and Adventureland Video each had about

600. National Video was large enough to negotiate a special arrangement with the studios: in 1986 it introduced a plan to offer 50 percent of rental revenue to suppliers in exchange for receiving titles ahead of its competitors and at as little as one-tenth the price.[26]

Even by 1984, established retail chains had begun to undercut the position of the small video specialty stores as the PRC market grew into a billion-dollar business. K-Mart and Waldenbooks began to sell and U-Haul to rent PRCs, adding a couple of thousand retail outlets. In addition, supermarket rental grew rapidly.[27] The entry of mass market retailers was stimulated by the appearance of PRCs, other than movies, that were inexpensive and/or more appealing for purchase and library building. For example, old television series began to be released in late 1984—over the objections of broadcast stations that were buying syndication rights to these series.[28] When music videos became widely available in 1983, record store chains began to compete with video stores in selling—not renting—music video; a Michael Jackson release in early 1984 increased the number of record stores carrying music video.[29]

Still, rental had been established and remained a low-cost option for consumers, even as the small retailers who pioneered it were squeezed out. The sell-through strategy of the studios did not increase sales relative to rentals.[30] In fact, it was being blamed by distributors for their shrinking profits as they lowered their prices to meet quotas set by the studios.[31]

The rental rebellion had two major effects: one on the introduction of videodisc and the consumer electronic corporations that tried to promote it, and the other on audiences for cable and broadcast television and for movies shown in theaters.

THE VIDEODISC FIASCO

One might reasonably assume that eight to ten giant corporations with annual sales of tens of billions of dollars and millions to invest in advertising would have the market power to create a demand for a new product and thus shape the leisure practices of millions of people. But just such a group of companies was unsuccessful in doing so with the videodisc and consequently wrote off several hundred million dollars in losses.

Videodisc is the visual equivalent of the audio record, as videotape is the visual equivalent of audio tape. Like record players, videodisc players are limited to playback of prerecorded discs, whereas VCRs can both record and play back. In 1979 three consortia of international electronics corporations, with combined U.S. assets of over $50 billion, each planned to manufacture and market a videodisc system in the United States.[32] In the first, RCA developed the technology and licensed Zenith and Sanyo to produce its player and CBS to produce discs for its system; CBS in turn formed a joint venture with MGM to produce films for these discs. Philips headed the second consortium; its wholly owned subsidiary Magnavox was to manufacture and market a laser disc player. MCA and IBM formed one joint venture to make discs for this system and another with Pioneer to manufacture laser disc players. MCA, Philips, and Pioneer formed yet another joint venture to produce films for these discs. The third consortium involved General Electric, Thorn EMI, and Matsushita/JVC in joint ventures to manufacture players and discs.

American and European companies had a special incentive to produce videodiscs for which they would hold the patents, because by the 1970s Japanese companies held most of the patents for videotape technology. RCA, the principal company in videodisc development, decided to invest because it expected videotape to remain an expensive specialty item for a select market. RCA hoped to produce a disc that could be sold cheaply to a mass market. Its expectations about VCRs were proved wrong when the drop in prices and the rental rebellion made the VCR a mass market item.

In late 1978 Philips-MCA was the first to test-market a videodisc system, priced at $775, and gradually expanded the number of cities in which it was sold. Nationwide marketing began in March 1981 when RCA tagged its system at $500 and spent $20 million to promote the new product.[33]

But problems arose immediately, and sales never really got off the ground. Only 157,000 players were delivered to dealers in 1981, compared with 1.3 million videocassette recorders. In 1982 things began to unravel. In February IBM and MCA closed the only U.S. plant manufacturing discs for the Philips system. The GE/Thorn/JVC system was delayed several times and then put on "indefinite hold" in November; it has never been marketed in the United States. RCA dropped its player price to $350 to stimulate sales, but in early 1983 Zenith and Sanyo stopped their production of players. As sales continued to be poor, RCA abruptly shut down its own player production in early April 1984. The Philips system continued to be marketed but only 100,000 had been sold by 1984. RCA's total sales were about 700,000 players.[34] RCA reported a $580 million loss on the total program; Philips and its partners had spent $400 million in developing and marketing; and total development costs for all three systems were reported to be over $1 billion.[35]

The root cause of the failure was poor timing. The development of videodisc technology was slow and proceeded in a series of starts and stops. CBS first demonstrated a system in 1966 but dropped its program in 1972 after investing $40 million. RCA's demonstration in 1969 was an embarrassing failure. Nevertheless, RCA, Telefunken, Zenith, MCA, and Philips announced their various systems in 1972; marketing was planned for the mid-1970s but repeatedly postponed.[36]

Meanwhile, Sony had introduced the first consumer videotape recorder and signed an agreement with Paramount for prerecorded programming. Videodisc development was put on hold at RCA and Zenith and delayed at Philips during 1977 as the success of videotape spread doubts about the rival system, and RCA and Zenith—the two largest television manufacturers—themselves entered the videotape recorder market.[37]

Even so, major corporations went on to invest hundreds of millions in videodisc during the late 1970s and early 1980s. What sealed its fate was the rental rebellion: just as videodisc began to be marketed, hundreds of movies became available to VCR owners at rental prices of two to three dollars. This, combined with the advantage of recording capability, which videodisc players lacked, made even a higher-priced VCR the better buy.

CHANGING PATTERNS IN THEATER AND TELEVISION AUDIENCES

VCRs and rental cassettes had to reach a high level of penetration before they affected the movie theaters, since most attendance is accounted for by the 25 percent of the population who attend movies at least once a month. In fact, no effect was apparent until 1984, when a slight drop in theater admissions occurred for the first time in twenty-five years; they dropped 12 percent in 1985 and another 2 percent in 1986, rose again by 6.5 percent in 1987, and declined 1 percent in 1989—a 9 percent drop in five years.[38]

Two independent surveys indicated a significant decrease in the theater attendance of persons under thirty at the same time that this age group was dramatically increasing its video rentals. By 1986, teenagers—traditionally the lightest users of television—were watching movies on VCRs with friends instead of going to a theater. Renting a cassette for a couple of dollars was an economical inducement to stay home, compared with five to seven dollars per person to go out to a theater.[39]

But the impact on theater attendance is still unclear. The drop in attendance may have been temporary and due to the tremendous VCR sales in 1985–86, or to demographic shrinkage of the movie-going, under-thirty age group. On the other hand, the 1987 rise in theater attendance may simply reflect changes made in movie content to attract the growing over-thirty age group, plus the opening of hundreds of new theaters in suburban locations, masking the effect of VCRs.[40]

What is clear is that the prerecorded cassette became a major factor, perhaps the major factor, in movie production. From 1983 to 1985 the number of PRC rentals skyrocketed from 30 million in 1983 to 262 million in 1985. In 1985 PRC rentals and sales ($4.55 billion) exceeded theatrical box office receipts ($3.75 billion) and accounted for almost two-thirds of total movie revenues by 1987. Even though the studios were not getting a cut of rentals, 1985 revenues from PRCs to program suppliers ($1.8 billion) nearly equaled revenues from theatrical film rentals ($1.82 billion). Thus, in the long run, PRCs fueled a Hollywood production boom.[41]

Whatever its effect on movie theaters, videocassette rental was part of general fundamental changes in the television industry and television use. The television audience and the mean hours of television viewing per household expanded: the average number of hours viewed per day per household increased consistently from 6.36 hours in 1980 to 7.10 hours in 1985. Cable subscribers watched much more television (21–30 hours per week) than nonsubscribers (11–20 hours). Nearly half of the subscribers reported increases in late-night viewing and decreases in going out to movies.[42]

Even so, the rapid rise of PRC rental slowed the growth of the pay-cable channels. A steady decline in new subscriptions to pay cable after the peak year of 1981 (see Table 11-2) was simultaneous

TABLE 11-2. Pay-Cable Growth: Net New Subscriptions

Year	Net New Subs. (millions)	Year	Net New Subs. (millions)
1975	0.33	1980	3.98
1976	0.55	1981	7.13
1977	0.71	1982	5.66
1978	1.85	1983	4.94
1979	2.83	1984	2.91

Source: Paul Kagan Associates, cited in "Pay TV Sees Its Growth Slow Down," *Marketing and Media Decisions*, August 1985, p. 22.

with the rise of the video rental business. Cable companies became sufficiently fearful of the effects of PRC rental to try to introduce a pay-per-view plan—requiring the rewiring of cable systems—which would, for a fee, deliver programs to viewers at times of their choosing, saving a trip to the video store.[43]

At the same time, hegemony of the commercial broadcast networks has lessened as their share of the audience declined dramatically. The three networks' share of the audience (the percentage of TV households with the television on and turned to network-affiliated stations) dropped steadily from 92 percent during the 1978–79 television season to 75 percent for 1986–87—51 percent in homes with pay cable.[44]

The drop in network share is due also to changes within broadcast television itself. Independent broadcast stations' share of the audience grew from 10 percent of total television viewing in 1975 to 21 percent in 1985—35 percent in the top ten markets. Average weekly viewing of all nonnetwork programming in noncable homes rose from 7.9 hours in 1979 to 12.7 hours in 1984,[45] thanks to the development of a variety of alternative programming sources, made feasible through satellite, that bypassed the networks and went beyond traditional syndication methods.[46]

CONCLUSION

The changes in leisure resulting from home video and other developments in television were not planned by capital so much as they were shaped by consumer choices and small retailers. Most important is the establishment of VCR instead of videodisc as the mass market home video product. Because the disc player cannot record, videodisc did not threaten broadcast or cable television to the degree that VCRs do. The VCR brought a new level of independence to people in their primary leisure activity, television viewing.

VCRs, together with cable, increased television use, reducing time spent in other pursuits. They have affected theater attendance and other activities outside the home. They may have increased privatization of the family, since TV use is almost exclusively in the home.[47] This is important because privatization may ultimately mean less community life on which class expression or resistance to hegemony might be based. We do not know yet what new patterns will emerge as VCRs become a more and more customary part of the household.

We do know that consumers' purchases and leisure choices have had a major impact on the industries involved and in turn on the purchasers' own leisure. Once hit movies were released on cassette and retailers offered them for rent, consumers responded in millions, fueling both the rental rebellion and VCR sales. No massive marketing campaign was needed to persuade them of the value of rental, whereas videodisc—even with such a campaign—was lost in the dust. Consumer electronics companies (primarily Japanese) benefited from VCR sales, but those who invested in disc (primarily American and European) lost; pay-cable growth slowed; and the theater became secondary to the videocassette as a movie exhibition outlet. Time-shifting fragmented audiences, and zapping threatened the basis of advertising for cable and broadcast television.

It was consumer decisions that established the videocassette recorder, the more liberating technology, and defeated corporate efforts to promote the less liberating videodisc player. With the VCR entrenched as the mass-market product, capital found it necessary to accept and serve it, thus supporting broadcast and cable television's loss of audience. Why were unorganized consumers able to do this?

For one thing, the involved companies and industries had at times conflicting, at times compatible interests. Consumer electronics companies' interests tended to coincide with the retailers' rental of tapes and with the consumers' purchase and use of VCRs and disc players. These were opposed to the interests of movie studios and theaters, cable and broadcast TV.

Although some were badly bruised, the large corporations were not so much defeated as denied the greater profits they expected. RCA hedged its bet on videodisc by becoming the major U.S. marketer for Matsushita's VHS format, selling a fifth of all VCRs in the United States. Over time, the movie studios gained handsomely ($1.8 billion gross revenues in 1985) from the overall growth of the PRC market that was stimulated by rental. Even the larger theater chains, undeterred by the drop in theater attendance, announced plans for expansion. Movie studios themselves reconstructed the vertical integration of their heyday in the 1940s by buying theater chains.[48] It appears that the losers were the smaller companies that did not diversify: specialty cinema theaters and the mom-and-pop video stores squeezed out by competition and large retail chains.

What, then, were the respective roles of capital and consumers in this reshaping of leisure? What did capital do; what did people do? What power did they wield? Consumers by the millions remade their own leisure—but the conditions that allowed them to contradict some corporate plans were not of their own making. There were no organized consumers' movements on these issues. Consumers wielded their purchase power as individuals. It was the combined effect of millions of individual decisions arrived at individually that created a product and market to serve their needs and to realize new uses of television and new control of what and when they could watch. Nor did their actions alone determine the outcome. It was because their actions coincided with the interests and actions of *some* companies and industries that these acted to protect the conditions (rental, first-sale doctrine) that were the basis for the new leisure built around the VCR.

This kind of consumer power is limited to operating within existing conditions, to making changes not planned or necessarily intended by the individuals involved. As individuals, they cannot pursue a positive agenda to bring about change. Thus, although consumers were not pawns in corporate plans—they did not act as some corporations wanted them to but pursued their own plans, wants, interests—at the same time they could not pursue a collective agenda of their own without some form of organization to coordinate their actions. Indeed, we might say it was the divisions within capital that limited its ability to control people's leisure. Contradictions in the development of capital and competition between sectors of capital created certain economic and legal conditions that gave small retailers the economic space to act against the will of their oligopolistic suppliers, providing an opportunity for consumers to reshape their use of television.

The case of the VCR, then, shows that hegemony is more complicated than capital versus consumers, class expression versus social control. The power of capital is limited by its internal conflicts—the differing interests of different corporations and industries—and by the individual actions of consumers. At the same time, people make their individual choices within the boundaries of conditions to a considerable degree created by the mix of capital decisions. It is only within a fortuitous sequence of circumstances that the unorganized consumer, as here, can have such an impact on the shape of leisure.

NOTES

1. For the various debates on domination and resistance, see James Curran, Michael Gurevitch, and Janet Woollacott, "The Study of the Media: Theoretical Approaches," in Michael Gurevitch et al., eds., *Culture, Society, and the Media* (London: Methuen, 1982); Alan Swingewood, *The Myth of Mass Culture* (Atlantic Highlands, N.J.: Humanities Press, 1977); William Muraskin, "The Social Control Theory in American History: A Critique," *Journal of Social History* 9 (Summer 1976): 559–69; Eileen and Stephen Yeo, "Ways of Seeing: Control and Leisure versus Class and Struggle," in Eileen

and Stephen Yeo, eds., *Popular Culture and Class Conflict* (Atlantic Highlands, N.J.: Humanities Press, 1981), 128–51.

2. "VCR Sales Down," *Variety*, 2 March 1988, p. 54. *Television: A World Survey* (Paris: UNESCO, 1953), 85, reports rates of U.S. television growth.

3. "The Coming VCR Glut," *Fortune*, 19 August 1985, p. 77; "VCR's: Ogre or Opportunity?" *Marketing and Media Decisions*, September 1984, p. 49; "VCR's Bring Big Changes in Use of Leisure," *New York Times*, 3 March 1985, p. 1.

4. Mark R. Levy, "Home Video Recorders: A User Survey," *Journal of Communication* 30 (Autumn 1980): 23; "A Crystal Ball on Homevideo vs TV Viewing," *Variety*, 25 June 1980, p. 5; "Tenth Annual Consumer Survey," *Merchandising*, May 1982, p. 22; "VCR's: Ogre or Opportunity?" 50; Opinion Research Corp., "Recent Media Trends: Television Programming as a Consumer Product," *Public Opinion Index*, June 1985, p. 2.

5. See Don Agostino & Associates, *Home Video: A Report on the Status, Projected Development, and Consumer Use of Videocassette Recorders and Videodisc Players in the U.S.*, prepared for the FCC Network Inquiry Special Staff (Washington, D.C.: Federal Communications Commission, 1979), 7–17. A new 8mm VCR format was on the horizon by 1986 but has been marketed as a separate camcorder technology for home "movies." See "8mm Is Bright at CES Meeting," *Variety*, 15 January 1986, p. 41. On the demise of Beta, see "Matsushita Takes the Lead in Video Recorders," *Fortune*, 16 July 1979, p. 110; "To the Beta End," *Forbes*, 16 December 1985, p. 178; "Beta's in Trouble Say Video Distribs; Some Hanging On," *Variety*, 15 January 1986, p. 41.

6. The A. C. Nielsen Co. claimed that households specialized in their uses of VCRs and identified three types: those that use the VCR with a video camera, those that use it primarily for time-shifting, and those that use it primarily for playing PRCs. See "Soaps Top Pix in VCR Taping, Per Nielsen Poll," *Variety*, 2 May 1984, p. 44. I have not discussed video camera use here, since it was a minor factor during this period: video camera sales from 1980 through 1984 totaled 1.5 million, or only about 2 percent of U.S. households. See *Consumer Electronics Annual Review, 1985* (Washington D.C.: Electronics Industry Association, 1985), 25.

7. "First Look at Cassette Audience," *Media Decisions*, March 1979, p. 147; "Home Tapers Tapping Cable Programming," *Advertising Age*, 31 May 1984, p. 40; Opinion Research Corp., "Recent Media Trends," 2; "Nets Audience May Be Widened by VCR Use," *Advertising Age*, 10 June 1985, p. 60.

8. "Consumer Survey," *Merchandising*, October 1979, p. 22; "VCR Usage Gains in America; Networks Account for 50% of Shows Taped," *Video Marketing Newsletter*, 4 November 1985, p. 2.

9. "First Look at Cassette Audience," 149; "Soaps Top Pix in VCR Taping," 44; Mark Levy, "Program Playback Preferences in VCR Households," *Journal of Broadcasting* 24 (Summer 1980): 332, 334; "VCR's: The Saga Continues," *Marketing and Media Decisions*, September 1985, p. 156.

10. "Nielsen Study Plays Back Videocassette Data," *Advertising Age*, 28 April 1980, p. 2; "VCR's," *Broadcasting*, 20 August 1984, p. 48; "Nielsen Attacks VCR Zap Factor," *Advertising Age*, 19 November 1984, p. 92; Opinion Research Corp., "Recent Media Trends," 2.

11. "Consumer Survey," *Merchandising*, October 1979, p. 22; "Tenth Annual Consumer Survey," *Merchandising*, May 1982, p. 22. In 1988 use of PRCs constituted 78 percent of adult VCR viewing. See "VCR Usage," *Broadcasting*, 11 July 1988, p. 63.

12. "Simultaneous Release of New Films, Prerecorded Tapes Due by Spring," *Merchandising*, February 1980, p. 58; *Home Video Yearbook, 1981–82* (White Plains, N.Y.: Knowledge Publications, 1981), 163; "MGM Film Forms Venture with CBS for Video Cassettes," *Wall Street Journal*, 5 June 1980, p. 17; "Fox's Magnetic Video Licenses 250 United Artists Feature Pix," *Variety*, 23 July 1980, p. 1.

13. "ITA Scouts Video Revolution; Film Majors Merit Biz Boom," *Variety*, 18 March 1981, pp. 277, 296. This survey reported an estimted 12,000 PRC titles—of all types, not just movies—available from 200 wholesale distributors. Another report estimated about 12,000 available for home use, of which some 5,000 were in the regular distribution flow through retailers. See "Homevideo, American Style: The Programs & Players," *Variety*, 12 May 1982, p. 408. Theatrical PRCs increased dramatically from 1981 to 1984, but the increase began to slow in 1985 as the Hollywood film libraries neared empty. See "U.S. Vid Library Keeps Growing; Over 40,000 Titles Now Available," *Variety*, 13 November 1985, p. 41.

14. "Videalers Prefer Rent to Sale, Two New Indie Surveys Show," *Variety*, 1 September 1982, p. 57.

15. "Consumer Survey," *Merchandising*, May 1980, p. 46. "See X-rated Sales as High as 70% of Total Prerecorded Market in '79," *Merchandising*, January 1980, p. 72. One source stated that by late 1980 X-rated accounted for only about 20–25 percent of the market. See "Incompatible Units Confuse Market," *Variety*, 1 October 1980, p. 1. *Adult Video News* reported a decline of adult videos' share from 33 percent in 1983 to 19 percent in 1985, even though the number of X-rated PRCs rose considerably. See "From Jane Fonda to 'Debbie Does Dallas,'" *Broadcasting*, 2 September 1985, p. 44. X-rated's share of the market continued to decline to about 9 percent in 1984. See "Twelfth Annual Consumer Survey," *Merchandising*, July 1984, p. 18. But 9 percent of a rapidly growing market was still a very lucrative business. See "X-Rated Vid Ain't Blue over '84 Sales," *Variety*, 30 January 1985, p. 37.

16. Heikki Hellman and Martti Soramaki, "Economic Concentration in the Videocassette Industry: A Cultural Comparison," *Journal of Communication* 35, no. 3 (1985): 127; "The Videocassette Market," *New York Times*, 19 September 1985, p. 1D; "Lorimar completes Karl Vid Acquisition," *Variety*, 31 October 1984, p. 49. As in the movie industry, the specific companies constituting the top four varied from year to year. Kartes Video, selling public-domain programming, was purchased by Scripps-Howard in late 1985. See "Scripps Howard Agrees to Buy Kartes Video; Founder Remains," *Variety*, 6 November 1985, p. 81. Vestron, formed in 1982, was the

only newcomer. See "Vestron Claims Major Status; Sees Sales, Catalog as Strength," *Variety*, 4 January 1984, p. 57.

17. "Videalers Prefer Rent to Sale," 57; "Home Truths for Hollywood," *Economist*, 30 July 1983, pp. 72–73. In 1985 the average inventory of video stores was still only 2,300 tapes and 1,600 titles. See "VSDA Survey Says Sales Volume 15%," *Variety*, 26 June 1985, p. 84.

18. Ironically, the major studios cooperated in initiating rental as a retail mode. In January 1979, Fotomat signed an agreement with Paramount to rent and sell several dozen movies; Video Corporation of America—later to become one of the largest distributors of PRCs—agreed in June 1978 with United Artists and shortly after with RKO and Avco Embassy to rent movie cassettes by mail. See "2 Movie Studios Join Prerecorded Rental Market," *Merchandising*, May 1979, p. 52. Columbia and several other majors also agreed to rent their films through Fotomat. See "Columbia Buys 42 Pics From Cinema 5 for Homevid Mart," *Variety*, 28 May 1980, p. 34.

19. "Firms Renting Videocassettes Worry Studios," *Wall Street Journal*, 27 March 1981, p. 31; "Rental Route as Copyright Hold," *Variety*, 11 November 1981, p. 1; "ITA Scouts Video Revolution; Film Majors Merit Biz Boom," *Variety*, 18 March 1981, pp. 277, 296; "Videalers Prefer Rent to Sale"; "3M Report Studies HV Rental Patterns," *Variety*, 19 September 1984, p. 113; "Coming Distractions," *Forbes*, 16 July 1984, p. 46; "Consumer Vid Spending in '85 Exceeds U.S. Theatrical B.O.; Hollywood Studios Reap $1.8 Bil," *Variety*, 15 January 1986, p. 218; "Col Survey Shows Vid Rentals Far Outdistancing Admissions; 'Staggering' VCR Growth Cited," *Variety*, 21 May 1986, p. 3.

20. "Home Truths for Hollywood," 72; "Disney's Rental-Only Cassettes Could Presage Industry Trend," *Variety*, 15 July 1981, p. 42; "Rental Route as Copyright Hold," *Variety*, 11 November 1981, p. 1; "MGM/CBS Video Introduces 'First Run' Rental Plan," *Merchandising*, January 1982, p. 46; *Video News*, 25 November 1981, p. 1.

21. "Videalers Prefer Rent to Sale," 57; "Warner Gets Mixed Reaction in Texas on Rental Program," *Merchandising*, December 1981, pp. 44, 63; "Much To-and-Fro Precedes Warner About Face," *Variety*, 6 January 1982, p. 39.

22. *Video News*, 21 December 1984, p. 4; "Media Plans Lowball Cassettes in Pitch at Pics Sell-Through," *Variety*, 23 May 1984, p. 47; "RCA/Col Pushes Sell-Through with Titles At $29.95 List Price," *Variety*, 17 April 1985, p. 27; "From Jane Fonda to 'Debbie Does Dallas,'" 43.

23. "Rental Wrangle Slows Market," *Variety*, 2 June 1982, pp. 37, 40. The Video Software Dealers Association (VSDA) formed in December 1981; another retail organization formed as well but folded in 1982. See *Video News*, 11 December 1981, p. 7. The American Video Association represented 350 retailers in objecting to Warner's rental plan. See "Warner Gets Mixed Reaction in Texas," 44.

The two largest independent suppliers, Vestron and Karl Homevideo, opposed the major studios' efforts to get Congress to repeal the first-sale doctrine on the ground that it would require dealers to invest more in stocking their shelves, with the result that the independents' tapes would be pushed off the shelves. See "Vestron and Karl Home Video Execs Claim First Sale Repeal Would Hinder, Not Aid Vid Biz," *Variety*, 13 June 1984, p. 37.

24. "Valenti, Wayman Trade Slams over First Sale in Warmup for Fall Legislative Battles," *Variety*, 31 August 1983, p. 34.

25. "Coming Distractions," 46; "Mom and Pop Videotape Shops Are Fading Out," *Business Week*, 2 September 1985, p. 34; "Rental Club Membership Fees Drop as Competition Swells in the Market," *Merchandising*, August 1984, p. 17, 26. In 1985 both the Video Retailer Association and the VSDA were pushing sell-through. See "RCA/Col Pushes Sell-Through," p. 27, and "VRA Pumping Up Video Sales Pitch," Variety, 17 April 1985, p. 26.

26. *Video Marketing Newsletter*, 1 July 1985, p. 7; "Mom and Pop Video Shops Are Fading Out," 35; *Billboard*, 7 December 1985, p. 32; "Majors to Share Video Rentals," *Variety*, 8 January 1986, p. 1.

27. "Debbie Does Exercises, Eyes K-Mart Sales Deal," *Variety*, 15 February 1984, p. 39; "U-Haul Sets Up Rental-Only Policy at 1,100 Outlets," *Variety*, 4 July 1984, p. 41; "Waldenbooks Set to Go Video after Tryout in Its 800 Stores," *Variety*, 11 July 1984, p. 32; "Supermarket Rentals Could Be Threatening Domain of Video Clubs and Specialty Outlets," *Merchandising*, December 1984, pp. 14, 19.

28. "TV to Homevid Will Get Boost Via Embassy, Paramount Release," *Variety*, 5 September 1984, p. 46; "Reruns Redux: Oldies Hit VCR's," *Advertising Age*, 7 January 1985, p. 64. On broadcast station reaction, see "Series Go Homevid; Stations Go Crazy," *Variety*, 27 March 1985, p. 41.

29. "Slow Start for Sony Vid 'Singles,'" *Variety*, 17 August 1983, p. 72; "Music Video on Rise at Retail," *Advertising Age*, 5 September 1983, p. 3; "Jackson's 'Thriller' Propelling Record Outlets into Video Biz," *Variety*, 4 January 1984, p. 57; "Music Vid Mkt Share Goes Flat," *Variety*, 1 April 1987, p. 1. Music video gained attention in 1981 with the appearance of MTV, where its primary purpose was to promote the sale of audio records. But it was slow to develop as a consumer product because there were few high-fidelity VCRs, and even in 1984 there were few high-fidelity music videos. See "Launch of VHS Hifi Is Sluggish due to Duplication Problems," *Merchandising*, August 1984, p. 17.

30. Rental increased its share of PRC revenues over sales from 74 percent of the total in 1984 to 79 percent in 1985. See "Consumer Vid Spending in '85 Exceeds U.S. Theatrical B.O.," 218. Sales did increase their share by 1987 to 37 percent of PRC revenues. See "More Wasn't Necessarily Better in '87," *Variety*, 6 January 1988, p. 5.

31. "Overblown Unit Projections for Pics May Backfire on Suppliers," *Variety*, 21 May 1986, p. 49; "Distributors Hear Analyst Forecast Shrinking Profits," *Variety*, 14 May 1986, p. 83.

32. "Video Discs: A Three-Way Race for a Billion-Dollar Jackpot," *Business Week*, 7 July 1980, p. 74; "The Fortune 500 Directory," *Fortune*, 5

May 1980, pp. 274–301. For an intra-corporate study see Margaret Graham, *RCA and the Video Disc: The Business of Research* (New York: Cambridge University Press, 1986).

33. "Special Report: Videodisk," *Broadcasting*, 2 February 1981, p. 36; "Videodisc: A Three Way Race," *Business Week*, 7 July 1980, pp. 72–74; "RCA's Biggest Gamble Ever," *Business Week*, 9 March 1981, p. 79; "Following a Slow Start, RCA Plans a New Push for Its Videodisc Player," *Wall Street Journal*, 13 October 1981, p. 35.

34. *Consumer Electronics Annual Review, 1985*, 25; "Vidisk Hour of Truth Approaching," *Variety*, 17 February 1982, pp. 43–44; "Third Vidisk System (JVC) Placed on 'Indefinite' U.S. & U.K. Hold," *Variety*, 24 November 1982, p. 31; "With Zenith's Exit, RCA Faces Lonely Haul in Vidisk Hardware," *Variety*, 26 January 1983, p. 39; "After RCA: Others to Exit U.S. Video Disk Player Mkt.," *Electronic News*, 16 April 1984, p. 20; "RCA's Rivals Still See Life in Videodiscs," *Business Week*, 23 April 1984, p. 89.

35. "RCA's Vidisk Losses," *Variety*, 10 March 1982, p. 35; "Philips Opens Books on LV; Messerschmitt Cites $400 Mi Marketing Development Tab," *Variety*, 10 March 1982, p. 35; "Home Videodisk Players Sell Slowly, So Firms Look to Industrial Market," *Wall Street Journal*, 18 May 1982, p. 33. The laser disc survived as a high-priced consumer technology. See "70–80,000 Laser Disk Players to Be Sold in '88, Sony Predicts," *Variety*, 24 August 1988, p. 88; "Videodisk Players Offer Double Value," *New York Times*, 5 February 1989, p. 25H.

36. *Broadcasting*, 21 March 1966, p. 160; "Videodisc: The Expensive Race to Be First," *Business Week*, 15 September 1975, pp. 58, 64, "Report RCA Makes Breakthrough in Videodisc Development Work," *Merchandising Week*, 31 July 1972, p. 9; "Philips Unveils Video Disk Unit," *Electronic News* 11 September 1972, p. 16; "MCA Enters Disk in Marketing Race for TV Playbacks," *Broadcasting*, 18 December 1972, p. 49; "Zenith in Big R&D Outlay on Video Discs," *Merchandising Week*, 30 April 1973, p. 3.

37. "See Betamax Moves Aimed at Disk," *Electronic News*, 21 February 1977; "Fear Philips Delay Fatal to Video Disk," *Electronic News*, 10 October 1977, p. 22.

38. "$4 Billion Plus B.O. Record Set in '84, But Ticket Sales Dropped," *Variety*, 9 January 1985, p. 24; *1985 U.S. Economic Review* (New York: Motion Picture Association of America, 1986), 2; "Box Office Year for the Record Books," *Variety*, 13 January 1988, p. 3; "U.S. Box Office Hits New High of $4.38 Bil. in 1988," *Variety*, 11 January 1989, p. 50.

39. "Col Survey Shows Vid Rentals Far Outdistance Admissions," pp. 3, 44; Opinion Research Corp., *Incidence of Motion Picture Attendance* (New York: MPAA, 1986), 1–4; "Teens Leaving Theaters for Homevid," *Variety*, 26 February 1986, p. 3; "VCR's Bring Big Changes in Use of Leisure," *New York Times*, 3 March 1985, p. 1.

40. "Say VCR Effect on Tix Sales Peaking," *Variety*, 15 January 1986, p. 36; "General Cinema on Construction Binge," *Variety*, 23 April 1986, p. 5; "MPAA Gives Pix Clean Bill of Health," *Variety*, 25 November 1987, p. 3.

41. "Col Survey Shows Vid Rentals Far Outdistance Admissions," p. 3; "Consumer Vid Spending in '85 Exceeds U.S. Theatrical B.O.," p. 41; "More Wasn't Better in '87," *Variety*, 6 January 1988, p. 5; "Prebuys Keep the Cameras Rolling," *Variety*, 4 November 1987, p. 3; "Filming Rolls to New High Mark," *Variety*, 13 January 1988, p. 1.

42. "The Impact of Cable Television on Subscriber and Non-subscriber Behavior," *Journal of Advertising Research 23*, no. 4 (August–September 1983): 15–23.

43. "Cable '85: The Indicators All Point Positive," *Broadcasting*, 2 December 1985, pp. 35, 36; "Pay Per View Sounds War Cry," *Variety*, 27 May 1987, p. 54.

44. "Chipping Away," *Broadcasting*, 6 January 1986, p. 26; personal communication, A. C. Nielsen Co., 29 April 1986. I was unable to obtain any reports on the network share in VCR homes.

45. "Viewing Trends from '50's to '80's," *Television/Radio Age*, 22 July 1985, p. 49; "Frazier, Gross Study Paints Rosy Picture for Independents," *Broadcasting*, 23 December 1985, p. 37; "Indie TV: It's Come a Long Way Baby," *Variety*, 1 January 1986, p. 29.

46. For examples, see "By-passing Networks Could Mean Big Profits," *Variety*, 25 August 1984, p. 1; "Is It Time for a Fourth Network?" New York Times, 28 August 1983, p. 1H; "M-E Joint Deal to Counter Webs," *Variety*, 19 January 1983, p. 77; "Program Suppliers Eye Satellites to Counter Nets," *Variety*, 30 September 1981, p. 60; "Fox Hatches Indie Web," *Variety*, 14 May 1986, p. 50.

47. Almost 15 percent of cable subscribers reported spending more time with the family and home entertaining, and driving fewer miles weekly. See "The Impact of Cable Television on Subscriber and Non-subscriber Behavior." As already noted, VCRs have contributed to people's spending more time at home, even teenagers.

48. "MCA Buys a Half Interest in Cineplex," *Variety*, 14 May 1986, p. 3; "Col to Buy Rest of Reade Chain," *Variety*, 25 September 1985, p. 5.

CONTRIBUTORS

RICHARD BUTSCH is Professor of Sociology at Rider College, Lawrenceville, New Jersey. His articles on the mass media portrayal of social class include "The Family as Portrayed on Television," in the Surgeon General's report, Television and Behavior: Ten Years of Scientific Progress. *His "Commodification of Leisure: The Case of the Model Airplane Hobby and Industry," in Vincent Mosco and Janet Wasko, eds.,* Popular Culture and Media Events, *documents the transformation of leisure by commercialization.*

JOHN CLARKE is Dean of the Faculty of Social Sciences in England's Open University. Among other books he is coauthor of The Devil Makes Work: Leisure in Capitalist Britain, *co-editor of* Working Class Culture: Studies in History and Theory, *and a contributor to Stuart Hall and Tony Jefferson, eds.,* Resistance through Rituals: Youth Cultures in Post-War Britain. *A collection of his essays in cultural studies,* Imperialism and Images, *is forthcoming.*

DOUGLAS GOMERY is Professor of Communication Arts and Theater at the University of Maryland, College Park, and Senior Re-

searcher in the Media Studies Project, Woodrow Wilson Center, Washington, D.C. His publications include The Hollywood Studio System, The Will Hays Papers, Film History: Theory and Practice *(with Robert C. Allen), and* American Media: The Wilson Quarterly Reader *(with Philip Cook and Lawrence Lichty), and articles in* Yale French Studies, Essays in Business and Economic History, *and* Journal of Communication. *He served on the Board of Trustees of the American Film Institute, 1986–88.*

L. SUE GREER is Assistant Professor of Sociology at Clinch Valley College of the University of Virginia. Her chapter continues the work of her dissertation, "Rationalization, Power, and the Forest Service: A Case Study of Conflict over the Mount Rogers National Recreation Area," which examined the connection between the development of corporate capitalism and the rationalization of the state, and its impact on community power.

STEPHEN HARDY is Associate Professor and Chair of Physical Education at the University of New Hampshire. He is the author of How Boston Played: Sport, Recreation, and Community, 1865–1915, *and articles in the* Journal of Social History, Journal of Sport History, *and* Theory, Culture, and Society.

GEORGE LIPSITZ is Assistant Professor of American Studies at the University of Minnesota. His many studies of popular culture include Class and Culture in Cold War America *and his most recent book,* A Life in the Struggle: Ivory Perry and the Culture of Opposition.

BRUCE A. McCONACHIE is Associate Professor of Theater and American Studies at the College of William and Mary. A fellow of the National Endowment for the Humanities, he has published several articles on nineteenth-century American theater and society and co-edited Theatre for Working Class Audiences in the United States, 1830–1980.

SHARON MAZZARELLA is Assistant Professor of Television-Radio at Ithaca College. She is currently completing her dissertation, an ethnographic study of the role of mass media in adolescent subcultures, for her Ph.D. from the University of Illinois Institute of Communications Research.

KATHY PEISS is Associate Professor of History and Women's

Studies at the University of Massachusetts, Amherst. Her publications on working women's leisure include her book Cheap Amusements: Working Women and Leisure in Turn-of-the-Century New York, and she is co-editor of Passion and Power: Sexuality in History.

ROBERT W. SNYDER was a predoctoral fellow of the Smithsonian Institution and earned his doctorate at New York University. He has taught at New York University and Princeton. Portions of his chapter have appeared in his Voice of the City: Vaudeville and Popular Culture in New York City.

ELLEN WARTELLA is Research Professor at the University of Illinois Institute of Communications Research. She has been a consultant to the Federal Communications Commission and the Federal Trade Commission and a Fellow at the Columbia University Gannett Center for Media Studies. She is co-author of How Children Learn to Buy and co-editor of Children Communicating. Her forthcoming book is titled Electronic Childhood.